A GUIDE TO SLOW TRAVEL IN THE MARCHES

by

Les Lumsdon

Logaston Press

LOGASTON PRESS
Little Logaston, Logaston,
Woonton, Almeley, Herefordshire HR3 6QH
www.logastonpress.co.uk

Published by Logaston Press 2011

ISBN 978 1 906663 53 7

Typeset by Logaston Press
and printed and bound in Poland
www.polskabook.pl

Front cover: Along the flanks of the Black Mountains in Herefordshire

*The guide is dedicated to Gladys and Leslie Lumsdon,
inveterate slow travellers, who explored the Herefordshire countryside
on foot and by cycle*

ACKNOWLEDGEMENTS

Grateful thanks are extended to the many people who helped in providing advice and information relating to the preparation of this guide. They include public transport and tourism staff from Herefordshire, Monmouthshire, Powys and Shropshire Councils, the Shropshire Hills and Wye Valley AONBs and the Brecon Beacons National Park. I am especially grateful to the following for making useful comments in the preparation of the final text: Clare and David Currant, Leila and Pat Lumsdon, Roger Furniss, Graham Lambert, Peta and Phil Sams and Les Williams. Special thanks also go to Andy Johnson at Logaston Press for additional information. Any errors or omissions are, of course, mine.

The photographs are by Chloe Lumsdon with the exception of those on pages 47, 60, 93, 112, 133 (top left), 142, 147 (both), 185, 198 (lower), 216, 222 and that on the front cover, which are supplied by Logaston Press.

FEEDBACK

If anyone wishes to suggest information for inclusion or correction in a future update of this book or on the website, then please either send this by letter to Logaston Press, Woonton, Hereford HR3 6QH, or via the email contact on the website: www.slowtraveluk.com

PAYBACK TIME

There's a tradition in places like the Alps or the English Lake District to encourage visitors to offer some form of payback to local communities at a destination to say 'thanks for the stay'. This is sometimes referred to as tourism payback. For every copy sold of the guide a small donation will be made to Ludlow 21, which promotes sustainable living in Ludlow and surrounding borders. That is my payback for the enjoyment of this outstanding borderland area.

CONTENTS

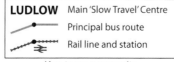

LUDLOW	Main 'Slow Travel' Centre
	Principal bus route
	Rail line and station

Key to map opposite

🚌	Bus Station, interchange or principal bus stop	🌿	National Trust property
●	Bus stop	🍺	Pub
⛺🚐	Camp site	🚂	Railway and station
🏰	Castle	**WC**	Toilets
✝	Cathedral, Abbey	*i*	Tourist information centre
✝✝✝	Churches, Chapel	**V**	Visitor centre
❀	Gardens	⋯	Walk route
Ⓜ	Museum		

Key to maps used in the text

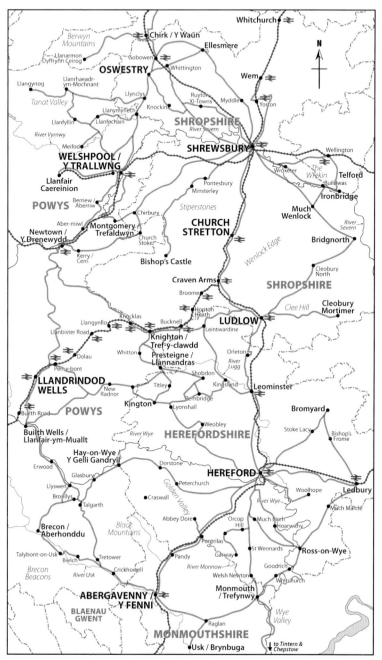

The Marches, showing the places covered and train and main bus routes used

SLOW TRAVEL

Some years ago I made a remarkable journey through the Marches on foot. It is possible, of course, to drive from one end to the other of this rural paradise in the time it takes to enjoy a leisurely lunch. But what pleasure is there in that? My idea was to turn the modern concept of travel on its head, to reject 'fast' and ease into a world which moves more slowly. The tour covered 110 miles and took ten days. Ten days of walking and on each and every day the pleasure grew as the story of the Marches unfolded. It unfolded in a landscape narrative that features ridges and valleys, etched out of bedrock limestone and rich red sandstones. It unfolded in meandering routes across water meadows, where paths run alongside sylvan rivers and their tree-like tributaries. It unfolded along lonely lanes leading to villages, hamlets and towns; towns where the locals rarely see the need to experience life outside their own place. Most of all, it unfolded in locality, in the vernacular, those abiding farmsteads, home orchards, corrugated barns and field patterns dating back to the days of enclosure.

The ten days of absorbing everyday life in this part of rural Britain turned out to be good. It involved capturing insights of a world which could only be gained when travelling slowly. The layered experience of walking through history was pieced into an intricate mosaic, sometimes one that raised uneasy subjects: of survival against the odds, of power and control, of ingrained rural poverty and of turbulent times, where the use of the sword and bow were commonplace. But these locales were also redolent of peaceful and fruitful times, when carpenters and stonemasons put their skills to good use and horse and cart plied between farm and field at harvest time.

These reflections were all scribbled down in a notepad to be unpicked at some future date. There was, for example, a cool breeze when treading the path of the ancient tribes along the Portway, and a haunting feeling of a township that failed to survive at Richard's Castle. This way of travel, of recalling the highlights of the day, was rounded off by a first person account of wayside inns, hostelries that have defied the tide of contemporary closure, the likes of The Mytton Arms at Habberley, The Dog Inn at Ewyas Harold, The Carpenter's Arms at Walterstone and The Goose and Cuckoo at Upper Llanover. These are memorable places offering local food and drink, places that serve their communities well.

Once the adventure was over I felt a need to share this unforgettable experience and several return visits later, an unofficial trail *Marches Way* was written up as a small token of gratitude, a payback for my enjoyment. It was also meant to encourage others to cast adrift and enjoy a way of life that is enhanced by gaining a sense of place and by doing things on foot, by cycling or sometimes with a little help from everyday buses and trains. But there remained a need to do more than to pen *Marches Way*; this book has been in the making for some years.

It has become increasingly obvious in recent years that travel *per se* has become somewhat unfashionable. Instead tourism talk is of fast transits, fast tracking, fast consumption and fast feedback on facebook. But be reassured, the tide is turning. There is something of a renaissance in slow travel, where the journey is as important as the destination and in some cases *is* the destination. It is coming back as a way of travel across Europe, not only in the Alps and across Italy, but also in northern Spain and France, Germany and Scandinavia too, where closeness to nature is treasured. We should join in this celebration of slow travel right here, right now and on our own patch. The Marches offer an entirely suitable destination. That is where *Slow Travel in the Marches* comes in.

This book explains how best to enjoy the Marches by engaging with the area rather than just driving through it. Instead, plan a walk across those hills, cycle down its lanes at a pace that suits or sit back on local buses and trains to admire those views and dream a little. Any one of these options might possibly take up two, three or more days, depending on your route and the extent to which you are willing to get side-tracked. The art of the detour is one which requires cultivation and the Marches is an ideal place to foster the habit.

Slow Travel in the Marches does not fit neatly into the image that comes to mind when you skip through the pages of a glossy holiday brochure. It's a way of travel that demands a different approach. Slow travel frees you, so that you can see more, talk with people and see what's going on in market towns. Most of all, it is about time. In its crudest sense, you are trading in distance for time. You might cover less ground but what you get is far richer. With slow travel there's no need to bag tourism trophies, no advantage in notching up mile after mile, and no hard sell package to keep up with as the week passes by. It's just a matter of relaxing and getting closer to culture and nature at the places you visit. That closeness brings a really satisfying feeling. It is also a desire to be released from constraints and day to day responsibilities so as to be more responsive to what comes along. Not that it is all spontaneity or relaxation. Every form of travel, from the donkey ride to the high speed train, brings pain as well as joy but as the doyen of travel writing Paul Theroux points out, it is the overall experience that counts at the end of the day. That includes the good, the bad and sometimes, admittedly, on very rare occasions, the ugly.

Michael Palin, travel explorer extraordinaire, has recently argued that home is a good starting point for any exploration; there's no need to travel thousands of miles when you have so much on your doorstep! He is right, and this book is as much for people who live in or near the Marches who want to learn more about their own patch as for those who want to take a look at someone else's corner of paradise. The Marches will give you an extra welcome as by travelling the slow way your carbon footprint will be light. The task of the book is to provide a basic toolkit for exploration of this part of the UK. The book is supported and updated by a website, www.slowtraveluk.com, so take a look at that too.

The main aim, however, is to rekindle an interest in slow travel. It follows a similar path to that of the Slow Food movement which campaigns for good, wholesome and fair food. Slow travel calls for us to put the travel experience back into the journey, to engage locally and with a light environmental touch. The book shows how you can do this; it is packed with ideas for holidays and days out that capture the very essence of slow travel. There is an opportunity to explore some of the very best of the Marches, to create your own story of time and place, in a way that stirs the imagination. Take the chance. It beats sitting in an airport lounge any day!

*Plate 1 The River Arrow at Eardisland on a dreamy day,
a village reachable by bus from Leominster*

Plate 2 The Marches are full of quiet spots

Plates 3-10 The Marches are ideal for slow travel: Above: buses in Acton Burnell (Shropshire) and Weobley (Herefordshire); and Shrewsbury Station in deep snow
Right: a steam special on the Marches line; pony trekking
Opposite: cycling near Ludlow, Shropshire; a cyclist, bikers and a pub in Herefordshire; a train on the Marches line with Stokesay Castle to the right, Shropshire

Plates 11-13 The Marches exude an atmosphere of calm and welcome you to join in. Above: the bar in the Bull's Head at Craswall, reachable after a good walk, pony trek or cycle ride from Hay

The towns offer a wide range of individual shops and cafés.
Plate 14 Above: Fodder Wholefood shop in Church Street, Hereford
Plate 15 Below: The Abergavenny Book Shop

Plate 16 Above: Maltsters Coffee Shop and Wigmores bakery, Monnmouth
Plate 17 Below: The Blue Note Café in Leominster

Plates 18-19 The Marches offer a huge variety of walking, from level paths by canals and rivers to the open hillsides of the Long Mynd and Black Mountains. Above, walkers descend the hills at Stowe with Knighton in the background

THE MARCHES

To the Victorians the railways were one of the main pillars of modernity. The arrival of the railway at any town of note was greeted with pomp and ceremony that would make many 21st-century opening ceremonies look a little on the meagre side. In the Marches, tourism came hot on the heels of the railways as destinations geared up to welcome visitors who had previously not had the wherewithal to travel. Places such as Church Stretton, Llandrindod Wells, and even the smaller settlements of Raglan and Tintern were all given a boost, much to the chagrin of residents reluctant to accept the new wave of visitors. But tourism had already arrived in the Marches; there had been a flurry some fifty or so years before with the growth of romanticism.

Travel writers have always been drawn here, even from the earliest days of tourism, when pilgrimages were giving way to the era of the grand tour. They came in their droves to write about their particular experience of this rural idyll. Painters and poets, the romantic picturesque movement; they all came to visit. In fact, it was a magnet to many of the great artistic names, the likes of Coleridge, Borrow, Gilpin, Wordsworth and Turner. They were all deeply enchanted by the place. Each one has trodden an ancient path or taken a carriage down green lanes to sketch or paint the scenery or to record their recollections on nature for posterity. Sculptors, classical composers, rock musicians and muses, diarists and designers have been attracted since; many chose to stay and that is as true now as in previous times. This place is good for creativity. The Marches has an enigmatic quality that is hard to put your finger on; it is there for those who reach out to it.

In this book, 'the Marches' (meaning 'Borderlands') is used to describe the diverse landscape where England meets Wales. The book concentrates on a geographical area that might be considered as the mid Marches, an area spanning the counties of Herefordshire, Shropshire, the eastern parts of Powys and Monmouthshire and a small wedge of rural Wrexham. To be geographically correct the area should be referred to as The Welsh Marches, to distinguish them from the Scottish or Italian Marches. In reality, it is an indeterminate area that has been contested by Welsh and Celtic tribes, Anglo Saxon kings and last, but certainly not least, the Normans. The struggle for power and ascendancy has left a cultural legacy that is unmistakable; there are more motte and bailey castles here per hectare than anywhere else in the UK.

In tourism circles the term 'The Marches' has been side-lined but it has never been entirely lost. If you 'google' the term on the internet, you'll find it is alive and well. Many of the old guide books chose to use the term and this book continues that tradition.

Landscape

The landscape of the Marches has a presence that draws the traveller in; nature and humans working together to create a patchwork that has an enduring appeal to those who tread its ways. It is a landscape that unravels in a way that demands attention. There are pockets of simple architectural brilliance, unique natural habitats and farming patterns that change from one village to the next. It is not only the appeal of those parched outlines, the bluffs, knolls and scarps that nudge toward the skyline but also the gentler, rolling hills. The Long Mynd and Hay Bluff, the Brecon Beacons and the Radnorshire Forest are for those who seek wilder parts where the wind is in your face. They are places for those with a sense of adventure, where mountain bikes, bivouacs and buzzards are the buzz-words. This is the high bare ground of the Welsh border and above all else, it is sheep farming country. Of the 32 million sheep reared each year in the UK it seems as if most of them are here on the green grass of the Marches.

The gentler escarpments and plateaux, found mainly in Herefordshire, Monmouthshire and Shropshire, have an equally stimulating appeal for those seeking to get closer to the outdoors and nature. The wooded slopes of Wenlock Edge, Grinshill, Woolhope Dome or Trelleck plateau have much to offer the geologist and naturalist seeking out hidden fossils and woodland habitats. Many of these hills remain the subject of folklore, places that evoke old legends, such as the Pyons in Herefordshire or the Stiperstones in the Shropshire Hills.

The valleys reveal the gentler side of the Marches. They present a peacefulness that can be unnerving; it is as if the tranquillity should never be broken. Even if the tractors are bigger and faster than we'd like and the agricultural wagons fill the road, they are only momentary distractions. There's no better place to gaze across than the farmland of the Clun or Golden Valleys; places where there is an enduring calm.

It is to the river valleys of the Marches that we look for refuge; they have done much to shape the settlements which we now seek to visit. The verdant canopy of the riverside revels in many shades of green where moss and ivy crowd the crumbling banks. The lesser known tributaries are constantly at work eroding banks and depositing sands or gravels downstream. These smaller rivers had much less potential for navigation and flow through narrower, steep-sided valleys so remain less populated, especially in their upper reaches. They include the Arrow, Cain, Cam, Clun, Ceiriog, Irfon, Ithon, Lugg, Monnow, Onny, and Teme. Each one has a distinctly different character, but in every case, fresh waters babble over the bedrock and meander by alders and marshy water meadows. These are the habitats of the otter and kingfisher, heron and water vole.

The Severn, Wye and Usk are the grand rivers of the borders, and forge their way between countries without ceremony. They have been the significant transport corridors over the centuries, initially for the early warrior, the medieval merchant and now the leisure traveller. The wide river plains have provided a fertile base for a mixed farming economy. However, it is to their tributaries that we return time and time again to absorb the true spirit of the Marches; they exhibit such diversity and just beg to be explored on foot or by bike.

The Marches landscape includes much ancient parkland where fallow deer roam and age-old oaks stand majestically apart. Fragments of the great hunting parks have survived from medieval times, for example, at Moccas in Herefordshire or Mortimer Forest near Ludlow. These harbour rich thickets and woodland where flora and wildlife flourish. They also illustrate land stewardship through the centuries for the production of wood, forest fruits, venison or other game. The many hedgerows, steeped in the history of enclosure, act as temporary refuges for wildlife and shape meadow, pasture and ploughed field alike into a tapestry that changes colour with the seasons. High hedgerows, more prevalent in the western reaches, include the fruit of yesteryear, the damson (including the suitably named Shropshire Prune), and the lesser known bullace, crab apple and cob nut.

In many parts of the Marches, orchards define the landscape character. The orderliness of the old cider or perry orchards, lined with tall standards, some of which are more than two hundred years old, deserves nothing less than admiration. Now this order is often broken by the wind, old age or neglect. But some trees still remain productive, ragged though they might be, if only to make a single batch of farmhouse cider to be matured in the barn. For the most part, standard orchards have been replaced by a contemporary mass bush planting. The modern orchard, row upon row of dwarf trees cultivated for ease of picking, still offers a haven for wildlife, especially if free from pesticides. They also look attractive. Orchards, to be honest, have come and gone over the ages with the variability of markets, but now there is real interest once more and a focus on the older, rarer local varieties too.

History of the Marches
The contrast between the richer soils of the lowlands, principally around the Severn and Wye plains, and the less fertile uplands of the Brecon Beacons, Black Mountains and Radnorshire Forest has had a great influence. It has determined to a certain extent the way in which the Marches has evolved as a contested and somewhat indeterminate borderland.

The earliest of settlers, the prehistoric tribes that frequented the ridges and wood covered plateaux, have left their mark in the Marches but it is something of a task to detail the succession of these early settlements. One marker is Arthur's Cave near Symond's Yat (estimated at 8000BC) but there are many sites spanning the Neolithic and Bronze ages through to the more numerous Iron Age sites (around 1000BC). These are fine examples of ancient camps, hillforts, or places of burial where you can gain some insights into a very different world of defence, trading and cultural change. These are evidenced on the ground at fortified camps such as Croft Ambrey and Sutton Walls in Herefordshire, Caer Caradoc at Church Stretton or the old Oswestry hillfort in Shropshire. These Iron Age forts represent the last bastions of Celtic occupation, places where the Cornovii and Dubonni tribes held sway.

The Celts were severely repressed during the Roman occupation, which lasted approximately three centuries from AD43 onwards, a period described by the late archaeologist C.S Stanford as being a short and untidy episode. Nevertheless, there are many Roman sites throughout the Marches. For the Romans this really was a frontier territory. Roman camps at Usk, Kenchester and Wroxeter illustrate their way of life; the latter is by far the most extensive site to visit. There are other pockets of evidence such as the Roman roads of Watling Street in Leintwardine and Church Stretton and mining at Llanymynech and Shelve in the Shropshire Hills.

The period beyond the Roman withdrawal, from about 400 through to 1066, is often referred to as The Dark Ages, although archaeologists argue that this is a misnomer as there were flourishing cultures across Britain. In relation to the Marches, it has been characterised as a world dominated by tribal princedoms in Wales and England, principally the two buffer zones of Powys and Mercia. It was a time when two early and remarkable boundary structures were built: Wat's Dyke, possibly in the 5th century and Offa's Dyke in the 8th century. This was also an age of Christian mission amid pagan culture, and early Saxon monasteries at Leominster and Much Wenlock were established. It was also a period of Anglo Saxon infiltration where disputed borderlands, the likes of New Radnor, became anglicised.

The Norman legacy in the Marches is impressive. The imprint of a new political and legal structure, characterised by manorial systems, is significant. The division of lands, patronage and payment of dues were inextricably linked to Norman control. This was signified by an almost standard layout of the motte and bailey castle, almost invariably with a Norman church and a walled settlement alongside. This form of planned development was contested by the native tribal enclaves, located mainly in the isolated uplands of Wales. For centuries they made violent incursions into this imposed order that sought to destroy a Welsh way of life. Even during the more peaceful interludes there were periods when the Marches suffered from infighting and political intrigue between the Norman lordships themselves.

It was only when the monarchs of England became more assertive and began to temper the aspirations of Marches lordships that some semblance of peace was established. The Norman influence is imprinted on almost every village and town of the Marches; there are hundreds of castle mounds to bear witness to their domination. However, the new order also meant a change in agricultural practices

CIDER AND PERRY

The Marches are partly defined by their orchards. They are renowned especially for the cultivation of the cider apple and the perry pear, picked each autumn to make traditional alcoholic beverages. Hereford is home to the giant producer, H.P. Bulmer, which is now part of the global Heineken corporation. Over the years H.P. Bulmer has planted many orchards and taken a real interest in the advocacy of cider as a pleasant beverage. The Marches is also home to an increasing number of small scale craft producers, the likes of Dunkertons Cider at Pembridge, Greg's Pit at Much Marcle, Olivers at Ocle Pychard, Ralph's at New Radnor and Ty-Bryn Cider in the Monnow Valley.

It is all about authenticity, or as some would say, the provenance of the product. This is no ordinary drink but one which has for centuries been crafted in the Marches with great skill. In recent years, a number of producers have joined together to ensure that a quality product survives for the future. For example, several perry producers have established a Three Counties Perry Slow Food Presidium that seeks to retain a product, almost unique to this area, for an increasingly discerning market. For more details about the Presidium and outlets for real perry (rather than the standard fizzy mass produced pear cider) take a look at www.slowfoodfoundation.com.

The making of these traditional beverages relies on a good supply of cider apples and perry pears. Many of the trees from which the varieties are picked are now old and rare and thus supply is limited. Some growers have begun to replant or re-invigorate orchards as demand for the real thing continues to grow. This can only help to improve local landscapes and biodiversity as these orchards tend to be planted with standard and half standard trees. Local councils and groups, such as The Marcher Apple Network, are also working alongside nurseries to re-kindle this traditional landscape (see www.marcherapple.net). Some villages have also joined in the process too. You can see the good work of community orchards at, for example, Eardisley, Kingsland and Knucklas.

and more extensive building. This brought about the depletion of the extensive tracts of woodlands across the Marches. These were replaced by pasture and arable farming, some already within the hands of ecclesiastical dynasties and others following more modest strip farming practices around the manorial villages. In due course, the monasteries, priories and monastic granges of medieval times gave way, during the Dissolution of the 16th century, to new forms of churches and education.

It was only in later medieval times that the fortified manor house signalled a major change in the borderland. A visit to Tretower Court in the Usk valley or Stokesay Castle near Craven Arms illustrates perfectly how land-owning families increasingly chose comfort over defence in the design of their houses. The turbulent medieval period was followed by more peaceful times under the Tudors and even more so during the prosperous Georgian era. This was the period of great houses and extensive parkland reflecting esteem and influence. It was an age when brick became more prevalent in buildings and glass came into more common use so as to make properties so much more light and airy. Merchants deployed their surplus wealth in the rebuilding of town houses throughout the settlements of the Marches. It was also a time when early industrial processes took shape and transport innovations brought increased business to all sectors. This was evidenced mainly in the larger towns but also the market towns.

Market towns and villages
In past times the market place was where you met others, mainly for the transaction of business and the buying of provisions. It was also a place where news was conveyed by word of mouth as literacy levels were low. Gossip in the taverns, inns and during later periods, coffee shops, was an integral part of market town life in the Marches. However, transport was a limiting factor. All of this had to be within a half day's walk or by horse or cart; thus market towns tend to be about 8-15 miles apart. Some of the least populated places eventually lost their market status when roads began to be improved and greater distances could be covered in a day; these include the old townships of Grosmont, Llanrhaedr-ym-Mochnant, Leintwardine and Pembridge.

Other towns gained ascendancy, for example, Abergavenny and Oswestry, as they reaped the early benefits of improved roads then railways. With a considerable improvement to public transport in the first part of the 20th century, followed by an inexorable rise of private car travel, patterns have changed. People now travel further than ever before to fulfil the simple things in life. Nevertheless, the market towns are holding their own as many people simply do not want to travel miles to do their everyday shopping.

Generally speaking the market towns retain their role as places to meet people and access local services. Many of the traditional cattle markets have moved out of town, although Bishop's Castle, Kington and Knighton are notable exceptions. Most still have a market day where stalls are set out in the streets but unfortunately, in many cases, these are now small affairs. Supermarkets and internet sales have made significant inroads on both high street shops and market traders. There are exceptions. The Tuesday market at Abergavenny seems to go from strength to strength and with the advent of slow food, butchers and bakers seem to be holding on remarkably well and greengrocers and delis are returning.

Each town brings a different character to the Marches. Some are more laid back in style, such as Bishop's Castle, Kington and Presteigne; others have a bustle to them, as at Brecon, Monmouth and Welshpool. There are those with a distinctly

Edwardian feel, principally Church Stretton and Llandrindod Wells, and several exude that era of Georgian prosperity as with Cleobury Mortimer, Leominster and Ross-on-Wye. Thus, despite the impact of communications and mobility, market towns retain their role as meeting places. Some have carved out new identities. Abergavenny and Ludlow are rated for their food festivals and Hay-on-Wye is the original 'book town'. Ludlow is undeniably the capital of the Marches in terms of heritage and Shrewsbury possesses one of the finest Tudor enclaves in the UK. Hereford is defined by its cathedral quarter and rejoices in its 1,200 years of ecclesiastical heritage.

The villages have fought, above all else, to hold on to the values of small scale, rural communities. Many have also sought to invest in their heritage, whether that it be a legacy of mining, as in the Ceiriog Valley, or the magical patterns of half-timbered carpentry, as in the Black and White Villages of Herefordshire. This is a positive and noticeable development across the Marches in recent years with improved information about places and more community-led facilities. Examples of this are the Angel public house in Grosmont, Wigmore Community stores and the Talgarth mill project. A growing number of projects seek to nurture commons and nature reserves across the area. The book seeks to encourage exploration of these places. In the end, it is a matter of choice as to where and how you explore what is on offer but it is good to know what is feasible on foot, cycle or public transport.

In the Marches you can still absorb elements of rural life long since gone or diminished elsewhere. There's still an opportunity to relish everyday ways of life in these communities by staying at a local bed and breakfast, camp site or holiday cottage. So many things about this part of the world appeal to the passions of the slow traveller: travel which means something, locality, slow food and the natural world. Enjoy the very best that the Marches have to offer.

HOW TO USE THE GUIDE

The guide is divided into eight sections based on key towns, all of which are served by a railway. They are as follows:

Shrewsbury
Oswestry (served by Gobowen)
Welshpool
Church Stretton
Ludlow
Llandrindod Wells
Hereford
Abergavenny

In each section there's a description of the town or city and a 'walk around' section to help you navigate about the place if you have not been before. This is an exploration on foot, but with some minor modifications these can be enjoyed by cycle. A main attraction is highlighted, although you may choose to differ and spend your time at another attraction or simply explore what appeals to you at the time. There is some information about other attractions and some pointers with regard to refreshment (these are simply a personal selection) and any additional information is provided in an 'extras' section.

From these key centres, a number of outings are recommended to places served by bus/ train or, in some cases, readily accessed by cycle. These are described as day outings and follow a similar format, for the most part, to the main centres described above. In some cases it is possible to travel to a day excursion destination from a wide range of locations. For example, a trip to Craven Arms could easily be made from the south (Ludlow, Hereford and Abergavenny) or the north (Church Stretton and Shrewsbury) as described. The information sources listed below as well as those provided on the slowtraveluk.com website will help you to navigate your way across the public transport network.

However, you may be tempted to stay at these places rather than just make a day visit; the choice is yours. For example, Brecon and Hay-on-Wye are popular haunts that can be reached by bus from the railheads of Hereford, Abergavenny or Newtown (mid Wales).

In each section opportunities for walking and cycling in the area are summarised. You might wish to walk one day and cycle the next, depending on place and facilities. However, the author appreciates that some readers will be here in the Marches for a tour and the cycling or walking route chosen will be the focus of the holiday. In that case, the guide provides background information.

SLOW TRAVEL NETWORK

The slow travel network combines all modes of transport that don't involve driving in your own tin box. Public transport, hire of cycles and walking holidays for the active traveller are provided by a wide range of companies and organisations. If you are looking for more detailed information then it will be necessary to look up the website for a specific company. For example, if you have a detailed enquiry about rail travel for the disabled passenger, then check it out on www.nationalrail.co.uk/disabled.

Here are the contact details for the main information providers and companies:

TRAINS

The information system for train travel is really good and you can easily check train times, fares and other matters such as how many bikes a train can take (usually two per train on most trains in the Marches).

There's one central enquiry number for all train times (24 hours daily) Tel: 08457 48 49 50.

There's one key website for all rail enquiries: www.nationalrail.co.uk. This provides core information and a journey planner.

When you need up-to-the-minute train information call Train Tracker: 0871 200 49 50.

Four principal train operating companies run the routes within the Marches:

Arriva Trains Wales: www.arrivatrainswales.co.uk.

Birmingham International to Aberystwyth and Pwllheli via Shrewsbury and Welshpool (Cambrian Line).

Cardiff to Merthyr Tydfil (for Brecon Beacons).

Cardiff to Gloucester via Chepstow.

Holyhead to Cardiff via Chester, Wrexham, Shrewsbury, Hereford and Abergavenny and intermediate stations.

Manchester to Carmarthen and Milford Haven via Crewe, Shrewsbury, Hereford, Abergavenny and intermediate stations (Marches Line).

Swansea to Shrewsbury via Llandrindod Wells (Heart of Wales Line).

First Great Western: www.firstgreatwestern.co.uk.

London Paddington to Swansea via Newport (change at Newport for the Marches Line).

London Paddington to Hereford via Ledbury.

London Midland: www.londonmidland.com.

Birmingham New Street to Hereford via Ledbury.

Birmingham to Shrewsbury via Wellington.

BUSES

The provision of bus services across the Marches lies in the hands of dozens of bus companies, ranging from corporate giants such as First Bus to small companies such as Abbey Cars in Herefordshire. Most bus companies operate with vehicles that accommodate disabled passengers but not all buses meet the needs, for example, of wheelchair users. It is best to check before you travel with the bus company concerned.

There are an increasing number of attractive day tickets available. The Powys Day Rover and Herefordshire Sunday Rover, for example, offer good value, as do some of the specific company day tickets.

Please note that many bus companies do not allow the carriage of animals and in some cases it remains at the discretion of the driver on duty. This is an important factor to bear in mind if you have a dog with you.

The information system for buses is called 'traveline', Tel: 0871 200 22 33. The website address for 'traveline' is www.traveline.info. It provides a journey planner and timetable information.

The main bus operators are as follows:

Arriva Midlands North: www.arrivabus.co.uk.
    Principal services are:
    Ludlow to
        Bridgnorth: Service number 141
        Knighton: Service number 738, 740
    Oswestry to
        Ellesmere: Service number 53
        Llanymynech: Service number 71
    Shrewsbury town services and park and ride
    Shrewsbury to
        Bishop's Castle (Sundays only): Service number 553
        Ironbridge: Service number 81
        Ellesmere (Sundays only): Service number 501
        Much Wenlock: Service number 436
        Pulverbatch (for Shropshire Hills): Service Number 546
        Oswestry: Service Number 71, 576
        Wellington: Service Number 96
        Wem: Service Number 511

Bryn Melyn Ltd: www.brynmelyn.co.uk.
    Shrewsbury to Ellesmere (Not Sundays) : Service Number 501

DRM: no website; Tel: (01885) 483219.
    Hereford to
        Bromyard: Service Number 420, 469
        Ledbury: Service Number 476

First Midland Red: www.firstgroup.com.
  Hereford town services (most of them)
  Hereford to
    Bromyard: Service Number 420
    Ludlow: Service Number 492 (Sundays only)
    Ludlow to Kidderminster via Cleobury Mortimer: Service Number 292 (Mondays to Saturdays only-Sunday service operated by Central Connect)

GHA Coaches: www.ghacoaches.co.uk
  Llangollen to Llanarmon via Chirk: Service Number 64/64A

Lugg Valley: no website. Tel: (01432) 356201,
  Hereford to Ludlow via Leominster: Service Number 492
      (Mondays to Saturdays only)
  Leominster town services
  Leominster to
    Hereford via Dinmore: Service Number 492
    Hereford via Canon Pyon: Service Number 501
    Hereford via Bodenham: Service Number 426
    Kington via Pembridge: Service Number 495-7
    Presteigne via Pembridge: Service Number 493/4

Minsterley Motors: www.minsterleymotors.co.uk.
  Ludlow to Pontesbury via Bishop's Castle: Service Number 745
  Shrewsbury to
    Bishop's Castle: Service Number 553 (Mondays to Saturdays only)
    Ludlow: Service Number 435
    Stiperstones: Service Number 552

Sargeant Brothers: www.sargeantsbros.com.
  Hereford to Llandrindod Wells via Kington and New Radnor:
      Service Number 461-463

Sixty Sixty Coaches: www.sixtysixty.co.uk.
  Abergavenny to Cardiff via Brecon: Service Number X43

Stagecoach (Wye and Dean/South Wales): www.stagecoachbus.com.
  Hereford to
    Brecon via Hay-on-Wye (Mondays to Saturdays only): Service Number 39
    Cardiff via Abergavenny: Service Number X4
    Garway: Service Number 412
    Monmouth: Service Number 416
    Ross-on-Wye: Service Number 38
  Monmouth to
    Chepstow (Sundays only): Service Number 69
    Newport (Sundays only): Service Number 60
  Ross-on-Wye to
    Ledbury: Service Number 45
    Monmouth: Service Number 34

Veolia Transport Cymru: www.veolia-transport.co.uk.
Abergavenny town services
Brecon town services
Abergavenny to Builth Wells: Service Number X12
Abergavenny to Monmouth: Service Number 83 (Mondays to Saturdays)
Kington to Newtown via Presteigne, Knighton and Beguildy: Service Number 41
Llandrindod Wells to Builth: Service Number 47
Ludlow to Builth Wells: Service Number X11

Yeomans Canyon Travel: no website. Tel: (01432) 356201
Hereford town services (some)
Hereford to
Brecon via Hay-on-Wye (Sundays only): Service Number 39A
Eardisley and Almeley: Service Number 446
Madley: Service Number 449
Woolhope: Service Number 453

Top Ten Scenic Bus Rides in The Marches			
Bus Route	Description	Bus Company	Days of operation
X11	Ludlow to Builth Wells	Veolia	Mon & Thurs only
X15/445	Hereford to Builth Wells	Veolia; Roy Brown's Coaches	Wed & Sat only
39/39A	Hereford to Brecon	Stagecoach, Yeomans	Daily
412	Hereford to Broad Oak via Garway	Stagecoach	Mon – Sat
461	Hereford to Llandrindod Wells	Sargeants Motors	Mon – Sat
493-7	Leominster to Kington/ Presteigne	Lugg Valley Primrose	Mon – Sat
552	Shrewsbury to Bishop's Castle	Minsterley Motors/ Arriva	Daily
745	Ludlow to Pontesbury	Minsterley Motors	Mon & Fri only
Offa's Dyke Flyer	Hay-on-Wye to Capel-y-ffin, Longtown and return	Roy Brown's Coaches	Summer Sun only
Shropshire Hills Shuttles	Church Stretton to the Long Mynd and Stiperstones	Shropshire Council	Summer weekends only

BUS AND TRAIN INFORMATION FROM LOCAL AUTHORITIES

The following local authorities provide public transport information and up to the minute local advice which can be very helpful.

Wrexham Borough County Council (for services around Chirk):
It is possible to download timetables from its web page: www.wrexham.gov.uk/english/travel/bus.

Shropshire Council:
provides printed timetable leaflets for those services which it supports financially. These are sometimes available in visitor information centres and libraries. Otherwise, the Council refers visitors to traveline (see above) or transport direct (www.transportdirect.info).

Powys County Council:
produces a Bus and Rail Guide, available free, from visitor information centres and libraries. The timetables are less easy to read than others but the book is packed with information. Up to the minute information can be obtained on www.powysbus.info.

Herefordshire Council:
produces three superb area bus and train timetables which are great for visitors. A small charge is made for each one. They are available at local tourist information offices or from Herefordshire Council: Public Transport Information, Transportation, Herefordshire Council, PO Box 236, Plough Lane, Hereford, HR4 OWZ. There is a charge for a set of timetables and updates. Tel: (01432) 260211. Information, contact details and updates available on www.herefordbus.info.

Monmouthshire County Council (for services around Abergavenny and Monmouth):
provides a great little pocket guide to bus services, available free from visitor information offices. Timetables are also available on www.monmouthshire.gov.uk. Look on the website menu for the 'transport and streets' section then 'Find your timetable'.

BUS AND RAIL TICKETS

The rail companies offer a range of single, return and season tickets in addition to rover tickets. They also offer seasonal special offers such as Arriva Trains Wales Club 55 promotion in the autumn.

By far the best ticket for holiday travel by train and bus through the Marches is the *Explore Wales Pass*, especially if you wish to extend your trip through Wales. Check it out at www.walesflexipass.com.

The main bus companies, Arriva, First and Stagecoach have a range of day travel tickets available but these are for use on their services only. There are some network tickets which can be used on a number of bus companies. The *Network Rider* ticket in South Wales offers great value and is available in the Abergavenny and Monmouth area as well as down to Cardiff. Another network ticket is the Powys Day Rover which is valid on most buses in Powys (including some cross border services except the 39 Hereford to Brecon and 445 Hereford to Llandrindod Wells service). See www slowtravelinthemarches.com for more detailed information regarding tickets. Bus tickets are usually available from the bus driver (although in some cases a company may accept the ticket but not issue it).

CANOES AND KAYAKS

There are several companies offering canoe or kayak holidays or day adventures, mainly on the River Wye but also on the River Severn and the Brecon and Monmouthshire Canal.

Here is a selection of companies that can help:

Adventure River: based in Monmouth, www.adventureriver.co.uk.

Black Mountain: based in Brecon Beacons, www.blackmountain.co.uk.

Celtic Canoes: located at Glasbury-on-Wye, www.celticcanoes.co.uk.

Monmouth Canoe Co: based at Monmouth, www.monmouthcanoe.co.uk.

Paddles & Pedals: located in Hay-on-Wye, www.paddlesandpedals.co.uk.

The Canoe Hire Company: based in Ross-on-Wye, www.thecanoehire.co.uk.

Wye Canoes: based at Symond's Yat, www.wyecanoes.com.

Wyedean Canoe and Adventure Centre, located at Symond's Yat, www.wyedean.co.uk.

COACHES

These are mainly from London to Hereford and Shrewsbury, but there are some other services, for example, from Birmingham to Abergavenny, Brecon, Monmouth, Oswestry and Welshpool.

The main scheduled coach operator is National Express: www.nationalexpress.com.

CYCLING

Most cycle routes in the Marches involve cycling along country lanes and in many cases you will encounter hills, although bikes with low gear ratios make this easier than first imagined. There are some off road leisure routes as in the Forest of Dean and The Peregrine Trail from Monmouth. There's a good 'rail trail' out of Govilon near Abergavenny using an old railway trackbed into the Clydach Valley.

By far the best way to look for routes to suit your needs is to log onto the wheelywonderfulcycling.co.uk website and press the 'maps' button. This highlights a range of guides, maps and itineraries available and for sale. These are ideal for planning a cycling break in the Marches.

Over the past 25 years many cycle tourism companies have come and gone. Standing out above all others are three companies that have spent much time developing cycling tourism in the Marches. Collectively they offer some great cycling opportunities. These are (in alphabetical order):

Bicycle Beano: who trade out of Erwood in the Wye Valley near to Builth Wells. They offer very special guided cycle tours, www.bicycle-beano.co.uk.

Pedalabikeaway: located in the village of Llangarron between Ross-on-Wye and Monmouth. They offer cycle tours but also have several day hire bases which include the Forest of Dean, Govilon and Monmouth, www.pedalabikeaway.co.uk.

Wheely Wonderful: based in an idyllic position amid orchards at Elton near Ludlow, offer cycle tours with flair and are renowned for their friendliness and detailed knowledge of the best cycling routes throughout the Marches, www.wheelywonderfulcycling.co.uk.

Other companies include:

Byways Breaks: offer self-guided cycle tours of the Marches, www.bywaysbreaks.co.uk

Drover Holidays: located at Hay-on-Wye, www.droverholidays.co.uk.

Walk or Bike Wales: based near Abergavenny, www.walkorbikewales.com.

Cycle hire and repair shops are listed at each destination.

HORSE RIDING

The guide does not feature opportunities for horse riding in any detail. There are a small number of exceptionally beautiful routes suitable for horse-riding and trekking, especially in the Brecon Beacons, Radnorshire and Shropshire Hills. Two long standing routes are Jack Mytton Way through Shropshire and the Radnor Loop. But the word is that it is best to talk to those offering stabling or holidays before you plump for a riding break as their detailed knowledge is second to none.

The following useful contacts are for those interested in taking a holiday on horseback:

Free Rein: Clyro near Hay-on-Wye, riding in the Radnorshire Hills and Wye Valley, www.free-rein.co.uk.

Ellesmere Riding Centre, Llangors, near Brecon, riding in the Brecon Beacons, www.ellesmereridingcentre.co.uk.

Lower Buckton Country House: riding in Mortimer Country, www.lowerbuckton.co.uk/bring_your_horse.htm.

Marches Horse Trails: riding the by ways of Shropshire Hills, www.marcheshorsetrails.co.uk.

Mill Farm Riding Centre: riding in and around Wenlock Edge, www.millfarmridingcentre.com.

Riding for the Disabled: riding at Baschurch near Shrewsbury, www.rda.org.uk.

Springhill Farm: situated near Chirk with routes in and around the Ceiriog Valley, www.atspringhill.co.uk.

Tregoyd Mountain Rides: near Hay-on-Wye and with routes in and around the Black Mountains, www.tregoydriding.co.uk.

TAXIS

Sometimes there's a need to get a taxi to accommodation or somewhere else not served by public transport. There's also the rare occasion when public transport fails so it is always useful to have the telephone number of a local taxi firm to hand. For up to the minute information check www.slowtraveluk.com.

WALKING

Footpaths, bridleways and roads used as public paths are managed by each respective local authority. The countryside and rights of way teams working in the Marches are doing a good job to open up the countryside for walking. These are the main long distance trails available:

Black and White Village Trail: 62 miles of gentle walking between Leominster and Kington. No special waymarks. Devised by David Gorvett and Les Lumsdon and written up in *The Black and White Village Trail* published by Scarthin Books.

Beacon's Way: 100 mile challenging walk across the Brecon Beacons from Abergavenny to Llangadog. Devised initially by the ex Brecon Beacons Park Society Secretary, the late John Sansom. Guide book available; path has special waymark roundels.

Herefordshire Trail: 150 mile circular walk devised by the Ramblers. Waymarked and guidebook available.

Glyndwr's Way: 135 mile national trail through very isolated countryside, dedicated to the Welsh warrior, Owain Glyndwr. Specially waymarked throughout route between Knighton and Welshpool.

Monnow Valley Walk: 40 mile walk from Hay-on-Wye and nearby source of River Monnow to its confluence with the River Wye at Monmouth. Specially waymarked; guide book available

Mortimer Trail: 30 mile specially signed ridge route between Ludlow and Kington. Guide book available.

Offa's Dyke National Trail: 177 mile, waymarked trail from Prestatyn in north Wales and Sedbury on the Severn estuary near Chepstow. Superb challenge that passes through the heart of the Marches.

Severn Valley Way: signed 210 mile route near to River Severn although the route in Shropshire follows mainly along back roads until Ironbridge.

Shropshire Way: there's great walking to be had on the Shropshire Way (Shropshire Hills) section, some 100 miles of waymarked routes from Shrewsbury south the Ludlow or Cleobury Mortimer. See www.shropshirewalking.co.uk for more detail.

Teme Valley Walk: 93 miles from the source, near Newtown to confluence at Worcester. No special waymarks; devised by David Milton and written up as *A Teme Valley Walk* published by Meridian Books

Usk Valley walk: 48 miles of walking between Brecon and Caerleon. Waymarked and with an official route guide available from bookshops and visitor information offices.

Wye Valley Walk: 136 mile walk from the source of the River Wye on the high ground of Plynlimon to its confluence with the River Severn near Chepstow. An astounding walk with great diversity. Guide book available.

There are a number of companies offering walking holidays in the Marches:

Byways Breaks: see cycling section for contact details.

Celtic Trails: located at Chepstow offering a wide range of walking holidays, www.celtrail.com.

Crown Border breaks: walking holidays based on the Crown Inn, Newcastle-on-Clun, www.ivyhousedesign.co.uk/borderbreaks.

Marches Walks: located in Glasbury-on-Wye, this long standing company offer a wide range of walking opportunities, www.marches-walks.co.uk.

Secret Hills Walking: based at Church Stretton, www.secrethillswalking. co.uk.

The Walking Holiday Company: based near Monmouth, www. thewalkingholidaycompany.co.uk.

Walk or Bike Wales: see cycling section for contact details.

Walk Herefordshire: based in Leominster and offers walking tours in the Marches, www.walkherefordshire.com.

Wheely Wonderful Cycling: also offer walking holidays, for example, on the Mortimer Trail – see cycling section for contact details.

SLOW TRAVEL WEBSITE

For more information about travel in the Marches you might also like to take a look at slowtraveluk.com. It is packed with slow travel ideas and updates about the slow travel network in the area.

SHREWSBURY

Shrewsbury is the largest of the Marches towns and shows to good effect the markers of its illustrious past as a central market and administrative seat of power. It was most certainly a Saxon settlement of note, presumably sited near to the fording points on the large loop of the Severn that literally contained development within the confines of the old town. What makes the place so special is a rich mixture of architectural styles dating from different periods and in such close proximity. There are so many listed buildings that it is scarcely believable that so many have survived.

The resilience of the merchant classes, who made money from wool and later from textiles and other manufactures, was a key factor. Their wealth endowed the town with Tudor, Georgian and Victorian properties, some of which fell to the ravages of 20th century development especially in the late 1950s and early 60s and with the advent of more recent industrial scale shopping centres, but many remain. Much of the town is superimposed on an earlier medieval grid. The passages and alleyways that thread between the main thoroughfares, the numerous churches and myriad of streets leading to and running along the old town walls are evidence enough of a centuries old layout. A mix of small independent shops, in the central area known as The Loop, combine to make this a major venue for those visiting the Marches.

The elegant façade of Shrewsbury railway station, dating from the 1850s, makes a fitting entrance to a town that combines architectural splendour with the functional necessities of contemporary city life. It oozes has a vibrancy that is not common in English towns. Perhaps it is the long list of festivals and events staged throughout the year, or maybe it can be put down simply to the hubbub of music and meetings in pubs, cafés and public venues that brings the town to life. Whatever the case, it has great riches to offer the slow traveller.

Shrewsbury remains as one of the great provincial hubs of train travel in England. Little trains leave from seemingly endless platforms to almost everywhere in the

The ornate façade of Shrewsbury railway station

Marches. There are regular services to Gobowen (for Oswestry), Welshpool, to Church Stretton, Ludlow, Leominster, Hereford and Abergavenny as well as the Heart of Wales line to Swansea via Craven Arms and Llandrindod Wells. Services operate every day of the week including Sundays. Shrewsbury is an even more important hub for radial, inter-town bus routes to places you'd really like to visit by train if only there were a station. These include Bishop's Castle, Ellesmere, Ironbridge, Montgomery, Much Wenlock, and Oswestry. Most of these bus services operate seven days a week, though not the one to Ironbridge – something of an irony given its tourism potential. The bus station is five minutes' walk from the railway station via Castle Gates and Meadow Place. As bus stations go, it is buzzing, but sorely needs a makeover, for it has neither the heritage appeal of a rail station nor contemporary style to be called attractive.

Walking around town

Walking is by far the best way to see Shrewsbury. From the strategic high ground of the medieval fortress, seen from the railway station, the town stretches towards the flowing waters of the Severn where trading of stock, wool and other agricultural products has brought wealth, at least in the good times, throughout the centuries. Shrewsbury has grown ever since, and most generations have added to the overall richness of the townscape. There have been some attempts to reduce traffic. There's an extensive park and ride system and this helps. To be frank, the street pattern confounds attempts to squeeze more cars in, but traffic planners seem hell-bent on building more highways around this lovely town. For the visitor, the closeness of the station to the town centre counts for much. Within a stone's throw of the station entrance you'll smell the products of an artisan bakery. What better welcome could there be?

The central quarter is five minutes walk from the railway station; it lies within a magnificent meander of the River Severn and thus is necessarily compact. Only when the river floods do the riverside paths and parks become waterlogged (and on occasion impassable) but there's still a maze of small streets sealed within the town walls

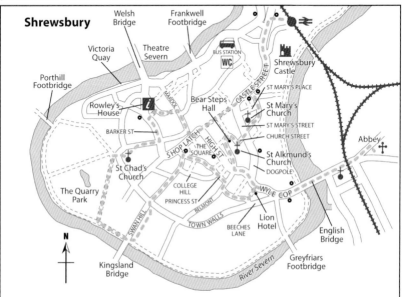

to discover. They offer hours of exploration. These narrow, historic thoroughfares and passageways (known as shuts) are packed with small, characterful shops that are likely to charm even the most reluctant of consumers.

There's a main route and a minor route into town. For the main route, from the station entrance, walk up to Castle Gates (by the pedestrian crossing where you turn left). Follow Castle Gates as it rises towards town. You pass beneath the walls of **Shrewsbury Castle**, built by Roger de Montgomery to defend a growing settlement. The heavily modified and restored red sandstone castle is now bedecked with floral displays and is also home to the **Shropshire Regimental Museum**. You then pass the handsome library building, at one time part of Shrewsbury School before it moved location and where Charles Darwin (the famous naturalist who rocked the scientific world with his book *On the Origin of Species*) spent his early years studying. There's a statue in the grounds to commemorate the fact. As you proceed into town, cut left along Windsor Place, passing by the timber-framed **Perche's Mansion** to St Mary's church. You also pass near to a retail arcade where there's an eclectic mix of shops. It is known as The Parade and is housed in the old Royal Salop Infirmary dating from the 1830s.

The alternative, minor, route is to make a sharp left at the end of the station entrance along a Victorian passage back towards the station, climb the steps and go left over the pedestrian bridge to the Dana where the last public hanging at Shrewsbury took place in 1868. There you'll catch sight of a fine bust of John Howard, the 18th-century penal reformer, appropriately balanced above the entrance to **Shrewsbury gaol**. The prison was considered to be a model by all accounts in the late 18th century, but all the same it's probably not advisable to loiter. At the corner, make your way down steps to the banks of the Severn. Turn right to walk beneath the enormous bleak bridge columns supporting part of Shrewsbury railway station above. On

The bust of John Howard, penal reformer, above the entrance to Shrewsbury gaol

reaching St Mary's Water Lane, go right to climb up to **St Mary's church**, with its tall spire reaching into the sky. The church is known for its fine stained glass, much of it made on the continent by artisans of the time. It also houses a range of monuments including one to Admiral John Benbow, born in 1653 at nearby Coton Hill. Despite his early upbringing in landlocked Shropshire he pursued a tempestuous career at sea, and Benbow died on board his flagship from wounds following engagement with the French navy near Jamaica in 1702.

Whichever route you select, you need to aim for Church Street. Cross over St Mary Street into Church Street where the Loggerheads public house stands to the left and the Prince Rupert Hotel is to your right. **St Alkmund's church** stands ahead, again with a tall spire that is much admired amid the low rise medieval buildings. Make your way around to the right and then left, in St Alkmund's Place, and opposite a café to the Bear Steps.

Main attraction

The main attraction in Shrewsbury is this older quarter of town where the medieval layout of streets and passages is very evident on the ground. It radiates out from this spot, i.e. from St Alkmund's church along Butcher Row and Fish Street. The **Bear Steps Hall and Gallery** (HQ of Shrewsbury Civic Trust) is a good place to start your exploration; it houses exhibitions where you can also admire the beautifully restored great hall. In this area, you will find many *shuts*, characteristic to Shrewsbury, including some with very un-pc names, such as Grope Lane (I'll leave that one to your own imagination) and Gullet Passage, as well as the others such as Coffee House Passage and Bear Steps. There are over 30 shuts in town and a good introduction to them has been posted by Proud Salopian on the Shrewsbury Forum blog (wwwshrewsburyforum.co.uk).

Some of the buildings in the older quarter

From St Alkmund's church, descend the Bear Steps and go left along Fish Street, beneath the tower of **St Julian's church**, another building of medieval origin which is now a centre for several religious denominations. It is wandering time from here onwards, among the shops located within 'The Loop'. Go left into Milk Street by Appleyards, packed with local food and drink and something of an institution. Make your way down into Wyle Cop, a lovely part of town spoilt only by the endless drone of traffic. The **Lion Hotel** is an impressive old coaching inn with a fine building adjacent,

Appleyards in 'The Loop' – packed with local food and drink

Shrewsbury Abbey: looking down the choir and the nave to the west end (left) and to the east end (right)

Henry Tudor House, where Henry VII is said to have stayed before the Battle of Bosworth in 1485.

Continue along Wyle Cop and cross the English Bridge to make your way to Shrewsbury Abbey Foregate. You pass beneath the railway. There is, by the way, a great view of **Shrewsbury Abbey** as the train approaches from the south. The asymmetrical position of the clock is a constant source of irritation to some but otherwise this much restored ecclesiastical survivor is a very pleasant distraction. The abbey offers an island of relative calm next to a thoroughfare, remodelled by Telford in the 1830s, which is now way too busy.

The entrance to the abbey, known also as the parish church of Holy Cross after the Dissolution in 1540, is at the south-facing door. It was founded as a Benedictine monastery in 1083 by Roger de Montgomery, a trusted relative of William the Conqueror who served the Norman empire until his death in 1094.

He was buried in the abbey and his effigy can be seen as you approach the Lady Chapel from the south aisle. The arches of the nave date from his time; they are the only remains from the 11th century above ground level. The abbey exhibits many fine examples of stained glass windows, some of which are dedicated, for example, to St Benedict and St Winefride. There are also numerous monuments throughout the abbey of past notables from this part of Shropshire from different periods. In more recent times, the abbey has been associated with *The Chronicles of Brother Cadfael*, novels written by Ellis Peters (the late Edith Pargeter) on which a popular television series, reflecting medieval times, was based.

Hidden among the greenness of the gardens surrounding the abbey, in the shade of a tree, is a monument to one of the most endearing of war poets, Wilfred Owen, who lived in Shrewsbury until he was posted to France. He met his untimely death in 1918.

The statue on the Old Market Hall – but whom it depicts remains a subject of debate

Step across the road to the **Shropshire Wildlife Trust**'s headquarters. It is located in the Old Infirmary and features exhibitions (and a shop) that reflect their superb work across the county. There's a Potato Day here every Spring at which you can learn about the humble spud and buy rare varieties of seed potatoes for the garden or allotment.

Across the car park is a pocket of railway history almost lost to the town, but not entirely so. Here you will find the old **Abbey Foregate railway station**, now the subject of a small scale restoration scheme; needless to say, you'll not see trains here again.

Retrace your steps back to Wyle Cop. Go left just before the Lion Hotel, by the Chocolate Gourmet, through Barracks Passage to Belmont Bank. Turn right here to climb up to Milk Street. Take a look back at the Lion Hotel. The Lion is there, neatly perched at the rear of the building. Turn right again at the top of Belmont Bank by the Old St Chad's Church and churchyard; this is a good place for a rest if you need one. Turn left into Princess Street to The Square. You'll pass by Golden Cross Passage, an intriguing little shut running through to High Street if you fancy a detour.

The Square is the location for many an event, including a thriving monthly farmer's market. Here you'll find the stone **Old Market Hall**, dating from the late 16th century, which is now a cinema and café. Look out for a statue said to be of the Duke of York in armour. It can be seen on the north side of the building. Pevsner suggested that the statue was of Edward, the Black Prince, but Richard of Shrewsbury, the first Duke of York seems more probable. Beyond the hall in The Square is a statue of Clive of India, at one time MP for Shrewsbury. Nearby stands the **Music Hall**, an elegant Grecian style building from the 19th century which, at the time of going to press, was still being redeveloped as a centre for contemporary art and culture. Take a look to see how they are getting on with this complex piece of restoration.

There's now a chance to detour to The Quarry. Go ahead to Market Street but before Shoplatch, turn left to walk over Swan Hill to Murivance, another intriguing medieval name. This is a site of the old town walls and it is possible to wander off along this street, known as **Town Walls**, to take a look at the rich mixture of architecture including an old watch tower dating originally from the 13th century and a mock gothic Roman Catholic Cathedral. It is a one-way street so there's traffic about.

If you are not inclined to wander along here, you might like to cross Town Walls to descend to the tranquillity of the flowing waters of the River Severn. The promenade is wide and pleasant. It dates from the early decades of the 18th century, but the line of lime trees are from the 19th century with replacement projects since

The old Shrewsbury coat of arms as displayed on the Loggerheads inn

The timber-framed King's Head in The Mardol, typical of many buildings around Shrewsbury

Charles Darwin was baptised here. The church is worth a closer look so go right to climb away from the river to St Chad's Terrace. The churchyard is a sanctuary for wildlife and has a curiosity lying beneath the trees, a gravestone dedicated to Ebenezer Scrooge, used for the filming of *A Christmas Carol*, a film buff's favourite, directed by Clive Donner and starring the late George C. Scott, in 1984.

You can cut through the churchyard to Claremont Hill to walk towards the town centre, but then go left and right into Barker Street where you'll find **Rowley's House**. This is a combination of a late 16th-century timber-framed building, possibly a brewery, meshed with an early 17th-century brick-built mansion. It was built for a wealthy merchant by the name of Rowley and is considered to be one of Shrewsbury's finest corners, saved for the municipality in the 1930s by the then borough surveyor. It stands apart from its surroundings, which are pretty drab. It is now home to the **Museum and Art Gallery** as well as temporary location for the Visitor Information Office. The aim is to move the latter back to the Music Hall.

OTHER ATTRACTIONS

Coleham Pumping Station is a 15-20 minute walk from the railway station via Wyle Cop and Greyfriars Bridge. Alternatively, bus 546 from Shrewsbury Bus Station runs through Coleham; ask for Longden Road. South of the river is a cluster of shops, cafés and pubs at Coleham. The main attraction here is a vintage pumping station which used to remove sewage from the town using two heavy steam-powered beam engines. The late disc jockey extraordinaire, John Peel, occasionally played a recording of the engines in full blast on his late night Radio One slot. The engines have been beautifully restored by the Shrewsbury Steam Trust.

Theatre Severn is located in Frankwell, offering a wide variety of entertainment and art throughout the year. The contemporary

then. You might catch sight of the tour boat (see Extras) which sails along this stretch of the river from Victoria Quay. Turn right along the promenade. The riverside includes several pleasant parks of which the jewel is **The Quarry** and within it The Dingle; these feature heavily in the annual flower show. The Dingle was very much the creation of the late Percy Thrower who was head gardener at Shrewsbury until his television career took off. There is a bust to commemorate his good work. The Quarry has a long history of staging plays over the centuries and to this day is the key location for events. There's a view over the river to **Shrewsbury School**, attended by many a celeb including Michael Palin, Richard Ingrams and the late Willie Rushton.

You'll see, on the right, **St Chad's church**, a neo-classical masterpiece with an unusual round nave which is said to have excellent acoustic qualities. It has fine stained glass dating from the 1840s, designed by local craftsman, David Evans.

building stands across the water from the Quantum Leap sculpture. This amazing piece of art commemorates the bicentenary of Charles Darwin in 2009. There's also a Charles Darwin's Riverside walk from outside the theatre that passes his home, The Mount, about a mile away. The way is signposted and takes about an hour or a little more depending on your pace.

WALKING

Shrewsbury is a great place to stay if you want to catch a bus or train out to a countryside location but it is less attractive for those who want to walk directly into the countryside, for there's a need to walk for a few miles first to escape the urban sprawl. By far the best access routes are the riverside paths out of town. To the east, the **Shropshire Way** and the **Severn Way** lend themselves to good linear walks. For example, it is possible to catch Bus 519 from Shrewsbury Bus Station to Haughmond Hill (ask for Haughmond Abbey, which is worth a visit too) where you can follow the Shropshire Way for four miles back to the railway station. Alternatively, catch buses 81 or 96 to Atcham and walk back along the Severn Way back into town. To the west, it is possible to catch the 70 bus to Montford Bridge and walk back along the Shropshire Way into town, by the Theatre Severn. These are all easy to follow half-day walks without any climbs.

CYCLING

Shrewsbury is also on the up when it comes to cycling too but it is not quite there yet. It is one of the UK's Cycling Towns and additional investment in facilities over recent years has brought increased resident cycle use. The riverside routes (shared with pedestrians) are a real attraction, although they narrow in places and care has to be taken with the number of walkers alongside. Cycling is also feasible on some of the quieter back streets around town, but you need to know these well. The rub is, then, that the dominant one-way

road system still remains very unpleasant and many would not contemplate cycling these highways until segregated routes are brought in as a continuous network. That is happening, slowly but surely, so it is hats off to the cycle team. In my book, cycling around central Shrewsbury is not as convenient or comfortable as walking. Nevertheless, if you fancy giving it a go then pick up *Shrewsbury Walking & Cycling Map*. It is packed with vital information for the cyclist in town.

On the other hand, the National Cycle Network offers a number of routes out of town into the near countryside – see the Shrewsbury Cycle Rides on the Cycle Shrewsbury website (www.cycleshrewsbury. co.uk). These include **Route 44** Six Castles Cycleway Shrewsbury to Leominster; **Route 81** Shrewsbury to Welshpool and **Route 45** (using Route 81 to Uffington from Shrewsbury) to Wem or to Ironbridge. Leaflets are usually available for these routes at Shrewsbury Railway Station or on the internet at www.shropshire.gov.uk/ cycling.nsf.

REFRESHMENTS

There's considerable choice in Shrewsbury. In all honesty it is difficult to do justice to all providers but here are listed some that are different:

Cafés And Restaurants
Café Retreat, 24 Castle Street is on the way into town from the railway station in an old church. Here you can sip coffee and eat homemade cake as you gaze across the street at Darwin's statue and the old school where he spent many an hour studying to good effect. The old church also houses a beauty sanctuary (www.serenityshrewsbury.com).

Old Market Hall café, The Square is an excellent place for coffee and light snacks, on the first floor of the ancient hall in the town centre, by the cinema entrance.

The Gallery Tea Shop on Princess Street is a traditional café that excels in making homemade cakes.

The Good Life Wholefood Restaurant is a must for lovers of good food. It is located on Barrack's Passage next to the Lion Hotel.

The Peach Tree on Abbey Foregate has a menu packed with delicious food, much of which is sourced locally.

There are many restaurants, including **Loch Fyne** on Princess Street for those who love fish (sustainably sourced; **La Dolce Vita** near to Rowley's House is a family run Italian restaurant where the fish dishes are rated; while **Café Saffron** on Hill's Lane has a good reputation for Indian cuisine. Take a look at the Eat Shrewsbury website for more information on what locals think about eating and drinking in their town (see www. eatshrewsbury.co.uk).

Pubs

Shrewsbury has many traditional pubs and below is a small selection:

The Loggerheads on Church Street is a good starting point when wandering through the medieval quarter.

The Three Fishes on Fish Street (many local beers on tap); like The Loggerheads it is a real pub with character.

The Admiral Benbow on Swan Hill (near The Square) is a haven of tranquillity offering a range of cask beers and ciders most of which come from the Marches.

The Armoury on Victoria Quay has a wide selection of ales and a growing reputation for food.

Local Produce

There are a small number of shops selling mainly organic and local produce including:

Appleyards, High Street

Indoor Market, off Pride Hill

Shrewsbury Bakehouse, Castle Gates

Shrewsbury Fairtrade shop, St John's Hill

The Fruit Bowl, Belmont

Wild Thyme wholefood shop, Castle Gates.

EXTRAS

Farmers Market: The Square, 1st Friday of the month.

Shrewsbury Civic Society, (2006) *Shrewsbury Town Trail*, Shrewsbury Civic Society Trust Ltd.

The Fair in The Square: 2nd Saturday in the month where local arts, craft and food are displayed and sold. See www. madeinshropshire.co.uk.

Visitor Information Centre, Rowley's House, Barker Street: Tel (01743) 281200.

Short **boat tours** of the river Severn loop depart from Victoria Quay (by the Welsh Bridge) (see www.sabrinaboat.co.uk).

PUBLIC TRANSPORT

Trains

There are direct trains from Birmingham, London, Cardiff and South Wales, Manchester and North Wales.

Buses In Shrewsbury

There is a network of services across most of the town. You'll find some time-table leaflets at the foyer in the railway station and a wider selection at the travel agents at the bus station. Buses are reasonably frequent in Shrewsbury but are reduced in the evenings and there's a reduced network on Sundays. The network is operated by Arriva.

A park and ride service is available on Mondays to Saturdays operating every 10-15 minutes from three sites:

Harlescott (near Tesco)

Meole Brace Retail Park

Oxon Business Park.

There is an extensive network of buses to all of the market towns in Shropshire which run daily (with the exception of buses to Ironbridge, Ludlow and Wem; they do not operate on Sundays and Bank Holidays). There are also direct buses to Llanfyllin, Montgomery and Welshpool (everyday except Sundays and Bank Holidays). They all depart from the main bus station in Barker Street.

EXCURSIONS FROM SHREWSBURY

BISHOP'S CASTLE AND THE STIPERSTONES

Ride to Bishop's Castle

The bus ride to Bishop's Castle through the Rea valley seems pleasant enough, but nothing to write home about. Then you catch sight of the rising hills of Pontesford and Earl's Hill and the passing scenery suddenly begins to grab your attention. **Earl's Hill** is a nature reserve managed by the Shropshire Wildlife Trust and it is possible to jump off the bus for a bit of an exploration. Ask for the Nag's Head public house stop in **Pontesbury**. To reach Earl's Hill turn left with your back to the stop and left again along the lane. Go left opposite Mary Webb school (named after an author who penned *The Golden Arrow* whilst living in the village). Soon, you cut left again on a footpath across a field and up a drive to the entrance of the reserve. It is about a 15 minute climb to the summit and the remains of the Iron Age hillfort defences, where you'll feel the breeze on your face as the superb views open up around you.

After Pontesbury, the bus passes through **Minsterley**, known for its dairy production. Tucked away is one of the most unusual churches in the Marches; it is principally red brick and dates from the late 17th century. The church houses a rare display of 18th-century maidens' garlands. These were placed on the coffin at the funerals of young girls who had died chaste; it was a customary token of respect of womanhood at the time. Once out of Minsterley, there are views across to the Stiperstones but the Bishop's Castle bus does not divert from the main road. If you intend to visit the Stiperstones, probably a day out in its own right, take a look at the Stiperstones section outlined below.

The Bishop's Castle bus begins to climb in earnest after the turning to the Stiperstones at Plox Green, through the narrow and wooded **Hope valley** where there's a nature reserve managed by the Shropshire Wildlife Trust. It then passes the hamlet of the appropriately named **Gravels** and onward to **White Grit**, both of which have been subject to the mining of minerals. There's an evocative reminder, mid-field to your right; there you'll spot the forlorn ruins of an engine house. On the moorland above, stands **Mitchell's Fold**, the remains of a Bronze Age stone circle, located alongside a ridgeway which also dates from prehistoric times. There are also exceptional views across to one of the most impressive hills around, Corndon (on the right), before the bus descends to Lydham and onward to the final destination of Bishop's Castle.

BISHOP'S CASTLE

Bishop's Castle is not actually in the Shropshire Hills Area of Outstanding Natural Beauty but is a great place to stay a while, especially if you enjoy walking on the wild side. The town still has, more or less, the same layout as determined by the Normans in the 12th century. The main route through, High Street, leads into Church Street and lesser thoroughfares peel off to the left and right in a rectangular pattern. The town's main core descends from higher ground, where the Norman castle was situated, down to the large parish church at the bottom of the town. Independent shops dominate and are mostly in the hands of local traders. A beautifully frank statement, in the tourism blurb, 'No IKEA, M&S or Boots here' says it all. What is quite remarkable is the resilience of the town to fight against the odds. It lost its political clout as a Rotten Borough in the 19th century, its railway as early as 1937 and has witnessed a steady decline in agriculture over the decades. Despite this, Bishop's Castle has become a leader in the 21st-century green revolution thanks to the enormous efforts of groups such as the Wasteless Society, tirelessly working towards sustainable development in the Marches. Amongst its residents was the late Pete Postlethwaite, an actor of exceptional talent who starred in the film *The Age of Stupid* (2009), a salutary reminder of the need to respond to the challenges of climate change.

The town's tourism association is just as keen to reduce the visitor carbon footprint. It is one of the few destinations that genuinely seek to attract visitors by public transport. This includes the bus from Shrewsbury whilst some B&Bs offer lifts from the railhead at Craven Arms and others luggage transfers for walkers. Bed and breakfast providers are, in the main, progressive and getting greener by the day. The Old Brickhouse, for example, goes out of its way to maintain every comfort while minimising its environmental impact. It is one of the few bed and breakfast providers that sets out its green policy (see www.oldbrick.co.uk). In fairness, others go out of their way to welcome walkers and cyclists and are greening their business. The same applies to some of the town's cafés and pubs which do their best to source local food supplies for their kitchens. So, the area is definitely a green tourism champion.

Bishop's Castle spices its tourism with a number of festivals and that's when the town really does let its hair down for a couple of days (or in the case of the beer festival, 24 hours of partying and music after which everyone sleeps, exhausted either by serving endless pints or imbibing the various beers on tap). What is pleasing to the visitor is the number of public houses for this size of the town (1,600 people); there are six remaining, and two breweries to boot, so you won't go thirsty. At non-festival times, there's a relative calm about the place; the laid back atmosphere soon becomes apparent.

Walking around town
The bus arrives at the Boars Head in Church Street. From here stroll to the church and the Six Bells public house, then return to the Boars Head where you continue ahead at the crossroads to climb High Street to the Market Square.

*The church clock
with its unusual single hand*

The **church of St John the Baptist** is of Norman origin but it was completely rebuilt in the 1860s. There are several monuments in the church, mainly effigies of local notables from the 17th and 19th centuries. The church tower houses six bells, mainly dating from the 18th century, and these chime beautifully. Take another look at the clock on the way out of the churchyard. What's unusual about it is that it only has one hand. Evidently, a clock with only one hand was not seen as a problem when it was installed in the last century. Industrial time (counting the minutes and seconds with precision) had evidently not arrived in Bishop's Castle. However, elsewhere in the Marches it's a very different story. At Llanymynech, the church clock face was actually enlarged so that the local workforce would not be late for a shift at the quarry, a clear reflection of the advent of industrialisation in these rural parts.

Main attraction
The main attraction of the town happens to be its two breweries. One is situated at the bottom of the town and the other at the top. Across the road from the parish church stands the **Six Bells public house** and one can guess why this might be. The inn once fronted an area which was used as a cattle market, but the herding of stock in the street is no longer a regular occurrence.

*The Six Bells inn and brewery at the
bottom of the town, near the church*

This homely inn offers a full range of brews. In terms of beer miles, these notch up mere beer yards (or metres), for the brewery is behind the pub. It really has been a case of putting to good use old buildings which had been little used for some time. It originally housed an old carriage works and forge, built in the early years of the 20th century; that was about the time when the inn stopped brewing its own beer. The pub also had its own orchard and made cider, but these have also long since gone.

But brewing came back onto the scene in 1997 when new equipment was installed. The landlord and brewer in chief is 'Big Nev', so there's no messing with him. His real name is Neville Richards and he has not looked back since those early days when the first brews were rolled out. The brewery has won several awards since. There are three principal beers: Big Nev's, Goldings BB and Cloud Nine which are augmented by monthly specials. Tours can be arranged but for groups only.

The other brewery is at the top of the town and your way is back up Church Street, which is lined with a mix of fine buildings from half-timbered through to Georgian town houses. It then becomes High Street and climbs up to the Town Hall. The character of the street changes, as there are more Victorian commercial buildings clustered here. As you approach the 18th-century brick Town Hall, look out for School Lane on the right where you'll find the **Bishop's Castle Railway Museum** in a small wooden-clad building; check opening times at www.bcrailway.co.uk. It tells the story of a much loved but, as was often the case, impecunious railway that operated from 1865 to 1935.

As you continue to climb up High Street you'll come across a cluster of shops from traditional clothing retailer to bookseller, delicatessen, furniture maker and gallery. It is a really good part of town to root around. Take the path on the left to walk along the cobbled pavement above the elegant **Porch House**; some parts of

*The Three Tuns inn and brewery
at the top end of town*

the half-timbered building date back to the 16th century. It is not open to visitors (other than groups) but the town tours usually call there (see Extras). Nearby is another half-timbered property, the **House on Crutches**, that stands partly on two pillars, hence the name. It is very crooked in places and the floors slope so it is not for people with limited mobility. This late medieval building is now a museum run by a trust and there are four principal rooms which house displays. These focus on business life, agriculture, the home and kitchen, and there's a range of artefacts and photographs which illustrate life in the town over the past two hundred years. The museum is closely associated with the Bishop's Castle Heritage Resource Centre which seeks to piece together more about the history of the town and surrounding area. The museum is open at weekends in the summer.

Your way is through Market Square, on the right, to Salop Street. Before you venture to the Three Tuns brewery, turn left into Bull Street and cut left along a path (waymarked as the Shropshire Way) up to the town's bowling green. You can just about see over the fence on your left; this is all that remains of the **castle**. There is, however, a splendidly restored club house on site which dates originally from the 18th century.

Retrace your steps into Salop Street and arrive at the **Three Tuns brewery**. This is something of a legendary affair as brewing started on this site in 1642 and has continued since with the exception of a few breaks for refurbishment or change of ownership. Alongside the likes of Shepherd Neame, this must be one of the oldest licensed breweries in the country. The magnificent brick tower you see today, however, dates from 1888. It is a splendid piece of brewery architecture featuring four storeys; it really does look the part in a small town like Bishop's Castle. The principle of the tower brewery is simple. Gravity is used to aid the brewing process. Raw materials are hoisted to the top of the tower and beer is crafted as it descends

from floor to floor. Casks of real ale then flow from the bottom floor where they have been settling in cool cellars. This style of brewery was commonplace in Victorian England but is a rarity now. This particular brewery was commissioned by a local man John Roberts, whose family continued to brew here for the best part of a hundred years. We owe them much for their perseverance when times were hard.

By the 1970s the Three Tuns brewery was one of only four brew pubs remaining in the UK, the others being the All Nations at Madeley, Blue Anchor at Helston, and the Olde Swan at Netherton. These became the sites of modern day beer pilgrimages with a steady flow of aficionados paying homage to a bye gone age. It nearly all came undone when a consortium, who also owned the pub next door, wanted to hive if off for housing. It was then that three stalwarts stepped in to save it and with the community right behind them. Thus, in 2003 the brewery was restored and the range of beers tweaked to meet a growing demand for tasty pale-coloured local brews (1642, XXX and Cleric's Cure are three mainstays of the range). The new owners have been true to their word and the Roberts family's heritage has not been lost. Their commitment to the brewery brings success after success to a town that loves a drop of beer. There is a brewery shop available, but tours can only be arranged for groups.

THE STIPERSTONES

En route to Bishop's Castle you will catch sight of the Stiperstones, a cutting edge of geology in Shropshire. The ridge comprises a grit-shale base, known as Mytton flags, capped by a quartzite outcrop laid down some 510 million years ago when this was no more than a sandy beach by a lapping shallow sea. Not only do the outcrops look magical but there's a rich folklore about the place. As to be expected, there's the almost obligatory tale about a rock known as the 'Devil's Chair', but perhaps more intriguing are the stories of early chieftain Saxon, Wild Edric. He led a resistance movement against the Norman incursions but then abandoned the cause, struck a deal with no less than William the Conqueror and effectively sold out his mates. His punishment, according to folklore, was eternal imprisonment beneath these very rocks; this would be his fate, it is chronicled, until justice is restored in the land. It'll be some time before we see him then.

This 'lore' landscape is formed of sandstone grains bound by quartz and known as quartzite. The weathered form presents a landmark that you cannot ignore. The erratic shapes are the result of freeze-thaw action during colder climatic periods thousands of years ago. These are the iconic skyline blocks, the centrepiece of The Stiperstones National Nature Reserve, managed by Natural England, from where swathes of heather, gorse and whinberries sweep away from the rocks. In order to conserve this moorland, there are projects afoot to remove some of the coniferous plantations and to create conditions to attract back a diversity of heathland plants.

The tourism blurb calls the Stiperstones 'a place of solitude', but this is not quite true. There's usually a crowd here on a fine day, milling around the Knoll Car Park, before making the painful pilgrimage (it really is hard under foot, even in boots let alone canvas shoes) to Cranberry rocks. Thirty minutes at most and there's an orderly retreat to the nearby **Bog Centre** (adjacent to the remains of the old Bog Lead Mine) for a little education, tea and cakes, and who can blame anyone for this? The food is very enticing and the displays here are always of interest. If you'd like to escape the madding crowd, however, then walk on through the heather and whinberries for 1.5 miles to **The Hollies** where the old approach to growing holly trees for winter feed is being restored by the Shropshire Wildlife Trust (see www.shropshirewildlifetrust.org.uk).

The area was also important for mining, principally for lead but also the extraction of other minerals such as zinc and barytes. The Shropshire Mines Trust manage two old mine sites, one at Snailbeach and the other at Tankerville. **The Snailbeach mine** is open to the public at weekends during the summer months. The interpretation begins to unfold a story of hope, speculation and financial success but mostly this dusty site exposes the harsh reality of mining. The process of extracting minerals which were then transported on the narrow gauge Snailbeach and District Railway, which once ran down to Pontesbury, is explained around the site. The mines were closed in 1955 with little or no business taking place after that year.

Ask the bus driver of the 552 bus to drop you at Snailbeach Village Hall; there's a stop by the toilets. Opposite is the short walk (five minutes) up to the principal mine. Further on is Lords Hill Chapel, dating from 1833, which was featured in Mary Webb's book *Gone to Earth*. You can continue on a walk up to the Stiperstones Ridge before dropping down Perkin's Beach to the Stiperstones Inn where there's a bus back into Shrewsbury (or use the Shropshire Hills Shuttle). Allow about two hours for the walk. It is not possible to travel directly between Bishop's Castle and the Stiperstones; you have to change buses (Bus 552/3) at Minsterley or Pontesbury (see public transport section on page 34).

WALKING

Another way to travel to Bishop's Castle from Shrewsbury is by walking on the **Shropshire Way**, a distance of approximately 25 miles. If you are up for it and not a long distance walker, you'll need to arrange an overnight stop at a mid-way point such as at Bridges, some 13 miles, or nearby Wentnor, then continue the walk on a second day. If you simply fancy a taste of the Shropshire Way then it is possible to catch the 553 bus from Shrewsbury to White Grit and walk onward to Bishop's Castle (see www.shropshirewalking.co.uk). This is an attractive walk that introduces you to some wilder parts of the Shropshire Hills AONB, including walking beneath

Linley Beeches, planted in the mid 18th century and, in recent years, subject to replanting as the ancient specimens fall. There are a number of climbs on the walk so you'll need to muster additional stamina for these.

One of the best ways to explore this remote border country is on foot and Bishop's Castle is a great base for this; it has signed up as a 'Walkers are Welcome' town. It is hardly surprising given the efforts of its long-standing walking group and the annual walking festival, which follows green guidelines by using local buses and minibuses wherever possible. There are walks through to the Stiperstones or to Clun, both of which are day walks and fairly strenuous.

There's also the **Kerry Ridgeway**, a ridge walk in very quiet and hilly countryside where sheep farming reigns supreme. The Ridgeway is partly on road and partly an old track. It leads to Offa's Dyke National Trail (see page 17). The Bishop's Castle Ring walk is a circular exploration of the Shropshire Hills. It is very remote and not well served by public transport. However, several local accommodation providers will set you down or pick you up at pre-arranged points. There's also a considerable choice of local footpaths to explore the near countryside around the town, so it is a good place if walking is your prime motivation. Local accommodation providers have a good knowledge of the paths so they can often advise on routes to take.

CYCLING

An alternative way to travel to Bishop's Castle is to cycle on the National Cycle Route from Craven Arms or Shrewsbury railway stations on **NCN Route 44**. This route follows back roads which are relatively traffic free. Brace yourself for the numerous climbs but there are some rather relaxing descents too. The cycle trip will take the best part of the day so it is best to book accommodation in advance.

Bishop's Castle has an active cycle campaign group that is keen to encourage visitors to the town by cycle. They campaigned for a traffic-free route on the old Bishop's Castle to Craven Arms railway track bed but this was thwarted by the lack of enthusiasm of local landowners in the Plowden area. Nevertheless, there are some good local rides through to Montgomery and Clun Valley which make pleasant outings, but you need to be able to handle the hills. They are written up in a leaflet *Bishop's Castle Cycle Rides* available locally.

REFRESHMENT

Cafés and restaurants

Capricho, High Street: café and gallery using local ingredients for homemade food.

Happy Burp, High Street: local and organic food served.

The Poppy House, Market Square: tea rooms and restaurant with great homemade cakes.

Yarborough House, Market Square: book shop, second hand classical LPs and a coffee shop with home made cakes.

Pubs

The Castle Hotel, The Square: good reputation for locally sourced food in traditional hotel which serves local beers.

The Six Bells, Church Street: sources local ingredients for its freshly cooked meals.

The Three Tuns public house, Salop Street: sells beer from the brewery next door and prides itself on providing locally sourced food.

Local Produce

Andrew J. Pugh, High Street: great sausages and pies from Reg Mays at Ditton Priors plus other local products.

Harvest Wholefoods at Lydham: long standing wholefood supplier and shop.

Sol Delicatessen, High Street: has some local produce on sale.

EXTRAS

For more visitor information see www. bishopscastle.co.uk.

Visitor information point is at Old Time on the High Street; maker of furniture, some from green ash in the workshop.

Bishop's Castle Railway Society: see www.bcrailway.co.uk for more detail about the railway and to check opening times of the museum (essentially weekend afternoons only during summer).

Bishop's Castle Ring Walk: see www.bcring.co.uk.

Blue Remembered Hills Bridleway: 38 mile route in Clun and Bishop's Castle area for horse riders.

Farmers Market: Town Hall and Market Square, 3rd Saturday of every month.

Towntours: guided tours of Bishop's Castle undertaken by knowledgeable locals – a great way to get a detailed insight into the town's history-www.towntour.co.uk.

PUBLIC TRANSPORT

Buses to Bishop's Castle
Shrewsbury Bus Station to Bishop's Castle (Boar's Head). 553. Six buses per day, four on Sundays. Travel time 1 hour. Operators: Minsterley Motors Monday – Saturday, Arriva on Sundays.

Market day bus from Bishop's Castle (Boar's Head) to Ludlow (Mon/Fri) Operator: Minsterley Motors. Travel time approximately 1-1.5 hours.

Buses to The Stiperstones
Shrewsbury Bus Station to Snailbeach and Stiperstones (Stiperstones Inn) 552. Six buses per day. Monday – Saturday only. Travel time 45 minutes. Operator: Minsterley Motors.

Long Mynd Shuttle
Church Stretton to Stiperstones via Bridges on summer weekends only; hourly with lunchtime gap. Travel time 50 minutes. Operator: Shropshire Fleet.

ELLESMERE AND MYDDLE

Ride to Ellesmere
The bus ride to Ellesmere is a dreamy affair. There's an initial round the houses loop out of Shrewsbury but then you are on your way. The bus meanders through fields of cereal and pastures, by brick and half-timbered cottages in hamlets, tucked away in a gently undulating landscape. This, of course, is a landscape rendered smooth by glacial deposits, followed by a good peri-glacial splash and topped out by clays and pebbles. After passing through Cockshutt, there are more mounds to be seen; they might even be drumlins and moraines, the stuff of geography textbooks. The hillocks highlight the green pastures that lie between woods and parkland. This is the land of meres, small, naturally formed lakes that characterise this part of Shropshire. They are often hidden by woods and located away from the main roads. Consequently, they are rich in wildlife and a few, like Colemere, are designated nature reserves.

Myddle church

Before reaching this north-western corner of Shropshire, you'll pass by two red sandstone escarpments, Pim Hill and Harmer Hill. These prominent tree-lined hillsides exhibit a different character to the lowland and have been quarried over the years for local building stone. This can be seen in several dwellings and field boundaries. You'll also pass one of the earliest organic farms in Shropshire, Pim Hill Farm, which mills a range of flour and cereals available in local shops.

Myddle is the most interesting of the settlements on the route out to Ellesmere. The parish was home to the 17th-century writer Richard Gough, who penned a chronicle of everyday life in the area. He tuned into the gossip and all was revealed in his work, published as *The History of Myddle* in 1701. There is a circular walk, one of *The Gough Walks*, designed by a group of local people from the area (see www.myddle.net), which introduces you to his patch. This includes a stroll through the hamlet of Newton-on-the-Hill, Gough's birthplace, returning through the woodlands of Harmer Hill. At Harmer, there were at one time cave dwellings, several of which were carved into the hillside. It is easy walking but you'll need a couple of hours to complete the circuit, which happens to be about right for onward bus times to Ellesmere.

Myddle Castle, built in the early years of the 14th century by the Le Strange family, was by all accounts in ruins by the late medieval period as it lacked strategic value to the Normans. It was in such a poor state that it did not figure in the English Civil War either. Even so, Gough noted that it suffered badly from an earthquake in 1688. Only scant earthworks and one piece of stonework, a hall stairway, now remain. Some of the stones are to be found in the adjacent farm and no doubt there's more in the village that has been put to good re-use. The castle can be found behind the parish church and Castle Farm; please note that it is on private ground but there's a public footpath passing near it. There are several historic buildings in the village

including the 17th-century Red Lion Inn and the bus stops are sited here too.

ELLESMERE

Ellesmere is a town which has managed to resist significant change to its town centre over the past centuries. It also seems to have tamed traffic to some extent so it is a pleasure to walk around the shops and cafés. The older quarter is higher up, on St John's Hill. There was almost certainly an Anglo-Saxon settlement on this high ground, perhaps near to the parish church, but as elsewhere in the Marches, the Norman invasion brought a **castle** and a planned town built in a grid format.

The town centre reflects a diversity of buildings dating mainly from the Georgian and Victorian periods, although there are also earlier timbered-framed houses to be seen. The **Town Hall** is the centrepiece. You cannot miss it. This Victorian masterpiece now houses a restaurant on the ground floor and has rooms for communal activities on the second level. The building illustrates the town's sustained importance in previous times, especially during the good agricultural years, times when wheat and farm produce came to market here from a rich agricultural hinterland.

The wealth that came to the town in later centuries is perhaps associated as much with its role as a transport hub. This was enhanced by the choice of **canal** route made by the Duke of Bridgewater; he brought the network to the very edge of town. The canal, of course, was superseded in the 1860s by the Oswestry, Ellesmere and Whitchurch railway, which in turn soon became absorbed into the Cambrian railway. The railway has long since gone but the canal still thrives with narrow boats making their way to Llangollen; there's also a popular annual boat event based at the wharf. Although the extensive water and transhipment areas are now lost to development, the towpath provides a charming conduit to the near countryside. Tourism flourishes in another part of town too. Less than half a mile from the centre, thou-

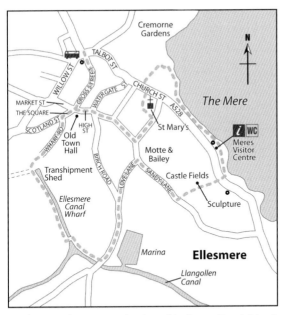

Cremorne Gardens

N

The Mere

St Mary's

Meres Visitor Centre

Motte & Bailey

Castle Fields

Sculpture

Marina

Ellesmere

Llangollen Canal

Old Town Hall

Transhipment Shed

Ellesmere Canal Wharf

MARKET ST
THE SQUARE

a meeting of roads with a number of fine buildings in the vicinity. In adjoining streets there are others to look out for, especially the Savings Bank and Market Hall in Scotland Street, both dating from the latter part of the 19th century.

Go right into Scotland Street then left into Wharf Road. However, it is worth a detour along Scotland Street to take a look at the **Market Hall** where stalls are still laden with goods on Tuesdays and Fridays. You might also visit **SPACE** (Supporting Potential Art Craft Enterprises) which houses an exhibition (and items for sale) of the work of local craftspeople. Make your way back to Wharf Road. It leads, as its name suggests, to the **old waterfront**. However, the approach is not what you might expect. Whilst there are a number of delightful seats in this public space, neatly placed in rows alongside a lone canal crane, it would hardly be accurate to describe it as a waterfront heritage site. The only building remaining is a solitary warehouse dating from the early 1800s. This is the former Shropshire Union Railways and Canal Company transhipment building which, unfortunately, is slowly decaying. It has cargo doors on both water and land sides and awnings in disrepair. The remaining land is subject to development. A supermarket has already been built across the water but it looks more 'urban north' than Shropshire vernacular. Nevertheless, there are plans to revitalise the remainder of the old Dairy Crest Creamery site in due course and this may bring an improvement.

It is certainly a far cry from the heyday of canal building. Trade was definitely given a boost by the completion of the Ellesmere canal, built in the late 1790s during a period when canal mania had

sands come to promenade alongside the tranquil waters of Ellesmere mere. Thus a walk around Ellesmere brings together two special water-based experiences, the canal and the mere, and that makes for a good day out.

Walking around town

From the bus stops in Cross Street, bear right to walk into the town centre. Cross Street widens and there are toilets and a little garden on the left. Here stands an unusual statue to commemorate the launch of Save the Children in 1919 by its co-founder, an Ellesmere-born lady called Eglantine Jebb. As you walk on towards the centre the sheer presence of the old **Town Hall** hits you immediately. It is taller than surrounding buildings and the Tuscan style of architecture is very bold. It was built from Grinshill stone (see Wem, Clive and Grinshill section) and is topped out with a large pediment projecting outwards over the square. It was funded by the Countess of Bridgewater as she thought it would befit the town in the 1830s. There is not actually a formal square here, but more

The canal wharf with its solitary remaining warehouse

just about peaked. There were many subscribers in favour of the project, but the canal was financed principally by the third Duke of Bridgewater, an inveterate supporter of waterways throughout the late 18th century. He also happened to own much of the land in the area, which helped ease a passage through prime agricultural pastures. The canal was engineered by the inseparable surveyor and engineer team, Thomas Telford and William Jessop, and was open for business by 1805. In the first decade it proved to be a major stimulus to the town and its supremacy as a form of goods transport remained unrivalled until the railway came some 50 years or so later.

Walk along the towpath away from the wharf. Cross the bridge at the junction with the Llangollen branch. Opposite stands **Beech House**, Italianate in style and at one time the headquarters of the Ellesmere Canal Company. Next door to it are a group of canal buildings, the old maintenance works. On the next section you will see a number of sculptures created each year as part of the annual **Sculpture in The Landscape Symposium** held in the town. There are more situated along the canal towpath which collectively form a sculpture trail. Many have been created by international sculptors who have attended past events. In each case they have been encouraged to use local materials.

Walk ahead along the towpath of the Shropshire Union canal to the next bridge, number 58, where you leave the canal to rise up to Birch Road. Go left (there's a marina across the road) and follow the road to a junction where you enter Love Lane on the right, a narrow walled way that leads up to St John's Hill. Turn right at the junction to walk along Sandy Lane but keep a look out for a footpath on the left. There are steps up to a stile and the path then proceeds through the earthworks of **Ellesmere Castle** – the secluded bowling green next door is said to have been rolled out on the motte, taking advantage of the Norman legacy.

The castle dates from the 1070s. The castle was built under the stewardship of Roger de Montgomery in the 1070s. It was given to the Peverel family by Henry I but taken back by Henry II who granted it to David, son of Owain Gwynedd, Prince of Wales in about 1177. It alternated between the English and Welsh crowns until the

1240s when it passed to the le Strange family whose origins were in Knockin, Shropshire. The castle fell into disrepair in the 14th century and all of its stonework has since gone, taken away by builders in later centuries to use elsewhere.

The path leads to the right, down a wild flower meadow, known as Castle Fields, where the outer bailey would have been. There are more sculptures located here as you make your way down to the main road, where you can cross to the Boathouse.

Main attraction

Ellesmere's tourism revolves around this superb stretch of water, the **Mere**, formed over 10,000 years back when ice gouged out a huge hollow. It is the largest of the glacial lakes in the area, but in comparison to Alpine lakes or even those in our very own Lake District, it is small, at some 114 acres. But small is beautiful and the setting is both soothing and engaging. Visitors pile in during the summer months to stroll along the waterside whilst geese and ducks waddle purposefully in anticipation of food.

The water's edge has been subject to sympathetic restoration in recent years including the refurbishment of the Boathouse Restaurant. The **Visitor Centre** is next door to the restaurant (and café) and houses a number of displays. It also offers a chance to catch a fascinating 'Big Brother' glimpse of the ongoing activity at the heronry located on Moscow Island during the summer month nesting period. Moscow Island was built in 1812, by unemployed locals, for the then owner of nearby Ellesmere House. They carted the soil across the ice to form the island, something of a perilous task. It was named 'Moscow' because that was the year that Napoleon retreated from Moscow in defeat. Evidently, the herons first colonised the island in the 1970s and have been coming back ever since. There are also many migrating birds to be seen on the lake in winter. There's boating for those who fancy trying their hand at rowing and fishing too. A tour of the lake can be made by a Victorian replica steamboat, *Lady Katherine*, a boat powered by recycled oil. Boating activities are mainly available in the summer season only.

It is about 15 minutes' walk back into town. You can continue to walk along the water's edge through Cremore Gardens (at one time a tannery) and around the lake to The Crimps; it does get much quieter at that end. But then the lakeside path stops and it is necessary to retrace your steps. However, it is possible to cut left before Cremore Gardens, away from the waterside, to walk through to Church Street. If you prefer a fairly level walk, you can go right here into Talbot Street and left into Watergate Street for the town centre. A more interesting route is to cross over Church Street by the Red Lion, an old coaching inn, then go left and right to enter the churchyard. **St Mary's church** dates from pre-Norman times but the building *in situ* now is mainly a Victorian restoration. There are a small number of medieval effigies in the church, including one of Sir Francis Kynaston and his wife on a tomb. Kynaston was a royal cupbearer to Queen Elizabeth 1 at a time when the serving of drinks in such quarters brought with it high status.

Walk up by the church to exit at the top churchyard gate. Go right to climb Church Hill; the bowling green on the castle site is to the left. At the top, turn right along St John's Hill, where you pass by the handsome 18th-century Sheraton House, described by Pevsner as the 'best house in the town'. Descend into The Square; fine Georgian houses give way to neat 19th-century cottages and town terraces.

WALKING

There are several local walks available. They are written up in leaflets available from the visitor information centre. One superb linear walk is to catch the 53 or 449 bus from Ellesmere (Cross Street) to the village of Welshampton and walk back along the **Shropshire Union Canal**. It is easy walking. You'll need to allow three hours or more, especially if you detour to Colemere. In **Welshampton**, there's a short road walk from the village by the church, along Lyneal Lane, to the canal. Go down steps to the towpath and turn right. Now keep ahead on the towpath through charming countryside to skirt **Colemere**. Here you'll catch sight of a small church built in 1867 to commemorate Lord Brownlow, a major landowner in the previous decades. One of his descendants became a well respected benefactor who gave the mere to the town. It is said that there was a church of earlier times on the site, ransacked by the Parliamentarians in the Civil War of the 17th century, but there's little to support this theory. Some say the bells from the older church lie at the bottom of the mere and you can hear them pealing in the dead of night. Continue along the towpath to pass Blakemere, tranquil and rich in wildlife. You might need a torch to negotiate the tunnel before reaching the sculpture trail and your return to the junction between the Ellesmere spur and Llangollen branch. Keep ahead to the wharf and for town.

CYCLING

The edge of the town centre is circled by traffic-laden roads; they are uninviting. However, there is a leaflet which includes five rides from Ellesmere following quieter back lanes in north Shropshire (see www. shropshirecycling.co.uk). The favourite has to be the ride out to Baschurch and Myddle, for it follows some very quiet back lanes. That is a day's cycle ride. A local electronic bulletin, *Mere News*, features ideas for both cycle rides and walks provided by local people and is worth a look. There's also a short ride (about 8-9 miles in total) to Colemere, via Birch Road to Lee Hall, then a left turn to Spunhill and across the main A528 (care needed) then on to Colemere to watch the geese, grebe and goldeneye. The return is by way of the same lanes.

REFRESHMENT

Cafés and restaurants
There are several local cafés, for example, the **Talgarth Tea Rooms** on Scotland Street, **The Corner House** on the way down from St John's Hill or **Pete's Sandwich bar** in Cross Street but my favourite is:

The Boathouse Restaurant: situated by the Mere, serves good food and has a policy of buying local. It has a 'walkers are welcome' message.

There are several pubs and inns but none stand out especially.

Local Produce
Vermeulens Bakery and Deli: located in Cross Street and offering local and organic products. Look out for the local 'Butter Bun'.

Top House Ice Cream: made in nearby Cockshutt and available in some shops.

EXTRAS

Mere News www.ellesmere.info/news.
Visitor Information Centre: Ellesmere Boathouse, The Mereside: Tel (01691) 622981.

PUBLIC TRANSPORT

Buses to Ellesmere
Shrewsbury Bus Station to Ellesmere (Cross Street) 501 Hourly on Mondays to Saturdays. Five buses on Sundays. Travel time 50 minutes. Operators: Bryn Melyn Monday – Saturday, Arriva on Sundays.

Other Buses into Ellesmere
It is also possible to travel from Oswestry (Bus Station) to Ellesmere (Cross Street) on Monday – Saturday. Buses 53 and 449. Bus 53 calls within 2 minutes walk of Gobowen Railway Station (Old Whittington Road).

Approximately hourly. Travel time 22-35 minutes. Some buses extend to Welshampton. Operators: Arriva 53; Tanat Valley Coaches 449.

IRONBRIDGE AND
THE WREKIN

Ride to the Wrekin
The journey from Shrewsbury to the Wrekin involves a ride by train and a then walk or cycle ride. One of the best ways to get there is via **Wellington**, a Walkers are Welcome town. The train trip from Shrewsbury to Wellington takes 13-14 minutes and is uneventful. It is an hour's walk from there to the Wrekin, initially on town paths and then through woodland, via The Ercall to Forest Glen (see www.slowtraveluk.com for a full description). These sites are managed by the Shropshire Wildlife Trust, which is keen to ensure that the special landscape of The Wrekin and its Iron Age hillfort are conserved for future generations.

There's a wide track from Forest Glen to the summit. It winds up to a long-standing outdoor tea room, known appropriately as Halfway House (open mainly at weekends but also in the week during the summer months). It's a good idea to call in for a breather as the next bit of the climb to the summit is strenuous and this last section can be something of a walkers' highway on a sunny day. Nevertheless, as every good guidebook writer points out, the effort will be rewarded by panoramic views. There's a telecommunication tower over there and yes, you are not the first to ask: 'how could they build it in such a lovely spot?' As you near the high ground of the prehistoric Cornovii tribe, the views are simply exquisite, so sit down and rest awhile.

THE WREKIN

Shropshire's very own mountain, the Wrekin, stands amid the low-lying pastures of the Severn Plain. At a modest height of 1,334 feet (or 406m) it is actually only the eighth highest point in Shropshire but definitely has that appeal to the eye. But it is not only the physical presence of this Precambrian remnant that impresses, but also how it represents the deep affection of place held by folk in these parts. The hill is even integrated in local language, for the phrase 'All round the Wrekin' refers to an indirect route or long-winded response. Evidence of early occupation can be found near the summit, where there's an outer enclosure and an inner enclosure dating from pre-Roman times. It is not easy to pick out the earthworks, but excavations indicate that a succession of tribes used it prior to its destruction by the Romans in the AD50s.

The Wrekin

While you are ticking off the landmarks there's a choice to be made. You can head back into **Wellington** (there's a variation of route available for the return) so as to catch the train back to Shrewsbury, or alternatively to catch the bus through to Ironbridge from Wellington Bus Station. Another option is to walk to Ironbridge (some 6 miles) on the Shropshire Way. If this is your chosen route then brace yourself for a sharp descent and some neat footwork; a stick will help you to keep your footing. Some locals refer to this as the dark side of the Wrekin, which says it all. It is certainly far quieter than the main drag up. The Shropshire Way descends through woodland to Spout Lane and it is somewhat less dramatic from there onwards into Ironbridge. You'll need to allow three hours to walk from the summit of the Wrekin to the Iron Bridge.

Ride to Ironbridge

Some people consider it best to just take a look at the Wrekin from afar and spend the day in Ironbridge instead. If that is your preference then catch bus 96 from Shrewsbury Bus Station to Ironbridge. Number 96 is a great route, the views are superb as it makes its way through this gentle countryside lapping against the Severn Valley. This particular bus serves a number of attractive places *en route* too. Firstly, it calls at Atcham where there's an easy walk in **Attingham Park** (about a mile walk from the gateway to the NT reception at Attingham Hall). Next, it runs through the **Roman fortress at Wroxeter**, one of the principal Roman settlements in the Marches, which can still be seen to good effect and is open to the public. There's a bus stop by the ruins. Nearby is a vineyard of the same name and it is about half a mile walk if you'd like to do as the Romans did and imbibe some of the nectar. It also passes near **Buildwas Abbey**, managed by English Heritage and offering a touch of serenity, if you can blank out the coal-fired power station looming in the background.

The Tontine Hotel

Of course, you can simply ride the bus direct to Ironbridge Gorge; it is about a 45 minute journey. There's a stop at the Museum of the Gorge and as luck would have it, the Ironbridge brewery is conveniently situated nearby for those in need of instant refreshment. On the other hand, you can alight more or less at the Iron Bridge. Ask for the Tontine Hotel, a handsome 18th-century hotel standing in the old Market Square.

IRONBRIDGE

Ironbridge Gorge has always been a fascination. The Industrial Revolution began here, and what a beautiful place these early entrepreneurs, ironmaster giants such as Darby and Wilkinson, chose to despoil! Fortunately, they failed in the long run. The cluster of historic factories, foundries, and workshops are packed tightly into the Gorge, as are the homely residences, all of which comprise this World Heritage Site, designated in 1986. The riverside, known as the **Wharfage**, by the Iron Bridge, is a place where people love to promenade, even when the sun is not beating down. It is a relatively tranquil setting and without too much traffic so people while away their time in admiration of the beauty of the river. Across the road is a mishmash of shops, cafés and public houses that have mushroomed over the years with the growing tourist trade.

Thomas Pritchard's and Abram Darby III's iron bridge

Main attraction

The **bridge**, designed on the basis of Thomas Pritchard's sketches and executed by Abram Darby III in 1779-80, all 380 tons of it, is the main attraction and worthy of more than a minute's gaze. This was the first iron bridge to be built in the world; it is an iconic symbol of the ingenuity of our forefathers and their ability to come up with innovative solutions. The bridge carried all manner of traffic and was built to allow a Severn trow to make its way upstream without downing the sail. On the south side is the old tollhouse. The list of tolls on one of the walls is a revelation. Members of the royal family, soldiers and the like, evidently still had to pay for a coach or

The tolls for crossing the bridge

horse. Even those in charge of a laden hearse had to cough up two shillings to cross, a fair amount at the time.

The Iron Bridge is one of ten exceptional museum sites dotted around the area; a great way to visit them is to use the Gorge Connect bus which runs at weekends and Bank Holiday Mondays between Easter and the end of October. An alternative option is to visit them by bike (see The Hub listed below) but expect some traffic and climbs. Each place offers a different experience. Nine are listed as follows (the tenth is the Iron Bridge itself):

Museum of the Gorge: this is the one you should visit first (the bus stops here) as it explains what happened in the Gorge during those pioneering days of the Industrial Revolution right up to its designation as a World Heritage Site.

Coalbrookdale Museum of Iron: the remains of a water-powered blast furnace that gives the low down on iron technology.

Darby Houses: explains the way of life for the Quaker Ironmasters who changed the industrial world, including original furniture and artefacts from their homes.

Engenuity: more of a design and innovation centre where the visitor gets hands on opportunities with technology.

Broseley Pipeworks: a time warp of a factory, still as it was in the 1950s when it was closed as a major centre for the production of clay tobacco pipes for smokers.

Coalport China Museum: housed in the old china works, it demonstrates traditional techniques of china making.

Jackfield Tile Museum: exhibits tiles from those used in the London tube to those designed for fashionable houses, offering a fabulous range of designs including a firm still making tiles on site.

Blists Hill Victorian Town: the one that every family loves as staff are dressed in costume and play the part. Education and fun result in this interpretation of life in Victorian times.

Tar Tunnel: amazingly, natural bitumen still seeps out of the tunnel walls into pools which you get to see first hand. Also on display are products such as pitch and medicines for rheumatics. A hard-hat job so it is really exciting stuff.

Other attractions

Green Wood Centre. A 10-minute walk from The Museum of the Gorge takes you to the Green Wood Centre in Station Road, open since 1985 and displaying wood working traditions in addition to having a café and small garden. It is worth the detour if you are interested in the crafting of products or use of wood for fuel; the centre offers a wide range of courses from charcoal burning to coracle making. It is also home to the Small Woods Association. Nearby is a **community orchard** situated in Coalbrookdale. It was planted by the Shropshire Apple Trust, in association with the Severn Gorge Countryside Trust which looks after over 50% of the open space across the World Heritage Site. The Trust's work can be seen on several local walks, or on a longer trek on The Shropshire Way and Severn Valley Walk.

WALKING

The Ironbridge Gorge offers many local walks, described in leaflets and booklets available from the Tourist Information office. They mostly involve climbs out of the wooded gorge to nearby industrial centres such as Broseley or Coalbrookdale. There is a good 6 mile circular walk to the National Trust property, **Bentham Hall**, a Tudor manor and parkland associated with a family of the same name written up in *Best Shropshire Walks* (see Extras).

The Shropshire Way enables a good half day walk to Wenlock; this has numerous climbs. The Severn Way allows river valley walking through to Wroxeter in one direction. This makes a good day ramble but much of it is on roads. In the other direction, there is a divine walk on the **Severn Way** to Bridgnorth, some 10 miles of riverside paths that brings you directly into this lovely old town. There are buses back to Ironbridge (Mon – Sat) or Shrewsbury (daily).

CYCLING

Another way to travel between Shrewsbury and The Wrekin and Ironbridge is by cycle on the National Cycle Network. You'll need to ride out of Shrewsbury via Uffington on **Route 81** as far as Upton Magna in the direction of Wellington. It is mostly free of traffic out of Shrewsbury along the riverside and then the old canal towpath. From Uffington, it follows back roads for the remainder of the way, although the level of traffic varies and you have to be on your mettle around Uffington and Atcham where traffic is more prevalent. From Upton Magna, you simply follow **Route 45** (Mercian Way) to The Wrekin and Ironbridge. This amounts to approximately 20 miles or so and thus offers an ideal day ride with a westerly wind behind you. It is then possible to continue on **NCN Route 55** (traffic free, for the most part, through Telford) to Telford Railway Station for a return trip by train. Alternatively, if you are staying in the Ironbridge area, then the **'All Round the Wrekin' cycle trail** is an ideal way to visit The Wrekin without climbing it. Bicycles can be hired at The Hub in Jackfield and the cycle trail follows back roads between Ironbridge and Wellington.

REFRESHMENTS

There's a wide range of provision at Ironbridge.

Atcham: **The Mytton and Mermaid Hotel** sources local food and beverages wherever possible.

EXTRAS

Ironbridge Visitor Information Centre, Museum of The Gorge, The Wharfage: Tel (01952) 884391

Lumsdon, Les (2010) *Best Shropshire Walks*, Sigma Press.

The Hub: located on NCN route 45 in Jackfield, a great cycle centre which offers sales, repairs and cycle hire. Check it out at www.thebicyclehub.co.uk.

PUBLIC TRANSPORT

Trains
Shrewsbury Railway Station to Wellington. Frequent trains on Monday – Saturday. Approximately hourly on Sunday. Travel time approximately 10-15 minutes.

Buses to Wellington
Shrewsbury Bus Station to Wellington Bus Station. 81. Four buses per day (Monday – Saturday only) Travel time 40 minutes. Operator: Arriva.

Buses to Ironbridge
Shrewsbury Bus Station to Ironbridge (Museum of the Gorge). 96. Two hourly (Monday – Saturday only) Travel time 40 minutes. Operator: Arriva.

There are also buses between Wellington and Ironbridge via Telford. Approximately hourly. There is a bus between Ironbridge and Much Wenlock, 88, Monday – Saturday. Four per day. Travel time about 30 minutes. Operator: Arriva.

MUCH WENLOCK AND WENLOCK EDGE

Ride to Much Wenlock

The bus ride to Much Wenlock leaves Shrewsbury by way of Shire Hall, the seat of county government, and outside the workaday building stands a fine monument, **Lord Hill's Column**. It was built in 1816 in the Greek revival tradition with dressed stone hewn from Grinshill. It is topped out with a statue of Lord Hill, hailed at the time as a tip-top military strategist in both the Peninsular and Napoleonic Wars. Hill came from Hawkstone Hall, near Wem and was a big man in the hunting and shooting set of north Shropshire, leading fox and otter hunts in his spare time.

On leaving town, the bus runs through the Severn Valley, on a road that parallels the old railway to Ironbridge and Bridgnorth, the Severn Valley line. The road was at one time the medieval highway to London via Bridgnorth which eventually became one of the major toll roads of the area. It passes through a number of pleasant villages at Cound, Cressage and Harley before rising up to Wenlock Edge, a section of road that was once known as Wenlock Pitch and which has suffered badly from landslips over the years.

MUCH WENLOCK

The town of Much Wenlock is an unassuming little place that is in the spotlight every time there's a run up to an Olympic Games, because it's where the ancient Greek concept of the Games was revitalised in 19th-century Britain. There's an **Olympian Trail** to celebrate the fact. It is easy to follow the trail around town from the Wenlock Museum/visitor information centre; follow the bronze marker plaques set in the pavement. However, it requires a bit of imagination to conjure up how life might have been for the young athletes of the time.

The centre of town lies a little to the east of a busy crossroads on the A458

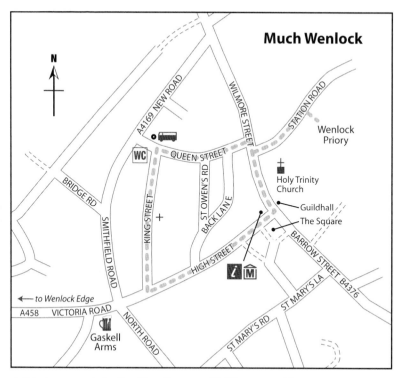

Much Wenlock

N

A4169 NEW ROAD

WILMORE STREET

STATION ROAD

Wenlock Priory

WC

QUEEN STREET

ST OWEN'S RD

Holy Trinity Church

BRIDGE RD

KING STREET

BACK LANE

Guildhall

The Square

SMITHFIELD ROAD

HIGH STREET

BARROW STREET B4376

ℹ 🅼

to Wenlock Edge

A458 VICTORIA ROAD

NORTH ROAD

ST MARY'S LA

ST MARY'S RD

Gaskell Arms

and this is somewhat off-putting if you are not in the know. Even the bus drops you off at the edge of the town centre in an easily forgotten spot. However, walk for two minutes and soon the medieval core of this magical little town is revealed. There is a cluster of old buildings nestled around the market place. These buildings include the half-timbered Guildhall and the Holy Trinity Church; they make the place very attractive. For many, however, the beauty of Wenlock priory, five minutes walk from the centre, is the main attraction. In many respects, the priory was the making of the town we see today. Throughout the medieval period the priory flourished and the town grew modestly to support its endeavours. It was at this time that the inner core around the Market Square was set out. The town is very much involved in the arts and there's wonderful poetry festival each year in July; this makes it a good time to visit.

Walking around town

From the bus stop in Queen Street, cross the road by the toilets and walk up King Street to High Street. Go left here and make your way into town. The prime building material was originally limestone hewn from Wenlock Edge and this is much in evidence, although brick has taken its place in later dwellings. There are a number of fine old buildings in this street including **Ashfield House**, said to have previously been part of St John's Hospital, dating from the 15th century. Its role was to look after 'lost and naked beggars'. Further along on the left is **Raynald's Mansion**, a 17th-century half-timbered town house of some character. Several of the pubs and other street scenes were featured in the film *Gone to Earth* (1949), the classic Pressburger and Powell production of Mary Webb's novel. Mary Webb lived for some time at The Grange just outside

The upper storey of the Guild Hall, a building which dates to 1540, with the church tower behind

Much Wenlock. A few scenes in the film which starred John Cleese as a headmaster, *Clockwise* (1980), were also filmed in the town.

There are three main streets leading to an open space often referred to as **The Square**, of which High Street is the principal one. There are also a number of passages linking streets too; you might notice Mutton Shut nearby. The area around The Square comprises the central part of town. A miniature clocktower is on the right in an open space; it dates from 1897 and is one of the many fine Victorian remnants throughout the town. The Square is a 20th-century feature replacing an area of rough ground and parking, much to the relief of residents.

Across the road is the small **Wenlock Museum** in the old **Market Hall**. It features three themes: geology, local history and the Olympian Movement. It is the starting point of the Olympian Trail, a tribute to the

importance of the revival movement that was started here principally by Dr William Penny Brookes. He was way ahead of his time on a number of matters including health care. Dr Brookes was also a founder of the Corn Market and **Agricultural Reading Room** located in High Street; this too dates back to the mid 19th century and is still a library. On some days local produce is sold beneath the bays where corn was once traded. Just across the street from The Square stands the magnificent half-timbered **Guild Hall** dating from 1540. This still houses a regular flea market. The market area sits beneath a courtroom and council chamber, adorned with exquisite wood panelling, funded by Dr Brookes in 1848. Above the judge's seat in the courtroom is an interesting inscription (in Latin) which has been translated as follows:

> This place abhors inequity
> Loves peace
> Punishes wrong doers
> Upholds the law
> Honours upright men

Dr Brookes was a very social philanthropist and his endless work in the town has been appreciated and admired over time.

Continue along Sheinton Street to see **Wenlock Pottery and craft centre** and there are also some historic almshouses in the vicinity. From here it is possible to walk via the Bull Ring to Wenlock Priory. On the way to the priory you'll pass by the large **Holy Trinity church**, built in Norman style during the 12th century under the influence of the priory. It is a large church which has had many modifications, principally Early English to Perpendicular changes in design that overlay a Norman structure. The nave, for example, was built in the 1150s by the priory monks and then modified in the late medieval period. The entire area remains a quiet quarter where time simply drifts along. It would have been busier in previous decades, no doubt, for the Bull Ring was the site of trading and bull baiting until it was banned in the early 1800s.

Main attraction

Many people visit Much Wenlock to enjoy the remains of the Cluniac **priory** which are administered by English Heritage; most of these romantic ruins date from the 13th century. They stand on the site of an early monastic building dating from the late 7th century, associated with Milburga, the daughter of the then King Merewald of Mercia. This earlier building was most probably sited on a Roman settlement, so this has been a favoured location throughout history. It was a wealthy establishment as Leofric, Earl of Mercia, devoted substantial funds to it. Some historians say that the Abbess Milburga was buried on site and that her remains were found in the early 12th century.

The Cluniac priory was established here by Roger de Montgomery in the late 11th century. He brought over monks to found a new priory that would be based on an existing priory at Cluny in Normandy. The only remains of the first building are beneath ground and what you see are re-builds and extensions made to earlier

Stonework in the chapter house at Much Wenlock Priory

structures, for the most part in the 13th century. This is especially the case with the priory church which is mainly Early English in style; the largest remaining structure is the south transept. Adjacent to it is the Chapter House, entered by a doorway with three orders of arches. The decoration of the arches is a reflection of the nature of this large room where the monks would have held meetings and communal readings of the bible. Another interesting part is the lavatorium, a rarity in the UK, although there are many examples remaining in French monasteries. This communal washroom with fountain retains a number of 12th-century carvings of the apostles and one of Christ's call to Peter. In St Michael's Chapel it is still possible to see decorative medieval tiles that have miraculously been saved from centuries of wear and tear.

The priory was dissolved in the winter of 1539-40 and much of the building was demolished for re-use throughout the town. The Prior's Lodge stands nearby (private property) and is considered to be the best preserved dwelling in the town; it dates from the 15th century. The house, now called Wenlock Abbey, was also part of the priory precinct but this too is a private dwelling.

WALKING

Wenlock Edge is one of the finest escarpments in the Marches, and its verdant scarp slope can be seen for miles. It stretches some 16 miles from the outskirts of Craven Arms through to the Severn Valley near Ironbridge. Covered in mixed woodland, comprising colonies of ash and oak, the wood is carpeted with an array of flowers, the likes of anemones, cowslips and orchids. Geologists world-wide adore the place for it was a tropical reef 420 million years ago, which means that crinoids and brachiopods are never far away. Some seven miles of the Edge are under the management of the National Trust that has recently acquired an old quarry which ceased extraction in 2009.

Much Wenlock is the only town located on Wenlock Edge and provides good access for walkers. There's nothing better than spending a day walking on the Edge from Much Wenlock to Easthope and the Wenlock Edge Inn at Hilltop (about 12 miles). Make your way along Victoria Road, which becomes Shrewsbury Road after the Gaskell Arms, a fine example of an old coaching inn that retains much of its traditional character. Climb up to a junction with Stretton Road where you turn left and then take the first right turn into a lane known as Blakeway Hollow. This gives out to a bridleway and you follow the **Shropshire Way** markers out to Easthope.The return stretch is via the Wenlock Edge Inn and Jack Mytton Way. Those keen to walk the entire length of the Edge might wish to stay at Wilderhope, an Elizabethan stone manor house in the quietest of spots, which was bequeathed to the National Trust but on the proviso that it would be used as a youth hostel. It is managed by the YHA and can be booked by phoning 0845 371 9149.

CYCLING

Much Wenlock is not the best place for cycling as many of the roads out of town, including the B4371 along the Edge, suffer badly from heavy and speeding traffic. The best way to access the Edge by cycle is from Craven Arms or possibly Ludlow for an outing into Corvedale. Some cyclists seek the off road bridleways along the Edge but there are currently no circuits of note.

REFRESHMENT

There are several cafés and pubs in Much Wenlock.

Pubs
Wenlock Edge Inn, Hill Top: great freshly prepared and locally sourced food and real ales.

EXTRAS

Farmers Market, Buttermarket: first and third Friday of the month.
Much Wenlock Visitor Information Centre: Museum, High Street, Tel: (01952) 727679.
Wenlock Poetry Festival in April (www. wenlockpoetryfestival.org). Attracts thousands with its big names in poetry, workshops and street performances. It is one of the best times to visit the town.

PUBLIC TRANSPORT

Buses to Much Wenlock
Shrewsbury Bus Station to Much Wenlock (Queen Street). 436. Hourly. Monday – Saturday. Six journey on Sunday. Travel time 35 minutes. Operator: Arriva.

The bus continues through to Bridgnorth.

WEM, CLIVE AND YORTON

Ride to Wem

It is a short ride by train to Wem via the village halt of Yorton. In all, it usually takes about 15 minutes. The journey has a number of highlights. The first is the departure from Shrewsbury station, with Howard's impressive gaol to your right and a glimpse of the Buttermarket, built in Grecian style in 1835 as a warehouse for the Shrewsbury Branch of the Shropshire Union Canal. However, take a look across to the left as the train moves off. On crossing the points immediately on departure, the train swings across the junction; the historic signal box on the left dates from 1884. It is a listed building as is the Severn Bridge Box located at the other end of the station. The signals are still operated by mechanical levers.

Now, take a glance to the right again to check the time. An original brick tower adorned with a clock dating from 1876 and proclaiming Morris Lubricants is invariably spot on. It was built originally as part of the Perseverance Iron Works. The train climbs an incline through the nondescript outskirts of Shrewsbury but at the urban fringe, on your left, is Battlefield Church and nearby is the site of the bloody Battle of Shrewsbury in 1403, when Henry IV and Price Hal defeated a force under Harry Hotspur who had rebelled against the throne, though with both sides sustaining heavy losses.

Some five minutes onward, on the right, is rich parkland and a late Georgian red brick house at Sansaw, obscured by leaf cover for much of the year. Then the train arrives at Yorton station, a halt used by stopping trains on request. If there's no one to alight or board, the train passes through at a snail's pace in case someone leaps out of the rustic waiting room at the very last moment. Next stop is Wem, a few minutes down the track, lying amid dairy green pastures. On the opposite side of the road to the railway station is the main bus stop in town for Shrewsbury, as it is also possible to travel to Wem, Clive and Yorton by bus 511 (Monday – Saturday) which follows a parallel route to the railway.

WEM

Wem is one of the smallest market towns in Shropshire and has seen better times. It had a large timber yard adjacent to the station, a corn mill and a major brewery right in the heart of town not that long ago, all of which employed many people from the locality. They are now gone, well almost; there's still a small brewery remaining in the town thanks to the efforts of Jack Hanby who upheld the tradition by brewing Wem ales in the 1990s. The Wem brewery is still going strong. The town's history may sound familiar. It first developed as a Saxon settlement but the Normans arrived and re-modelled it following the Conquest. Other than the narrow streets and a High Street which curves gently, little remains from this period despite there having been a castle and town walls *in situ*. There are, however, several handsome Georgian and Victorian buildings in town.

The town is home to the **Sweet Pea Festival**, an annual event usually held over a few days in July. The event is managed by the Eckford Sweet Pea Society of Wem, established to honour the work of William Eckford (1823-1905) who lived in the town for much of his life. During this time he worked tirelessly on developing hybrid varieties of sweet peas, some of which adorn contemporary gardens. At festival time there are usually displays in shops and plants available for sale including some of the Victorian favourites grown by the society's membership. Among other celebrities associated with Wem are two actors: the late Peter Jones and Peter Vaughan (of Porridge fame) who grew up in the area.

Walking around Town

Turn left from the station platform into Aston Street which heads into town. Pass by the **Millennium Garden**, where a mock Gothic chapel, dating from 1853, is situated on the left. Soon after, you'll walk by the **Morgan Library and Reading Room** dating from 1905. The library was given to the town by a notable JP in the 1920s and it is now Mythstories, a **Museum of Myth and Fable** devoted to storytelling. You are more or less in the town centre where there are a number of buildings of note, especially the old coaching inns with fine porches supported by solid Doric columns. On one of them sits a neat model of a castle. There's also the town hall and old post office dating from the early 1900s though their architectural merit is almost lost at street level.

It is best to cross the road at the top of High Street to take a closer look at the **church of St Peter and St Paul**, which is something of a centre-piece. This is the quiet end of town, interrupted only by passing traffic. Enter the churchyard through a lovely traditional gateway; the craftsmanship is impressive as the wrought iron gates are held by pillars adorned by Grecian vases. The church tower is medieval but the remainder is mainly a Victorian overhaul. From here you can walk down Mill Street to admire the old corn mill, standing alongside the shallow waters of the River Roden. It is a miracle that there was ever sufficient water to power the mill; evidently there were a succession of projects put in place to supplement the watermill using wind, steam, gas and finally electric power. The mill closed some years back and has been converted into apartments. There is no main attraction in Wem; it simply remains a sleepy town which has an old-fashioned feel about it.

CLIVE AND YORTON

The villages of Clive and Yorton can be visited *en route* to Wem. They make for a good half day walking tour. The villages are served by the railway station at Yorton, a request stop, or alternatively you can catch bus 511 to the post office in Clive. Trains call on a two-hourly schedule (approximately) including evenings and also Sunday, when they are less frequent. The

Clive church

Shrewsbury to Whitchurch bus also calls at Clive (approximately hourly Monday – Saturday until early evening).

The four mile walking tour involves a climb to the red sandstone escarpment of **Grinshill** where there are views across heathland towards Wales. This is the main attraction here; the views are exquisite. Assuming that you have arrived at Yorton railway station, it is possible to walk up to Clive by passing the Railway Hotel, a very traditional public house that is well worth the visit, and then ahead along Station Road. The alternative is to turn right on the lane from the entrance to Yorton Railway Station and take a path on the left, just beyond Yorton Farm, through fields to Clive. The fields have been cordoned off to secure horses but the path is clear enough. The feature to aim for is Clive church with its unusually tall spire. This was a late Victorian addition funded by the then owner of Sansaw Hall, a mercantilist who had a penchant for rolling out the money in pursuit of conspicuous wealth. The result is a much restored Victorian church dedicated to All Saints.

Grinshill

Just beyond the church entrance is a sunken lane, known locally as the Glat, which leads up to Grinshill and Corbet Wood. Tread lightly, for beneath your feet are sealed shafts; this was at one time Shrophire's most extensive copper mine. You can walk a circuit along Grinshill edge to Corbet Wood and then follow a path which curves down through the old quarry workings; the stone has been used extensively across Shropshire including at Attingham Hall and to build the English and Welsh bridges in Shrewsbury. It is said that the stonework around that famous doorway, Number 10 Downing Street, is also from Grinshill so take a look next time it is on News At Ten.

Continue your walk along the old cartway to the hamlet of Grinshill. There are several fine houses clustered around the road here, each one dating from a different period and exuding exceptional architectural use of the nearby source of stone. The grand Tuscan porch across the road is a timely reminder of the need for refreshment at the Inn at Grinshill. It welcomes walkers into its Elephant and Castle bar. There's a bridleway back to Clive church where you can wander down to the Railway Hotel at Yorton before your return to the station or bus stop (at the junction on the other side of the railway underbridge). Allow 2 hours for your exploration and longer if you call in somewhere.

WALKING

There's a pleasant 20-minute walk from Wem along the banks of the River Roden to the village of Tilley, where there are several prominent half-timbered houses nestled around the Tilley Raven public house. The walk branches off right along a track, opposite Wem Mill. The track gives out by a dwelling at a kissing gate into a large field. Follow the riverside around to a bridge by a confluence of two waters.

Go over the bridge, then ahead through another kissing gate to a road. Turn left here for the village. If you prefer not to walk back to Wem and would like to catch the bus you can continue ahead (as the village road bends left) along a no through road. Cross the railway tracks with care and then proceed to the main road. The bus stop on the opposite side is for Clive and Shrewsbury. If you fancy a longer walk then continue on the Shropshire Way to Grinshill. It is about seven miles, waymarked and passing through pleasant but not spectacular countryside.

CYCLING

An alternative way to travel to Wem is to cycle on the National Cycle Route between Shrewsbury and Upton Magna (Route 81). At this point, you go left on Route 45 north to the hamlet of Booley where there's a recommended route via Lee Brockhurst through to Wem. This route follows quiet roads, which are relatively traffic free but not entirely so, and there are two major highways to be crossed, so care is needed. The cycle trip is approximately 17 miles in length (one way) but the going is easy and it makes for a great day out. There's an option to catch the train out to Wem with your cycle and ride back.

REFRESHMENT

Wem

There are a few cafés or pubs but none which merit specific mention.

Pub

Tilley Raven Public House: the pub prides itself in using local produce and sourcing traditional beers, cider and perry from the Marches in the main.

Local Produce

T.O. Williams: situated on the High Street, this well known delicatessen specialises in bakery products and a wide range of cheeses including many local varieties.

Clive

Inn at Grinshill: this hotel prides itself in using locally produced ingredients wherever possible.

Station Hotel, Yorton: very traditional public house with local beers served.

EXTRAS

Jack Davies Cycles, High Street; sells parts and undertakes repairs.

Wem Farmers Market: 2nd Saturday of the month, Leek Street.

PUBLIC TRANSPORT

Trains
Shrewsbury Railway Station to Yorton and Wem. Yorton is a request stop. Approximately two hourly on Monday – Saturday. Six trains on Sunday. Travel time 10-15 minutes.

Buses to Clive, Yorton and Wem
Shrewsbury Bus Station to Wem via Clive and Yorton. Mainly hourly. Monday – Saturday only. Travel time 25-45 minutes. Operator: Arriva.

OSWESTRY

Lying between the Welsh foothills and the Shropshire Plain, Oswestry is one of those borderland places where rival forces have clashed swords on many occasions. Perhaps the explanation lies in the fact that until the 1700s the town was decidedly Welsh in character rather than English. However, curiously enough, its name is not of Welsh derivation. The name Oswestry comes from the phrase 'Oswald's Tree'. If the story is to be believed Oswald, King of Northumbria, was slain here and then dismembered and hung on a tree by Penda of Mercia. This gesture was evidently merely a warning to others intent on challenging him; it was nothing personal against Oswald. From then onwards, Oswestry held a strategic borderland position, and this brought endless trouble through to the 15th century, a period in which sacking and burning became the order of the day.

A major change swept through the place in the 19th century. A wave of urban expansion followed the arrival of the Cambrian Railways in the 1860s, especially after the company decided to make the town its headquarters and construct a significant manufacture and repair works in the locality. The outer shell of the old works is now being restored and the interior converted to apartments. But the development of the railway was a sobering shock to the system, especially for those who had intended Oswestry to stay as a cosy market town. The town's custodians had resisted numerous attempts by the Shrewsbury and Chester Railway to put it on the rail map some 20 years earlier. The Cambrian Railway, however, was made more welcome. There had been a mellowing effect and a train service was no longer so frowned upon.

The result is that there are in effect two towns, one centred on the old medieval quarter and the other reflecting a 19th-century railway sprawl of mixed terraced housing and industrial warehouses near to sidings. The two towns do not blend particularly well, and late 20th-century highway developments simply thwart attempts to

One attraction of Oswestry is the range of individual shops and cafés

hold on to the heritage of the town. The one-way system and the constant flow of traffic make it unpleasant in some places. The main advantage of staying in Oswestry is that it is exceptionally well positioned to access the Offa's Dyke Path and the Welsh foothills for walking and cycling.

Walking around town

First stop from the bus station is the old **Cambrian Railway Station**, just across Oswald Road. The Cambrian Railway Heritage Company is at the heart of the Cambrian Railway revival with a little help from partner organisations. The aim is to open a steam railway between Gobowen and Nantmawr; the latter was a branch line that was more successful in clinging onto life than the main route to Welshpool or the Tanat Valley spur. As part of the overall project, the Cambrian Railway buildings at Oswestry have been revitalised. The station is one of the finest Victorian buildings in town; there's now a café and information centre here. There's a museum (open daily 1 - 4pm) located in one of the old goods sheds next door which is a treasure trove of railway memorabilia and a great place to browse around.

Make your way up Oswald Road, passing the Oswestry Technical Institute on the right and the imposing classical-style Presbyterian Chapel of 1888 on the left, to a crossroads with Leg Street. Cross carefully over to Cross Street towards the centre of town. As you approach The Cross; you're bound to catch sight of a jettied, half-timbered building on the right.

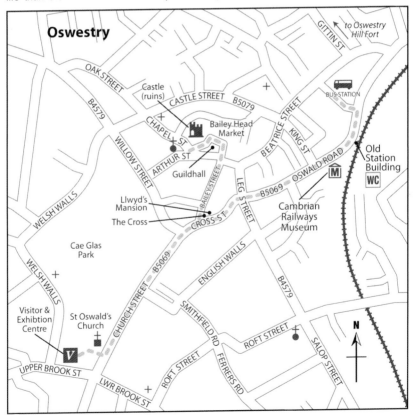

Llwyd's Mansion, Cross Street

This is **Llwyd's Mansion**, a splendid survival dating mainly from the 17th century but with earlier medieval features. There is actually a cross at The Cross. It was restored in 1862 and continues to be one of the key meeting places in town.

Keep ahead into Church Street, by far the most pleasant street, wide, decked with flowers and leading to **St Oswald's church** on the right and a fetching cluster of Georgian houses beyond. The church is thought to be on the site of a previous Saxon church of which there are no remains. Nor is there much of a legacy when it comes to the Norman period as only the tower is of Norman origin. The remainder dates from an extensive rebuild in the 1660s after the destruction of the English Civil War, or from a major restoration in the 19th century. There's an unusual monument in the church to the 17th-century Yale family, who emigrated to found Yale University.

You can walk through the churchyard, where there are exceptionally fine gate piers and wrought iron to admire. There's also a plaque to war poet **Wilfred Owen**,

The Cross

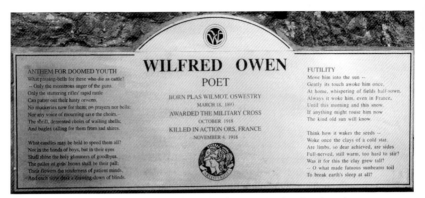

The plaque to Wilfred Owen by the gates to the churchyard

who was born in the town, before reaching the Heritage Centre and café. Return along Church Street to The Cross. On your right is the town's main hotel, the Wynnstay, an 18th-century red brick coaching inn with a porch that reflects the elegance of the period. On the left is **Bellan House**, a handsome late 18th-century town house and next door is **Cae Glas park**, a well-tended park which is a popular haunt for lunchtime strollers.

From The Cross, walk up Bailey Street to Bailey Head, a square full of pubs and at its best when market stalls fill the place. To the left, at the top of the square, stands the **Guildhall**, a late Victorian municipal building built of Grinshill sandstone. Walk by it to gain access to **Oswestry Castle**. It is hard to believe that the castle earthworks remain here given the changes of land use around it. There's a small amount of stonework, thought to be part of an early keep although some dispute this and argue that these fragments could be remnants of the old town wall.

The castle was built in the late 12th century by Lord Rainald and passed on to the Fitzalan family who strengthened it in the 13th century, for Oswestry was perceived as being paramount to the borderline defence against the Welsh (see Extras). This was the case for over three centuries but it was reported as being in disrepair by the 15th century. Its fate was sealed in the English Civil War after the

Parliamentarians repulsed a Royalist siege here after which the castle was dismantled for good. It is possible to climb up steps to walk the perimeter of the motte so as to admire the views. Look over to the east as there's a mix of buildings throughout town. The view to the west highlights Old Oswestry hillfort (see main attraction) above the roof tops, but the foreground is something of a disappointment. The castle now stands in a car park; this must be disheartening for those in Oswestry campaigning to retain its rich heritage. Return to Bailey Head and turn left into Albion Street and left again to follow Beatrice Street back to the bus station sandwiched between two supermarkets.

Main attraction

The main attraction sits somewhat aloof from it all on high ground near to the edge of town. It is one super-size version of an Iron Age fortification, known as **Old Oswestry hillfort**, which spreads across 40 acres of ground. Admittedly, the Marches have their fair share of prehistoric sites but the scale and intricate nature of these earthworks make them rather special. The ramparts and ditches are clearly delineated on the site and as you tread the earth here you can feel the power of the ancients beneath your feet.

From Oswestry it is a 20-minute walk to the site as there's no bus. It is not entirely tiresome but is best described

The prominent outlines of the multivallate ramparts of Old Oswestry hillfort

as workaday. From the bus station turn right into Beatrice Street and after a few metres, turn left into Gittin Street. Follow this across Liverpool Road and by a school to your right. On the left there are some very productive allotments. Keep right to walk into Gatacre Avenue and this gives out into a car park and interpretation board about the fort. A path runs along the edge of the recreational ground to the road by the fort (although there's also a path diagonally across the next field which offers an alternative). Go left on the road and right to enter the site of the fort.

It is worth mentioning that there's another route to the fort, from Gobowen. You can cycle the 4-5 miles from Gobowen railway station on NCN Route 31 via the farmsteads of Trewern (interesting Italianate style of buildings here evidently built in the 19th century), Lower Hengoed and Cross Lanes along roads that see little traffic. There's a first mundane stretch from Gobowen railway station along the B5096 where care has to be taken. There is also a walk from the station which, like the cycle trip, is urban for the first half mile but then the path leaves the road through a copse to traverse a pleasant pastoral landscape. You join Wat's Dyke Way, a lightly trodden path leading to the fort. This long distance trail follows the line of the old dyke, some 61 miles, between the River Dee and Llanymynech.

Wat's Dyke is one of those features which remain something of a mystery. There's little known about this linear borderland earthwork which runs for miles, virtually parallel to Offa's Dyke. However, a small number of archaeological digs have unearthed evidence which suggests

that Wat's Dyke was built in the 5th century rather than the mid 8th century as had previously been thought. The reason for its existence may well have been to restrain the Cornovii tribe at that time. The view of the hillfort from the penultimate field before reaching the monument shows to good effect the size of the fortification and what it must have been like to take courage before attacking a site that looks so formidable.

Other attractions

Whittington Castle. Whittington is on the main bus route 70 from Shrewsbury to Oswestry and it might be worth getting off for a while to explore the restored castle ruins and moat sitting comfortably in the middle of the village. The bus stop is called Three Trees, by a village green and it is two minutes walk from there to the castle. Like Oswestry it was rated as a key link in the borderland defence. The FitzWarin family became entrenched here in the 13th century and strengthened it against attacks by Llewelyn I. The FitzWarins were in residence for at least two centuries. In the late 14th century, however, the castle began to decay and it was derelict until it came into the hands of the Lloyd family in the early 1800s. It was during this period that the mock drum towers and drawbridge over the moat were reconstructed purely for aesthetic reasons, and this is your way in. The castle is now leased and managed by the community trust in Whittington. It is doing a great job in raising funds to restore and improve interpretation of the castle (see www.whittingtoncastle.co.uk for opening times of castle and café).

WALKING

Oswestry has a wide range of walking opportunities, from gentle canalside walking on the Montgomery or Llangollen canals, to hill walking on the Welsh borders. It is possible to walk from town, either via Broomhall lane and paths to **Offa's Dyke Path** at Candy Mill or via Bwlch to Oswestry Racecourse. A good day's walk is to catch the bus or train to Chirk then walk via **Maelor's Way** to join Offa's Dyke Path at Bronygarth for a 10 mile walk back to Oswestry.

CYCLING

There are four local cycle routes, varying from 13 to 31 miles, that offer superb day rides into the countryside and villages near Oswestry. They use quiet lanes for the most part and select the least busy routes out of town. Three of them cover routes to the west and south, as the A5 has become a major barrier to both walking and cycling routes to the north. These routes are written up in *Oswestry Cycle Rides* available from Oswestry Heritage centre or on line at www.shropshire.gov.uk/cycling. nsf. Some of the routes involve crossing very busy main roads so care is needed at these locations.

REFRESHMENTS

There are plenty of cafés (many of which are fairtrade devotees) and pubs in Oswestry. Here are three favourites:

Cafés and Restaurants

Booka Bookshop and café, Church Street; a contemporary café serving fairtrade coffee and organic teas amid a wide selection of books. Open daily.

Brooks Restaurant, Church Street: specialises in fish and vegetarian dishes using locally sourced ingredients wherever possible.

Gilhams, Church Street: a deli and coffee shop which promotes local food heroes.

Shropshire Poacher at the Heritage Centre: old fashioned tea rooms.

Pubs

There are a fair number of pubs in Oswestry but there's none that stand out.

Local Produce

A legendary wholefood shop, **Honeysuckle Wholefoods**, 53 Church Street, is an amazing cooperative retailer set up in 1978 and still going strong.

EXTRAS

Farmers Market, Bailey Head: 1st Friday of each month.

Burtscher, Michael (2008) *The Fitzalans, Earls of Arundel and Surrey, Lords of the Welsh Marches (1267-1415)*, Logaston Press.

Lewis, P. (2009) *Wats Dyke Heritage Trail*, Alyn Books.

Os21: environmental group seeking sustainable development of Oswestry. Visitors welcome to meetings and events. Contact www.oswestry21.co.uk.

Oswestry Town Guided Tours: all year-check visitor information centre for details.

Oswestry Town Visitor Information Centre: Heritage Centre, Church Terrace, Tel: 01691 662753.

Stuart Barkley Cycles, Salop Road: cycle sales and repair.

Wat's Dyke Way: wwwwatsdykeway. org.

PUBLIC TRANSPORT

Trains

Gobowen is served directly by trains from Chester and North Wales, Shrewsbury and Birmingham and the Midlands as well as London. Gobowen Railway Station is currently the railhead for Oswestry.

It is possible to catch a regular bus from the Post Office, Gobowen (out of the station and right into Old Whittington Road where the bus stop for Oswestry is by the fish and chip shop).

Buses 2 and 53. Approximately every 30 minutes on Monday – Saturday. It is a 10-minute ride into town. Operator: Arriva. Taxis also meet most trains.

Buses

Oswestry Bus Station is also served by a daily bus service from Shrewsbury. The buses arrive in a bus station sandwiched between two supermarkets on the edge of the central quarter.

There are two routes from Shrewsbury. Bus 70 is the frequent, mainline bus that operates via Nesscliffe (The Old Three Pigeons), ideal for accessing Nesscliffe Country Park, great walking territory.

The other route 576 is roughly two hourly and passes through Ruyton-XI-Towns, Knockin and Maesbury Marsh. Mon – Sat only. Operator: Arriva.

EXCURSIONS FROM OSWESTRY

CHIRK AND THE CEIRIOG VALLEY

Ride to Chirk

Chirk is less than 10 minutes down the track from **Gobowen**, a place where the residents were once known as 'gobs'. It is currently the railhead for Oswestry. The station was built for the Shrewsbury and Chester Railway in 1848 and is something of a masterpiece. It is probably the main reason you would decide to visit **Gobowen. The station building**, lovingly restored in 1989, has beautifully proportioned curved windows and an apse and square tower that give it a touch of refinement not to be seen at many rural stations. The styling is Italianate or more precisely of a classical Florentine nature. At first glance, the white stuccoed rendering might look a little over the top, but then both design and finish begin to win you over with their freshness.

On the Shrewsbury platform you will find more historic buildings, built by the Great Western Railway in the 1860s. Umbrella awnings extend along each platform, reminiscent of a railway era long since gone. The revival of Gobowen Station was inspired by the late David Lloyd, a teacher who set out to prove the importance of the railway to his community. His good work has encouraged others to follow on, and a booking office is now managed by Severn-Dee Travel. At the south end of Platform One, there's a forlorn, single buffer dropping to the ground at an angle alongside the bay platform. This is where trains once departed for Oswestry, and the hope is that they will return. The replica GWR board indicates that this is the place to change for Oswestry; it is an omen, perhaps, that the 'flyer' may be back soon. That would be great.

The short trip to Chirk is uneventful except for the very last minute when the train hurtles out of a cutting over the 16 arches of **Chirk viaduct**, standing high above the Afon Ceiriog valley. It is 100 feet above the river so, if you do not like heights, close your eyes. The ceremony of placing the last keystone, in order to lock the stonework of the viaduct together, took place in 1848, sealing the work of engineer Henry Robertson and his loyal workers for centuries to come. Upstream, but actually 30 feet lower than the railway viaduct, is the aqueduct designed and built by William Jessop and Thomas Telford between 1975 and 1801. This carries the Llangollen branch of the Shropshire Union Canal and is much loved by walkers and boaters alike. Initially, the canal builders envisaged a massive embankment but the then owner of Chirk Castle remonstrated that his views would be severely curtailed and asked the engineers to reconsider. They responded and to good effect.

It is also possible to travel by bus from Oswestry Bus Station to Chirk (Hand Hotel). The 20-minute journey is pleasant enough. Whichever way you travel, the Afon Ceiriog marks a very beautiful boundary between England and Wales. From Chirk railway station it is five minutes' walk along Station Avenue to the centre of town where the bus stops are located either side of the Hand Hotel.

Walking around town

Chirk stands on a bluff, an obvious site for defence. This is where the first castle was built in the 1130s; it stood near to the parish church of St Mary which was originally dedicated to the Celtic saint, Tysilio. It is now the focal point of a town conservation area. The main street, Holyhead Road, is a good example of how to calm down traffic by using different road surfaces. It makes the place tolerable. At the junction with Station Avenue there's a large coronation oak planted in a small public garden and behind it is a curious little plaque on a wall. This is a tribute to Billy Meredith, one of football's first superstars, who started his career with Chirk FC. It was one of earliest clubs founded in Wales and the team is still known as the Colliers, a reflection of a time when there were strong mining connections here.

Main Attraction

The main attraction is **Chirk Castle**, a formidable fortress, now partly in the hands of the National Trust. Built to serve the needs of the Marcher overlord Roger

Chirk Castle

Mortimer of Chirk, head of a branch of the Mortimer family of Wigmore, in the early days of the 13th century, it is recorded as the last castle in Wales to be built within the reign of Edward I. In the late 16th century it was purchased by Thomas Myddelton, establishing a lineage associated with the castle to this day.

The best way to reach the castle is a mile walk from the railway station. Go right across the railway bridge and ahead to the gates on this back lane. The old entrance gates date from the 1720s. Such a munificence of wrought iron is rarely seen. This is not your way, however. Keep right to pass a couple of entrances and then there's a path to the left, much more of a subdued tradesmen's entrance. This is a permissive walkers' route across the estate, marked by kissing gates and posts topped out in white. You can use them only between 1st April and the last day in September, and the route guides you to Home Farm.

The parkland is attributed to the 18th-century landscape gardener William Emes, who made a name for himself principally in mid-England, working to similar design principles to Capability Brown. Emes made a number of forays into Wales including work at the Erddig estate near Wrexham and, of course, his masterpiece here. On reaching Home Farm there's a farm shop, refreshments including locally made icecream and an information centre where you buy tickets for the castle or gardens and tower only.

The castle itself is a revelation. The thick exterior walls show that this was a defensive site not to be assailed easily. Inside, there are remnants of an earlier inner core. What could be more medieval than a tower and dungeon? However, there is also an opportunity to admire a number of stately rooms for those with more refined taste. In particular, spend time in the long gallery dating from the 17th and 18th centuries. This defines what is meant by stately rooms. Each room highlights the incremental modifications made by the Myddelton family throughout the ages to make this a salubrious home within the constraints of a fortified castle. The where-withal to do so came from the extensive mining rights and agricultural tenancies associated with the estate. The gardens are splendid, especially if you are into yew trees in a big way. The hedges are enormous. The mix of borders and shrubs bring a challenging complexity to the surprisingly sheltered gardens. There's a hawk house too, reflecting a time when hunting with birds of prey was a popular pursuit.

It is possible to follow a different walking route back. There is a path down to Castle Mills on the road to Glyn Ceiriog; it is no more than a mile. The permissive path cuts away to the right from the exit road by the junction to the castle. It descends through woodland to a pasture where you can see quite clearly the earthworks of Offa's Dyke. There's then a steep section descending to the valley road where you'll find a bus stop for Chirk (or stand on the opposite side for Glyn Ceiriog). Otherwise, there's a longer walk back, about 3 miles more. Cross the road and proceed ahead. There's an interesting plaque on the bridge parapet highlighting the battle of Grogen in 1165 between Henry II and Owain Gwynedd. Rise up to a junction where you turn left to head for Chirk using the Ceiriog Valley Walk – see walking section below for details.

THE CEIRIOG VALLEY

If it had not been for the eloquence and passion of the speeches of Liberal politician Lloyd George, the Ceiriog Valley would have been flooded in order to supply water to England, or more exactly to the brewing town of Warrington. One slogan at the time was that 'The English are taking the W out of Wales and turning it to ales'. The impassioned speeches of the former Prime Minister to a packed Parliament in 1923 put the project on hold, and from then onwards its backers lost momentum and finally withdrew the proposal. There is now a determined cry from local communities to counter proposals for large scale wind

farms on the surrounding hills which drop steeply to the valley floor.

The deeply incised valley of the Afon Ceiriog has a certain romance about it; the dappled waters and overhanging trees make it cool and lovely on a summer's day. There's an air of tranquillity which pervades the place. It is known locally as the valley of the poets having been home to at least three writers cited in Welsh literature: Huw Morris, the Reverend Robert Ellis and John 'Ceiriog' Hughes. Of the three, Ceiriog Hughes is perhaps the best known and his work is still celebrated in the Ceiriog Memorial Institute (Neuadd Gloffa Ceiriog) in the High Street at Glyn Ceiriog. There are other displays reflecting local Welsh culture at the Institute, but opening times are limited.

The ride on the bus up the valley is delightful. For much of the run there are glimpses of the fast flowing river and you'll most probably see a heron waiting for its catch on the way. The bus allows you to take in the beauty of the valley, the way hill pastures and woodland give way to rough moorland. It also passes through the villages of Pontfadog and Dolywern to Glyn Ceiriog, although none are particularly pretty.

Glyn Ceiriog

This is the main settlement in the valley. Sitting outside the Glyn Valley Hotel and watching the world go by is a pleasant enough pastime. There's not much traffic on the road and there's a stillness that is soothing. The Memorial Institute (Neuadd Goffa Ceiriog) is on High Street, about two or three minutes away, and the Theo Davies wood workshop is a similar distance. It is open to the public if you'd like to call in. Otherwise, it is the countryside that counts here for walking, riding or cycling.

The bus stop for Llanarmon is by the old railway shed belonging to the **Glyn Ceiriog Tramway** and there are plans to develop this site in order to explain the heritage of the line in the valley. There were several stone and slate quarries and these were served by the Glyn Ceiriog Tramway, an operation that lasted from 1872 until 1935. At first, this was a horse-drawn tramway and then it was converted for steam traction in 1887. The gauge was most unusual being 2 feet 4.5 inches whereas many were built at 2 feet 6 inches. Glyn Ceiriog was the hub of the system and tracks ran along the village streets from outlying quarries down to the main line in the valley bottom.

The loss of passenger trade to the emergent bus network and a reduction of freight brought closure as early as 1935. In more recent times, the Glyn Valley Tramway Group has unveiled ambitious plans to interpret the history of the 6 mile line from Chirk to the quarries beyond Glyn Ceiriog. This might possibly work out as a trail based on the old trackbed. Some parts can be walked at present, like the section at Pandy, which is in the ownership of the National Trust. However, there's a greater scheme in the offing. The aim is to recreate an operating tramway again between Chirk Railway Station and Pontfaen or possibly just beyond to the Chirk Trout Farm and Smokery. Given that the line has been closed for more than 65 years this is likely to be something of a financial struggle. Nevertheless, it would be great to see the dream come true and passengers arrive in the valley by tram.

Llanarmon Dyffryn Ceiriog (DC)

The bus ride up to Llanarmon DC is really worth it. The road climbs up the valley as it narrows towards Pandy. There's a **fulling mill** here, established in the 15th century and, having been a pub for some time, it is now a gallery. Some of the largest quarries were excavated nearby but the scars have been covered by nature in the 70-year interlude since closure. It is quite a revelation to look at pictures of the industrial scale of quarrying in the 19th century and see how green it all is now.

Soon the views open up as you approach the last settlement of any size in the valley. This really is the end of the road (well, the B4500). There was once an old trading route across the Berwyn Mountains, and the walking from Llanarmon is ideal for those who enjoy a wild, windswept landscape that challenged the Welsh drover. Perhaps the best known is a track leading up to the upper reaches of the River Ceiriog which then climbs over moorland to Llandrillo, near Bala. If you want the rough stuff then this is for you. There's a daily bus service back to Wrexham (and onward to Chirk) from Bala.

Llanarmon DC developed as a staging post and river crossing where drovers would rest overnight before continuing to markets in Chirk and Oswestry. Llanarmon has not grown much since those days; it still remains a small Welsh village where guests stay before or after their big adventure. The Hand public house stands on the left and the West Arms Hotel on the right as you enter the village. Both are welcoming hostelries. Walk along to the Victorian **church of St Garmon** and you will see the remains of a Bronze Age burial mound by the entrance to the churchyard. Beyond is farmland where buzzards and red kite can be seen above the farmsteads on the valley slopes, a reminder that this is a truly remote upland area.

The Hand inn at Llanarmon

The West Arms Hotel at Llanarmon

WALKING

In some respects the best way to experience both the natural beauty and the industrial heritage of the valley is on foot. The views unfold almost at every turn, and there are several trails to follow. By far the best is *The Ceiriog Valley Walk* which offers walks between bus stops in each of the communities in the valley. It is possible to take the bus up to Llanarmon and walk the 12 miles back to Chirk. This makes for a splendid day's walking. Otherwise, it lends itself to linear walks between villages. The walk has a white waymark on a red-orange background.

Offa's Dyke National Trail crosses the valley at Castle Mill, near Chirk Castle, where the bus will set down. From here it is possible to follow Offa's Dyke Trail, over the bridge to join the Maelor Way which you follow back into Chirk via Chirk Bank. The final section is on the canal towpath for the walk across Chirk aqueduct and through Chirk Tunnel (torch required) back to the railway station – first path on the right after the tunnel. This route leads through a mosaic of pasture, semi-natural woodland and riverside by the fast flowing,

pure waters which offer an ideal habitat for trout. It is about three miles with some climbs so it is best to allow two hours.

The **Maelor Way** is worthy of further exploration. It starts at Grindley Brook, near Whitchurch in Cheshire, where it connects with the Sandstone Trail, Shropshire Way and South Cheshire Way. For some 24 miles it passes through pleasant and relatively unknown territory to Bronygarth (near Castle Mill) where it joins Offa's Dyke National Trail.

*The Chirk Tunnel on the canal
– torch needed!*

CYCLING AND HORSE RIDING

The **Ceiriog** (14 miles) and **Upper Ceiriog** (23 miles) **trails** are designed for multi-use and they are well used, in parts, by both horse riders and mountain bikers (see Extras). These are not particularly easy walking routes and the wet patches can be difficult to negotiate. Cyclists might also seek out the **Ceiriog Cycle Route**, established in the early 2000s by Groundwork. This 27 mile circuit out of Chirk is strenuous and is suited to the experienced cyclist. Some prefer to ride on the main road up the valley on the B4500 although note that the traffic can be heavy and there are real and sometimes continuous climbs on the outward leg.

REFRESHMENT

Chirk

Pubs
The Hand Hotel, Holyhead Road: with its fine portico entrance, this traditional hotel is open for coffee as well as meals and drinks.

Local produce
McCardles, a traditional butcher and Eccleston's bakery, both of which supply refreshments as does the café across the road.

Glyn Ceiriog Valley

Pubs
The Glyn Valley Hotel: open all day and serves homemade food. There are some splendid pictorial references to the old tramway inside.

The Oak: open at lunchtimes during the weekend and evenings and is very much into local seasonal food. The view from the deck across the valley is stunning.

The Golden Pheasant Hotel: a mile or so from Glyn Ceiriog village; it sources local seasonal produce for its restaurant.

Llanarmon DC

Pubs
Hand Inn and **West Arms Hotel** are Good Beer Guide entries which offer refreshment and use local suppliers.

Local Produce
Chirk Trout Farm and smokery (near Castle Mill).

EXTRAS
Glyn Ceiriog: Tourist information is available at the post office on the Oswestry road.

The Memorial Hall is open on the first and third Saturday of the month between April and the end of September.

The Ceiriog Valley Walk is a project of the Chirk and Ceiriog Valley Partnership and a booklet is available from local outlets.

The Pandy Mill Gallery displays many fine examples of contemporary stained glass work.

There are a number of **equestrian centres** in the valley: see www.atspringhill.co.uk, an organic farm, 2.5 miles from Glyn Ceiriog, for details.

PUBLIC TRANSPORT

Trains
Gobowen Railway Station to Chirk. Approximately hourly on Monday – Saturday and at least two hourly on Sunday. Travel time 6 minutes.

Buses to Chirk
Oswestry Bus Station to Chirk (Hand Hotel). 2/2A Half hourly. Monday – Saturday only. Travel time 20 minutes. Operator: Arriva

Buses in the Ceiriog Valley
Chirk (Holyhead Road) to Llanarmon via Glyn Ceiriog. 64 Monday – Saturday. Hourly to Glyn Ceiriog, two hourly to Llanarmon. Travel time 20-30 minutes. Operator: GHA Coaches.

LLANYMYNECH AND LLANFYLLIN

Ride to Llanfyllin

The bus to Llanymynech from Oswestry runs between the higher ground of Sweeney Mountain, Llynclys and Llanymynech hills to the west and the lower lying rich pasture land to the east. The bus reaches Llynclys (at the White Lion), the stop for railway heritage aficionados as this is where the Cambrian Heritage Railways station is located. It is a five-minute walk from the main road crossroads (the main road is a hard one to cross so take care). Trains operate between Llynclys South railway station and Pen-y-Garreg halt. From Pen-y-Garreg it is a pleasant walk along the old tramway path linking to the canal towpath into Llanymynech. It is a nice way to arrive. It takes about an hour in total.

Llanymynech is something of a crossroads for buses and it is possible to travel on to Welshpool and Shrewsbury from here if needs be. The bus service to Llanfyllin from Llanymynech is less frequent, so a little planning is required to tie the two destinations together. The scenery on the road up to Llanfyllin is green and varied. It includes flood meadows of the River Vyrnwy (Afon Efyrnwy) and alongside the waters of the Cain (pronounced Kine). The River Cain (Afon Cain) is renowned for its salmon fishing and there have been projects in recent years to reduce pollution in the river to improve habitats for salmonoids.

LLANYMYNECH

Llanymynech lies at the very edge of the Severn Plain, just to the north of the River Vyrnwy which is joined a few miles upstream by the tributaries of the Cain and Tanat and downstream by the River Morda (Afona Morda). The Vyrnwy continues to meander through flood meadows to a confluence with the River Severn at Melverley. The village is overshadowed by a limestone escarpment known as **Llanymynech Hill** and the view west from the top, across the Tanat Valley to the hills of Moelydd and Mynydd-y-Bryn and the Berwyns, is something of a contrast to the surrounding lowlands of the east. It is easy enough to follow Offa's Dyke Path up from the bridge over the canal on the main street through the village (A483) to enjoy that view. The plateau at the top has been given over to a golf course so beware of those little white missiles.

The Hoffman lime kiln at Llanymynech, with added pieces of artwork

Main attraction

The main attraction in Llanymynech is its rich **industrial heritage** located in the main alongside the Montgomery Canal and the old Cambrian railway line. This area is easily accessed from the main crossroads at the centre of the village. From The Cross Keys Hotel turn right to rise up to the Montgomery Canal (in the direction of Welshpool). Take the next turning right through the car park to the heritage site. There are several limekilns here that have been restored to good effect. The **Hoffman lime kiln**, one of only three surviving in the UK, is an amazing sight amid a jungle setting of undergrowth; nature has been recapturing these slopes in recent years with vitality. The kiln, built in the last decade of the 19th century, burned material on a continuous basis. Evidently using less coal and producing a finer lime, it was considered to be a major breakthrough in relation to the output of the older, inverted bottle-shaped kilns of the time. Men working in shifts would feed the kiln on a 24-hour basis, and a draught and smoke release was provided by a 140 foot (42 metre) tall chimney. The kiln has been beautifully restored and the re-constructed pathways allow exploration of the historic artefacts.

It is also worth climbing up the old tramway on the incline plane to the site of the winding house. It is quite a gradient and you'll need sturdy shoes or boots. At the top you can go left to the Welsh **quarry** face or right for the English quarry face as the boundary runs right through the middle of it all. Llanymynech Hill was inhabited by prehistoric tribes and there are remains of a **Bronze Age hillfort**. Historians point out that there was early mining of minerals especially by the Romans. However, the big story is how limestone was quarried on a large scale from the 18th century through to the early years of the 20th century. Once transported down the hill it was burnt as lime and then was ready for despatch by wagon or narrowboat (the canal opened to this point in 1796) and, in due course, by the railway which came in 1863. The main uses of the slaked lime were for agriculture but also as lime mortar for the building trade and for flux in the ironmaking foundries of the Black Country. Other parts of the heritage area can be explored and there's a useful leaflet describing a walk which links the various parts (see Extras).

Llanfyllin church

LLANFYLLIN

This small town, en route to Lake Vrynwy, is nestled around the large Georgian brick **church of St Myllins**. The church is associated with the Celtic saint said to have been baptised in St Myllins well, located nearby. The town received a Welsh charter in 1293 and as part of the 700 year celebrations a tapestry was made and this is housed in the church. The bus stops outside or opposite the Lower Cross Keys pub and from here you can potter around the town; the central area is the main attraction but note that even a slow perambulation does not take long. Given the very quiet nature of Llanfyllin, it is hard to believe that it had its own railway branch from Llanymynech, and like the Tanat valley line it survived on freight rather than passengers. The old Cambrian railway station is still *in situ* (now private property); it is surrounded by an industrial estate.

On the way into town you might have noticed the **Old Workhouse** (known in Welsh as Y Dolydd), which was built in 1838 to house the poorest of the poor from 20 local parishes in accordance with the harsh Poor Law regime that existed in the 19th century. The buildings fell into disrepair in the 1980s but are being restored to house galleries, a café and accommodation. They will also be the venue for courses and events of which the Green Fayre (held in August or September) is a brilliant example of the innovation associated with the place. If you want to hop off here, ask the driver well before you arrive into town. You can then walk into town afterwards; it takes about 5-10 minutes.

WALKING

Offa's Dyke Path passes through Llanymynech and it is possible to walk back to Oswestry (about 12 miles) cutting off from the dyke at Candy Mill for a local path into Oswestry. For those wanting a shorter walk it is possible to follow the Offa's Dyke Path up to Llanymynech Hill then return via Pant back to the old canal, some 4 miles.

There are a number of local walks from Llanfyllin to the wooded hillsides surrounding the town. There's a great 3-4 mile walk across Jericho Hill to Llanfechain where you can catch the bus back into Oswestry, but you'll need to map it out as the walk is not written up.

CYCLING

East of Llanymynech there is a network of country lanes that make for a very pleasant day's leisure cycling. Ride out of the village on the B4398 towards Maesbury but then make an anti-clockwise loop through to Melverley, Kinnerley and Knockin. Alternatively follow Route 3 in the *Oswestry Cycle Rides* leaflet which covers similar ground but involves a longer 28 mile ride.

REFRESHMENTS

Llanymynech

Pubs
Bradford Arms Hotel uses local ingredients and purveys local real ales.

Cross Keys Hotel offers dishes using locally sourced food and local real ales.

Llanfyllin

Pubs
In the 19th century there was a saying that 'Old ale fills Llanfyllin with young widows' This does not seem to be the case any more as the town ceased brewing many decades ago. There are only a few places offering refreshment in town.

Cain Valley Hotel, High Street offers coffee as well as light refreshments.

Local Produce
'**Down To Earth**' wholefood shop is situated on Stryd Fawr; sources local products.

EXTRAS

The Workhouse: community driven project, see www.llanfyllinworkshouse.org.

Down to Earth wholefood shop in Llanfyllin

PUBLIC TRANSPORT

Buses to Llanfyllin (via Llanymynech)
Oswestry Bus Station to Llanfyllin (Cross Keys). Buses 445/6. Monday – Saturday only three buses per day but if you catch the 0945 (446) bus it allows a couple of hours before a return to Llanymynech or Oswestry. Travel time 35 minutes.

There is also an afternoon return journey from Llanfyllin to Llanymynech on the D74 bus and also journeys into Welshpool for those planning a ride around this area. Operator: All services operated by Tanat Valley Coaches.

Buses to Llanymynech
Oswestry Bus Station to Llanymynech (near old Lion Hotel). Buses 71, D71. Monday – Saturday. Approximately half hourly. Travel time 20 minutes. Operators: Arriva/Tanat Valley Coaches.

TANAT VALLEY

Ride to Llangynog
The 55-minute ride from Oswestry is one of the loveliest introductions to this quieter part of the Marches reaching out into mid-Wales. There's a rich green freshness about the landscape and always a promise of high hills ahead. The bus passes through the Tanat valley to Llangedwyn where a mix of parkland and pasture lead to rolling foothills. You can just catch a glimpse of the beautifully terraced gardens as you pass by the Tudor **Llangedwyn Hall** on approaching the centre of the village. The bus then diverts into the Rhaeadr Valley for a few miles.

The next settlement of note on the old 18th-century turnpike road is **Llanrhaeadr-ym-mochnant**. Llanrhaeadr has a neat square with local shop and the notable King's Head Hotel. On reflection, the square looks decidedly triangular from the bus. The village shot into fame in 1995 when it became the backdrop for some of the filming of *An Englishman Who Went Up a Hill but Came Down a Mountain* (who thought up that title?) starring Hugh Grant. The **church**, dedicated to St Dogfan, is a modest looking place of worship but has

Sculpture of a Welsh Mountain ram in Llanrhaeadr-ym-mochnant

attracted many literary clergymen including William Morgan, who completed a translation of the Bible into Welsh in 1588. Scholars suggest that his work provided a major stimulant to the Welsh language and culture at that time.

Another vicar of note was Dr William Worthington, who encouraged tourism to the area by promoting the turnpike road of 1756 and the establishment of tea rooms at Pistyll Rhaeadr. Llanrhaeadr is one of the stopping places for those *en route* to Pistyll Rhaeadr, a waterfall with a wonderful drop of 240 feet, a formidable sight after a wet spell. Unfortunately, there's no bus up that valley and the single track road has its hair-raising moments even with a modest influx of traffic so as to make cycling or walking less comfortable; that is why the mountain walk from Llangynog is suggested as a good way to discover the waterfall (see below).

You'll be on board the bus for another 15 minutes on the last stretch of valley road to Llangynog, a settlement that sits neatly beneath Graig Rhiwarth at a point where the Eirth and Tanat rivers meet. These small rivers drain flat-bottomed valleys hewn by glacial activity in the last Ice Age. It is a fertile valley that is given over to agriculture now. There are remnants of prehistoric settlements throughout the valley, perhaps most tangibly exposed in Iron Age hillforts. They stand defiantly along the mountain tops but you can only just pick out the ramparts from this distance.

Llangynog

The village of Llangynog grew up around the **church of St Cynog**, which has a round churchyard, a sign of early origin although there have been many re-builds over the centuries. There are several chapels in the community too as non-conformity was all the rage in 19th-century Wales. At the turn of the 20th century, Llangynog became known for its harp making and many accomplished harpists lived in the village.

However, the most visible aspect of history is the industrial waste of mining at Llangynog. The extraction of rock, lead and phosphates shaped the village. It's a legacy that is unmistakable. Nature has not hidden the piles of shales, mudstones and discarded slate tipped on the hillsides one hundred years ago. They are reminders of the period of heavy extraction which began in earnest in the latter decades of the 19th century. Both stone and minerals were transported out of the valley by horse and cart to the River Severn at Pool Quay for onward transhipment by boat; that must have been a tortuous journey. From 1904-1952 there was an alternative, the Tanat Valley Light Railway, although not much was shipped out in later decades. The line's formation still exists and so do some of the old station halts. The former terminus is now hidden by a caravan site. Like the train, the bus has always terminated at Llangynog. It happens to be a classic end of the valley route. The Berwyn mountains have always been a barrier to communication.

Main attraction

The main attraction has to be the waterfall of **Pistyll Rhaeadr** and what better way to come upon this natural feature than to walk to it. There's a classic walk from Llangynog to Pistyll Rhaeadr via Cwm Glan-Hafon and across the slopes of Y Clogydd, a walk described in a leaflet written up for Powys Council (see Extras). This is a strenuous walk requiring stamina and outdoor garments to suit all weathers. The return walk can be done in approximately 4 hours between the arrival of the morning bus and mid afternoon departure (without diverting to viewpoints or the path above the waterfall). Make time to take a rest and refreshment at the tea room near the waterfall before the return trek. There is also a 'retreat' campsite where people can really chill out for a few days in these exquisite surroundings (see Extras).

A more leisurely pace can be made, of course, if you elect to stay in the valley; that's a good option. There's bed and breakfast available in Llangynog and also at Llanrhaeadr-ym-mochnant. The views across the Berwyns from the watershed from Y Clogydd are spectacular. But the loveliest part of the walk is the last half mile as you inch your way through woodland by the waterfall. You hear the water cascading first, then come across it all of a sudden beyond the leaf cover, something of a spectacle on this classic walk.

WALKING

Besides the walk to Pistyll Rhaeadr, there are a number of superb local walks. **Pennant Melangell** is an easier walk through the valley of Cwm Pennant, some 4 miles from Llangynog. Here you'll come across one of the remotest churches in the Marches, a simple Romanesque structure which fits its surroundings perfectly. It is shrouded in legend too. The encounter of the young virgin Melangell with Brochwell, Prince of Powys, is told by every Welsh storyteller. Hunted by a young prince, a hare took refuge in her garments. The Prince was so taken aback by her authority and purity that he made land available so that she could establish an ecclesiastical site here. Hence the formation of this beautifully secluded church. The story is told in a decorative border of the 15th-century screen and there's a restored shrine of St Melangell which is a wonder in this Romanesque church.

You will need about three hours at least to walk to Pennant Melangell and back along the back lanes from Llangynog. There's a longer 15 mile linear walk between Pont Llogel and Llangynog outlined in a booklet *Pererindod Melangell* available at tourist information offices in Powys.

CYCLING

The ride from Oswestry to the Tanat valley is approximately 20 miles and with some real climbs *en route* so requires a little training for those who are not regular cyclists. The B4391 is relatively quiet and there are opportunities for rides up to Pennant Melangell and down the valley to Llanrhaeadr.

REFRESHMENT

Llangynog
Tanat Valley Hotel: a long-standing Good Beer Guide entry which offers local Welsh dishes.

Tan-y-Pistyll: a café, restaurant, bed and breakfast and a camping retreat (there are special rules). Check it out on www. pistyllrhaeadr.co.uk.

Llanrhaeadr-ym-Mochnant
The Plough Inn: is where the bus turns round and is a much loved community local.

The village stores sign in Llanrhaeadr

EXTRAS

Pistyll Rhaeadr Walk leaflet is available to download at simonholtmarketing. co.uk.

PUBLIC TRANSPORT

Buses to Llangynog via Llanrhaeadr -ym-mochnant.
Oswestry Bus Station to Llangynog (Car Park). Bus D79. Mondays to Saturdays. Only three buses per day but if you catch the 0850 bus it allows 4-5 hours before a return to Oswestry. 55 minutes travel time. Operator: Tanat Valley Coaches.

Plates 20-21 Panoramic views across Ludlow (above) and over Montgomery (below)

*Plates 22-23 Looking over Church Stretton from the head of the Townbrook valley
(above) and across the Sveren Plain from Caer Caradoc (below)*

Plates 24-25 *The flanks of the Black Mountains betyween Hay and Craswall (above) and Llandegley Rocks between Kington and Llandrindod Wells (below)*

Plate 26 *Garway Church, reached by bus from Hereford*

Plate 27 *Kington in north-west Herefordshire*

Plate 28 The Old House in High Town, Hereford

Plate 29 The entrance to Tretower Court, reached by bus from Abergavenny

Plate 30 Church Lane, Ledbury

Plate 31 One of the shuts in Shrewsbury

Plates 32-33 Festivals, events and shows abound in the Marches,
especially in the spring and summer:
music at the Royal Oak, Lingen (above)
and Burwarton Show (below)

WELSHPOOL

Welshpool grew up as a defensive site chosen by the Normans to defend a strategic river crossing. The location of the motte and bailey, Domen Castell, is very near to the railway station but hidden by trees. The town was so successful that it was granted Borough status in 1263, when it was known as Burgus de Pola, and remained under the jurisdiction of the princes of Powys. Welshpool continued to gain ascendancy as a trading town throughout the ensuing centuries and it still is a market place for villages around. Its medieval layout is discernible, especially Broad Street leading into High Street (which then becomes Mount Street), where there are several half-timbered buildings.

As you walk up these streets there are also narrow passages and lanes leading off the main thoroughfare, many of which originate from this early period. Unfortunately, most now exit disappointingly into car parks rather than uncovering secret corners of what was an intriguing old town. One worthwhile short deviation is to walk into New Street where an old six-sided cockpit, dating from the early 18th century, stands as a reminder of the barbarity of the period. Cock-fighting attracted over a hundred spectators at any one time; Lord John Russell's government eventually outlawed this extremely cruel and ritualistic pastime in 1849, and that put paid to this cockpit.

The importance of the town as a market for Welsh sheep remains to this day, although the agricultural market is now out of town. In the 18th and 19th centuries, Welshpool became a big-time producer of flannel, with several mills in town such as the old Red Lion Flannel factory in Church Street, which was then used as a cinema until 1945. Just beyond is St Mary's church and **Grace Evans' cottage**. Grace was granted this for her part in helping Lady Nithsdale carry out a cunning plot to release Lord Nithsdale from the Tower of London in the 18th century. The Nithsdales absconded to Rome and Grace to Welshpool.

The arrival of the railway opened up the town to more development, and the Cambrian Railway Company heralded Welshpool as its major junction for traffic between Oswestry and Shrewsbury to the Welsh coast, hence the money spent on the station design. The other railway to Llanfair Caereinion was a marvel in its day and is still very much part of the town. It originally ran through the streets of Welshpool from the main line to its current terminus in Raven Square, but the town section has long since gone.

Walking around town

Stepping off the train at Welshpool is not a memorable experience. The station is literally cut off from civil society by an industrial estate to the south and a bypass on the other side. From central platforms you climb over the pedestrian bridge where you snatch an envious glance at the marvellous railway station building now disconnected from its rails. The old **Cambrian station** is now a retail outlet. The bridge curves down to a roundabout near to the town's latest supermarket. But do not despair; once across you'll be a few minutes' walk from a small town which offers more than you might expect.

Walk along the wide avenue, Severn Street, to pass over the Montgomery Canal and by the Powysland Museum (see below) to a crossroads, where the handsome Royal Oak Hotel stands on the right. Continue ahead along High Street and you can make a detour to the cockpit in New Street. Walk back into High Street and pass by the Victorian Town Hall, with a distinctive clock tower capped by a château-style roof. Continue to walk ahead but then cut next left into Park Lane.

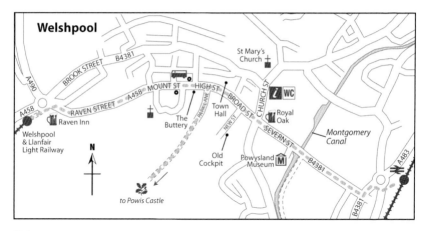

Main attraction

The walk down Park Lane and through the parkland of **Powis Castle** (National Trust) brings a momentous lift in mood, for soon you pass between ancient trees of considerable age and stature. It is then that you get sight of the imposing scale of the fortress that stands on high ground, admittedly rather aloof from the town, but the site is dramatic. It is a climb up to the castle and it soon becomes apparent why the princes of Powys first built a keep on this spot; it was a really good natural defensive site. There are some similarities to Chirk Castle in site and style. Rather like Chirk, this medieval fortification has been the subject of almost constant change, according to the fashion of the time, for at least 600 years. It is difficult to digest all of the architectural styles exposed to the eye when you walk around the place. The Herbert family resided here from 1578 onwards and this period heralded the making of the castle into a more comfortable abode. It was the marriage of Henrietta Herbert to Lord Clive (the eldest son of Clive of India) that brought the power of the Herbert-Clive dynasty to the castle. Lord Clive ploughed much of his wealth, or at least his wife did, into making the place even more opulent than it was hitherto. There were, of course, bad times in between, such as during the English Civil War and almost a

century later, when a disastrous fire swept through the place. But for the most part the castle has enjoyed the fruits of affluence now reflected in the paintings and sculptures that are displayed in the stately rooms. Of note is the Clive collection in the old ballroom, with artefacts and treasures brought home from Clive of India's reign over that mystical sub-continent.

For many it is the Italianate gardens that make the day. The Tuscan-style terraces, set against the red sandstone arches (the castle is also called Red Castle), and decorated with original statues, are as fine as any gardens to be seen anywhere. The statue of Hercules by John Van Nost is a particularly fine example. The gardens also reflect elements of French design, for in the late 17th century the layout was inspired by the grounds of Château St Germain-en-laye near Paris. Some of the surrounding landscape parkland is attributed to William Emes, who also had a hand in the landscaping of extensive tracts of Chirk Castle. This is heritage and horticulture at their best. It really is worth setting aside some time to appreciate the aesthetic elements of this superb pocket of the Marches.

Other attractions

The Powysland Museum is a modest little museum, housed in a beautifully restored canal warehouse, and the story behind it is fascinating. The Powysland Club was established in 1867 by local residents who were keen on investigating local history. Many club members had gained their own collections and they decided to bring them together as a museum in 1884. Thus, much of what you see today is thanks to the generosity of these Victorian historians. There is a wide range of displays, some reflecting agriculture and some more industrial exploits such as canal and railway development. The old photographs around the museum are worth the visit alone.

The **Welshpool and Llanfair Railway** is a must for the slow traveller. See the description of the Llanfair Caereinon outing for more detail. Even if you decide not to visit Llanfair Caereinion, a walk up to Raven Square to see the railway in operation is a good idea.

WALKING

Welshpool is at a crossroads for walkers. It is a good place to start or finish a walk on one of the national trails through the Marches. **Offa's Dyke Path** passes nearby at Buttington. It is possible to catch the 71B

Near the entrance to the Powysland Museum ...

bus to Forden and walk back to Buttington on the trail (the X75 bus runs back into Welshpool from here). Alternatively you can continue the walk to the Montgomery Canal and go left to return into Welshpool along the towpath (approximately 8-10 miles with some climbs).

It is also the starting point for **Glyndwr's Way**, (opposite side of the road to the Powysland Museum in Severn Street). There's a great section, as a taster, from Meifod to Welshpool (11 miles with climbs). You can catch the D76 bus (Mon – Sat) to Meifod and walk back. The third trail is the **Severn Way**, which runs from source to sea and in this area along the Montgomery Canal – see the description of the outing to Berriew (page 74).

There are some great walks on the **Breidden Hill**, capped by Rodney's Pillar, a tribute to the 18th-century Admiral Rodney who spent his career at sea commanding part of the British navy. His major achievement was the defeat of a better armed French fleet at the Battle of the Saintes during the American War of Independence in which he captured five ships. The climb of some 900 feet requires a commitment, but the walking is great and the views spectacular. It is best to start the walk from Middletown, served by the X75 bus on Mondays to Saturdays.

CYCLING

Welshpool is on one of the *Montgomery Cycle Rides* (see Montgomery section) offering a good day's circular ride. It is also on the **NCN Lôn Cambria Route 81** from Shrewsbury through to Newtown. The hardest part is getting through Welshpool itself, especially near to the railway station. Otherwise the route follows mainly very quiet roads. There are some climbs.

REFRESHMENTS

Cafés and Restaurants
It is difficult to do justice to all providers but some that are different are listed below:

The **National Milk Bar**, Church Street: offers homemade food and is something of a treasure in that the concept was devised by a mid-Wales farmer in the 1930s. These places were the biz in the late '50s and '60s and have survived the invasion of the multi-national owned coffee shops. National Milk Bars may be coming back into fashion given the retail renaissance of vintage in recent years.

Pinewood, Broad Street: Bakery that sells homemade bread and cakes.

Pubs

There are several pubs in Welshpool. A good place to sample local real ales is **The Royal Oak Hotel**, but premium prices are charged.

Local Produce

New Leaf Wholefood Shop, High Street: wholefood shop serving the area.

EXTRAS

Brooks Cycles, Severn Street: for repairs, hire and sales.

Farmers market, Town Hall: 1st Friday of each month.

Natur (Montgomeryshire Wildlife Trust): has an office and shop in Severn Street which provides information.

PUBLIC TRANSPORT

Welshpool is served directly by trains daily from Shrewsbury and the Midlands approximately every 2 hours. The station is a 5 minute walk into town along Severn Street.

Buses

Welshpool is also served by the X75 bus service from Shrewsbury Monday – Saturday. Approximately two hourly. Travel time 45 minutes. There are also services from Llanfyllin and Oswestry on Monday – Saturday to facilitate day outings. Operator: Tanat Valley Coaches.

EXCURSIONS FROM WELSHPOOL

BERRIEW

Ride to Berriew

If you decide to use the X75 bus, the 15-minute ride speeds you through the Severn flood plain to Berriew, but unfortunately you cannot see the magnificent oxbows and meanders from the main road. There are many back lanes leading off this highway to ancient farmsteads, and to fords which are rarely traversed, even when the waters are low. In medieval times these would have been places of significance. For example, at Rhydwhyman ford, Llywelyn ap Gruffud and Henry III signed the Treaty of Montgomery (1267), no doubt watched by dozens of their men on foot and horse-back. The wooded hills to the right of the bus offer a contrasting landscape with fairly dispersed farms surrounded by a patchwork of fields hemmed in by hawthorn hedges. Rather than taking the bus, you may wish to walk or cycle to Berriew as the distance is just right for a day visit – see below.

BERRIEW

Berriew is an attractive riverside village which has been touched by tourism throughout the 20th century but in a pleasing way. There are a number of half-timbered dwellings, many of which date from the 16th and 17th centuries, clustered around a church with red clay tiles topping the tower, unusual for these parts and presumably a replacement for a Montgomery wood tower. The **church** is dedicated to St Bueno and it is said that the ecclesiastical ground was gifted to him in the 6th century. He did not stay long as he was evidently not pleased with the increasing Saxon linguistic influence spreading northwards across the Severn. What you see today is a 19th-century version of the earlier building; little survives from earlier times. Walk by

The church of St Bueno in Berriew with the Lychgate café on the left

the Lion Hotel and Lychgate café to the bridge over the River Rhiw where trickles of water flow over the cataracts seen to the right. Go left to pass by the Talbot Hotel and the **Andrew Logan Museum of Sculpture** (see www.andrewlogan. com for opening times). This is housed in a contemporary building on the right. It displays a mixture of portraits, water-colours and a wide range of sculptures reflecting the sculptor's versatility.

Main attraction

Glansevern Hall Gardens is not open every day so check out current opening times before you visit at www.glansevern. co.uk. The short walk along the tree-lined drive to Glansevern Hall is suitably shady on hot summer days and the entrance to the gardens is by way of a gift shop cum boutique. This leads into a beautiful court-yard where your self-guided walking tour begins. The walk comprises three parts. Firstly, you are invited to explore the paths surrounding the lake. Here you'll come across numerous unusual trees identi-fied in most cases with a marker. The lake is a very tranquil location. You can

weave thoughts under the softness of the canopy or simply sit by the water's edge, entertained by ducks and swans dancing (not ducking) and diving between the lilies. There are small islands too. One hosts an interesting contemporary sculp-ture, *Embarkation*, by a borderland artist, Frances Carlisle.

The second part of the walk is more of an optional diversion through a folly garden and then across a watermeadow to a point near the confluence of the Rhiw and Severn rivers. There's a hide here where you can observe birds on the river. Then, it's back for a final promenade around the more formal gardens next to the hall, including a small but visually appealing white orangery. There are some citrus fruits growing in pots. The walled garden is the last stop but is something of a disappoint-ment if you expect the trees to be espal-iered, fanned or labelled to any degree of perfection. The café makes up for this with tea and exquisite homemade cake or possibly something more substantial.

The hall, however, is not open to the public. It dates from the first years of the 19th century and has a frontage of five bays and four pilasters. The vista looks particularly attractive as you make your way from the lake but the *Haslam* guide begs to differ, describing it as somewhat austere. Perhaps it depends on whether you favour simpler forms of the Greek Revival style or not. Nevertheless, there's something about Glansevern Hall that infuses formality with the charm of the informal and that is perhaps the secret of its success. It is also host to an annual **Welsh Food Festival** (held in early September) which brings together many local producers of food and beverages, mainly from Powys.

WALK TO BERRIEW

A good way to visit Berriew is to walk out to this lovely village and catch the bus back. Alternatively, it might suit to do it the other way around depending on your plan for the day. The walk follows the long distance path, the **Severn Way**, along the Montgomery Canal. This green belt offers a divide between the hills of Belan and Brithdir and the flood plain of the Severn. The path alongside the canal can be picked up at the Powysland Museum in Severn Street, Welshpool. It leads directly to Berriew so you cannot go far wrong on an easy 5-6 mile saunter without climbs or stiles. The first ten minutes of walking is the least attractive, but as soon as you pass beneath the highway at Whitebridge Nature Reserve, the landscape unfolds in an intricate and engaging way. The path soon reaches Belan locks, where there are ornate half-timbered cottages nearby. From here onwards, the gentle angle of the navigational curves, overhanging trees and rich canalside vegetation bring much diversity within a few miles. The water's edge is packed with yellow irises, red campion and water plantain. They are companions for most of the way.

From Belan onwards, you will also observe the frolics of damsel and dragonflies skimming the still water surface during the warm summer months. This is an increasingly rare sight as these beautiful insects are facing a rapid decline

elsewhere, partly as a consequence of loss of habitats and partly through exposure to pesticides. On passing the historic settlement of **Upper and Lower Luggy** (prehistoric burial mound site and motte and bailey in nearby fields) you might decide to adjourn to an old stabling pub, The Horsehoes. It is a stone's throw from the canal, near to limekilns which once shipped out slaked lime decades ago. There are other canalside structures to admire too. The lock keepers' cottages and other small buildings dotted alongside the canal, including an old stabling yard at Revel on the last stretch into Berriew village, will be poetry to those who enjoy these bucolic and historic landscapes. Collectively, they build a picture of a thriving rural canal which served the agricultural economy of the mid Severn Valley well for a century or so.

On reaching Berriew, cross the aqueduct and cut left down to a small recreation area and a leafy lane. Once on the lane, go left again under the Cuckoo Bridge and walk by the Andrew Logan Museum and Talbot Hotel into the centre of the village. However, if you are walking on to Glansevern Hall Gardens (about half a mile), there's a good footpath immediately to the left before crossing the aqueduct. This drops down to a path by the Afon Rhiw and you cut left through meadows. Follow this through to the main A483 which you need to cross with care. Turn right and walk along the path to the entrance leading into the estate.

CYCLING TO BERRIEW

The cycle ride out to Berriew from Welshpool follows **National Cycle Route 81**. This passes Welshpool Railway Station (real care is needed to cross the roundabout), then leads into the relatively sedate Severn Street. It cuts left on the canal towpath by the Powysland Museum. The route is sufficiently clear throughout with waymarking at junctions only. This section of Route 81 amounts to 5-6 miles and has some climbs, mainly beyond the entrance to Powis Castle, so take that into account.

One recipe for a good day's cycling is to go for the 23 mile circular route between Welshpool and Berriew described in the *Montgomery Cycle Rides* leaflet. For the most part the route follows lightly trafficked lanes but there are a number of junctions and crossings where you need to concentrate. Your debut in Berriew is at the bridge over the river with the café and hotels on hand for that well earned break. Once over the bridge, the way to Glansevern Hall Gardens is left, and onward to a junction with the A483. There's a 50mph speed limit but it is still safer to dismount and push your steed to the footpath on the other side of the road rather than making a pedal dash. Go right and left into the drive. Afterwards you can retrace the route back to Berriew and continue on the circular ride outlined in the leaflet.

REFRESHMENT

Lychgate Cottage Tea Room and Deli, Berriew: serves home made food and local products.

EXTRAS

Berriew Cider, Argoed Berriew: is available at some local outlets and farmers markets.

Silver Scenes, producers of fine pewter and silverware, is open to the public.

Haslam, Richard (1979) *The Buildings of Wales: Powys*, Penguin.

Montgomery Cycle Rides published by Montgomery Town Council. Available at Welshpool Tourist Information Centre. Tel (01938) 552043.

PUBLIC TRANSPORT

Buses from Welshpool to Berriew
Welshpool (High Street) to Berriew (Lion). X75. Monday – Saturday. Approximately two hourly. 14 minutes travel time. Operator: Tanat Valley Coaches.

LLANFAIR CAEREINION

The ride to Llanfair Caereinion

The railway is not only the best way to enjoy a day out to Llanfair Caereinion, the journey is the main reason for travelling there. It is a very rural, narrow gauge line and one wonders why it was built at all. Even in the heady days of railway mania of the 19th century this one must have looked to be a poor return on investment especially as it was such a late arrival on the railway scene. The line opened for passengers on a rainy day in 1903 and managed to survive for 53 years until it was closed by British Railways. Fortunately a group of diligent volunteers set about bringing the line back to life and within 7 years it was back on track.

The train departs from Raven Square Station. The buildings, by the way, were originally those built at Eardisley on the Hereford to Brecon railway line, located in Herefordshire (see Black and White villages). People begin to gather fairly early for the arrival of an inbound train at Welshpool. If demand for the day looks promising, one of the original Great Western railway tank engines, the *Earl* or the *Countess*, is usually deployed to attach an extra carriage to the train before departure. Every slow movement of this coupling operation is watched by the gathering crowd; it makes the eventual departure of the morning run even more special.

The small tank engines are lovingly coaxed into service each day by drivers and firemen who know the track well and the engine's capability too. There's a real skill in generating just enough steam and at the right time to propel the train up a gradient. Coal is imported from Portugal and Russia but there's talk of real Welsh black stuff being available again in the future. Burning coal is devilish when it comes to Co_2 emissions but every passenger secretly hopes that the small amount used for heritage railways will be excused when carbon rationing hits the streets.

The train climbs out of Welshpool to the flanks of Y Golfa hill. It is a sustained climb

The platform and signal box at Castle Caereinion

and you can hear the engine working hard as it rises alongside the Sylfaen brook to the first halt at Sylfaen. The train pauses at station halts like this, partly to see if there's anyone around and so that the crew can get up steam for the next leg. There's nothing here, just a farm back along the road. The stillness is very soothing. There are plenty of people on board but nothing happens much; stillness reigns. Then, the flag-raising ritual gets into full swing, steam rises and the train is off again. These halts are seldom used. They are mainly the haunt of walkers who catch the train out and walk back – see Extras. Such linear walks are very attractive.

Next stop is **Castle Caereinion**. This station has more of a presence about it than the halts and it is the only intermediate platform with a signal box. It is a rare one too. It is in fact the only one of its kind *in situ* in the UK. It was commissioned in 1907 when a loop was added here to enable trains to pass. It was in use until 1911 when, out of the blue, it was mothballed. One hundred years later it is in remarkable condition. The station serves the village of Castle

Caereinion which is about half a mile away, nestled around the Victorian church of St Garmon. There's a mound in the churchyard, assumed to have been part of the original **Castell Caer Einion**, named after an unidentified prehistoric camp, but little remains of the bailey. The castle was built by Madog up Maredudd in the 1150s but ransacked in the same century by the Normans with the help of Welsh collaborator, Owain Cyfeiliog.

There tends to be a slightly longer stop at Castle Caereinion to sort out the crossing gates. The train guard says that the village has a post office and shop called *Not Open All Hours*, a play on the title of the classic comedy television series dating back to 1976 and starring Ronnie Barker. There's also the Red Lion, a community pub that attracts walkers from the line and cyclists too. Soon the train traverses the watershed and glides into the Banwy Valley. The river happens to be known as the Einion as well as the Banwy. This is the loveliest section of the route; the engine runs effortlessly alongside the babbling waters of the river where you can spot pied wagtails and kingfishers. The river is particularly attractive here, rich in wildlife and providing suitable habitats for spawning trout. For the rest of the journey, some 5 to 10 minutes, the Banwy remains your constant companion. There are no more climbs until the return trip. The triumphant arrival at Llanfair is heralded with another blow of that haunting whistle as the train squeezes by the engine and carriage sheds to the station platform. Passengers now know it is time to gather their belongings.

LLANFAIR CAEREINION

The small town of Llanfair Caereinion is the principal settlement for miles around; in fact it is the only settlement of any size in the Banwy valley. The way to travel to town is by train; the journey is one of the slowest in the Marches. Alternatively, there is the 87 bus from Welshpool, which offers access when the railway is closed for business in the deep winter months. The bus service tends to be provided with a small and fairly uncomfortable vehicle.

Walking around town
The Llanfair railway stops at the edge of the town. There's a 10-minute walk from the station, across the Afon Banwy, then through pockets of housing into the centre of the town. This is far more pleasant than the pavement alongside the dusty main A458. The centre of town is where Bridge Street meets Broad Street at what is still described as the Market Square, although there's no longer a market here. It is best described as the space where the Red Lion fronts on to the Black Lion public house. There are a few shops and cafés but Llanfair Caereinion is not as busy as it used to be.

A lovely edge to the town is the **Goat Field** and **Deri Woods**. Walk along Broad Street into High Street where you pass the long-standing Good Beer Guide entry, the Goat Hotel. Beyond the Ebenezer chapel, on the right, is a path down to the Goat Field and Deri Woods. In the Goat Field

are wooden sculptures by David Millward which tell the story of **The Taliesin**. It is said that Ceridwen gave birth to a son so repulsive to humankind that she set about preparing a potion to give him greatness and wisdom. Gwion, son of Gwreang of Llanfair Caereinion, was asked to stir the potion for one year and one day with a blind man, Morda. However, one day Gwion spilt some potion on himself and this gave him insight into the dark powers of Ceridwen. He hid from her, turned himself into a hare and she into a greyhound, to a fish and she an otter, he a bird and then she to a hawk. He then chose to be a grain and she chose to be a hen that ate him. Nine months later she gave birth to the most handsome child, Taliesin; she could not bear to kill and therefore cast him into the sea. He was found by Elphin and grew up to be one of the great Welsh bards. That is the story, and there is also a Taliesin sculpture in Broad Street by the church.

Taliesin sculpture in Broad Street, Llanfair Caereinion

WALKING

There are many lovely walks between the halts on the railway line. If you fancy a day's walk then you may choose to catch the train out to Llanfair and walk back. It is approximately 10-12 miles depending on which paths or bridleways you select. There's a superb walking book, *Off The Rails,* detailing these walks. It is available from the railway. On the other hand, you might like to walk between two of the stations on the line.

CYCLING

Another option is to cycle to Llanfair following **National Cycle Route 81** to the B4385 (as described in the Berriew section) but then turning right to Castle Caereinion. Before the village there's a turning to the left for Ty Top followed by a fairly steep descent into Llanfair. It is possible to travel back on the Welshpool and Llanfair railway but they require 24 hours' notice for bikes so call them the day before you travel. Otherwise, it is a matter of returning on the outward route, some 25 miles with several climbs, so it will take up the best part of the day unless you happen to be super-fit. There are also eight local cycle routes promoted in the Llanfair Caereinion area – see Extras.

REFRESHMENT

Tea Room, Llanfair Caereinion Railway Station: homemade cakes are very enticing.
The Goat Hotel: long-standing Good Beer Guide entry that serves home cooked food.

EXTRAS

Page, Steve *Off The Rails,* The Welshpool and Llanfair Light Railway.
Llanfair Caereinion and District Forum *Cycle Routes around Llanfair Caereinion* available from Welshpool Tourist Information Office.

PUBLIC TRANSPORT

Trains to Llanfair Caereinion
Daily during summer months (with the exception of some Fridays). Weekends at other times except January through to March. 3-5 trips per day. Travel time 50 minutes. Operator: Welshpool and Llanfair Light Railway.

Buses to Llanfair Caereinion
Welshpool to Llanfair (Bridge Street). 87. Monday – Saturday. Only three buses per day. Travel time 25 minutes. Operator: Border Community Transport.

MONTGOMERY (TREFALDWYN)

The Ride to Montgomery

The bus ride out to Montgomery from Welshpool takes about 25 minutes and is a slow but steady climb out of the Severn Valley to Leighton, an estate village beneath the wooded slopes of Moel-y-Mab, Long Mountain and the remains of the prehistoric camp at Beacon Ring. The bus continues to **Forden**, where you can alight for a walk along Offa's Dyke Path back into Welshpool via Buttington. The road from Forden is straight as a dye and gives credence to its Roman origin. It runs through to Montgomery, dipping down at first into the Camlad valley and then rising up beneath a bluff where Montgomery castle oversees the lands that lie below.

MONTGOMERY

Travel writer J.C. Moore, making his way on foot through the Marches in the early 1930s penned the following note on arrival in the town: 'I discovered that Montgomery had been dead for a very long time.

Ruin and decay had come to it ... I try to describe Montgomery, and I remember only that it was a miserable little town set on a wooded hill.'

Perhaps Mr Moore was having a bad day, either that or matters have changed for the better in the intervening years. The town is certainly quiet but to describe it as miserable would be a travesty. Montgomery, named originally in honour of the Norman Earl of Shrewsbury, Roger de Montgomery, was the county town of Montgomeryshire until a local government shake up in 1974 meant it was absorbed into Powys. The handsome **Town Hall**, built in 1748, has been host to many a civic occasion as well as being a court-room and market place at different times. It rightly occupies the top position in the aptly named Broad Street, more akin to a market square than a wide street and used as such. In the past the partly cobbled pavements were used to pen animals for sale on market days; that must have been a sight. All buses arrive and leave at a stop (marked only on the road) by the Town Hall; best to be there 5 minutes before!

Looking over the church of St Nicholas in Montgomery

Walking around town

The layout of the town is mediaeval and has been barely altered for the best part of 800 years. There would have been several town gates and a curtain wall in those early days but these perished when defence became less of a need for the townspeople. The town now reflects the prosperity of the Georgian and Victorian periods, properties built to last when times were good. They have survived the intrusion of 20th-century highways, a major achievement.

There are many notable buildings packed into this inner area. **The Dragon Hotel**, just behind the Town Hall, is a fine example of an old coaching inn of substantial character. It is possible to be misled by the look of the building; the half-timbered effect actually dates from a revamp at the turn of the 20th century although the history of the place spans several centuries. It is possible that some of the wooden beams and stonework of the inn came from Montgomery Castle, brought down the lane by cart in the early days of the 17th century. The inn was a calling point for the *Dart* stagecoach, which served the county town and spa towns to the south, places that the discerning traveller planned to visit for a quiet retreat in mid Wales. It was also a favourite stop-over for her majesty's executioner; he stayed there the night before the very last public hanging in Montgomery, when hundreds gathered in the streets to observe the macabre event.

A few paces down Arthur Street leads to the **Old Bell Museum** (see below) and then on the right it is difficult to miss the characterful façade of Bunner's amazing shop, retailing since 1892, and stacked from floor to ceiling with all manner of hardware and ironmongery. A walk in a different direction along Broad Street leads into Church Bank and the **church of St Nicholas**. The church dates from the same period as the castle and houses a font from the 13th century and many fine tombs and effigies from later periods, including, it is believed, the tomb of Edmund Mortimer, defeated and captured by Owain Glyndwr, who then joined with him and married one of his daugthers. You could just sneak a look in the churchyard to find an unmarked grave, a mere cross to denote the resting place of John Davies, hung for alleged assault and robbery. He protested that he was a scapegoat for skulduggery perpetrated by others, and pledged that grass would not grow on his resting place for well over one hundred years. A little white cross marks the spot.

The entrance to the inner bailey at Montgomery Castle

Main attraction

The main attraction is **Montgomery Castle**. There's a footpath off to the left after the Blue Bell which leads to the castle ground. Otherwise, follow the lane after the Dragon Hotel up to a car park and entrance. The first castle to be built, however, was a wooden motte and bailey structure located at Hen-Domen and referred to as Castell Domen. This was one of the many fortresses situated near to the River Severn (Afon Hafren) in order to protect a river crossing at Rhydwhyman.

The present castle, approximately one mile south of Hen-Domen and perched on the edge of the hill high above the town of Montgomery, was built during the reign of Henry III. Several historical references pinpoint a date of 1223 for the inauguration of a new castle which took several decades to complete. Speed's map of 1611 illustrates a magnificent structure, but by the time of the map's publication the castle would have been much reduced following its partial demolition in the late 1640s. The story of the castle is one of constant demolition. As soon as stonework had been laid down by the master craftsmen, the castle was subject to the demolition activities of invading forces. There was a good reason for this. The Normans had planned for Montgomery to be a key site, but opposed to this were the princes of Powys. In the aftermath of the start of construction, full scale assaults were the order of the day, and the town was ransacked on each and every occasion even when the town walls were *in situ*. In short, life was pretty grim for Montgomery folk.

However by 1343, not much more than a century on, the castle had been rendered virtually redundant. The Welsh Marches had become a more peaceful place, though not entirely. During the ensuing decades the Mortimers (of Wigmore and Ludlow repute) restored Montgomery Castle, and a more substantial dwelling was added later by the Herberts, a family associated with Powis Castle. This investment was to no avail. The castle was damaged during the Battle of Montgomery in 1644, the major battle of the English Civil Wars fought in Wales. The castle was held irresolutely for the king, and was quickly surrendered to a Parliamentarian army when it appeared in September 1644. The Royalists regrouped and managed to surprise the Parliamentarians, some of whom took refuge in the castle, whilst the others fled to Shrewsbury. Here they in turn regrouped, gathered reinforcements and headed back to Montgomery once more. The final battle raged for little more than an hour, but in that short time, over 500 Royalist troops died in the encounter and over 1,500 were taken prisoner. This really was a rout and fortunately the last conflict witnessed at Montgomery Castle. Parliament ordered it to be partly dismantled afterwards.

From the castle outer ramparts and the inner ward there are excellent views across to the Shropshire hills to the east and looking down on the Camlad and Severn valleys to the north-east. There's more detail available at the interpretation board provided by the Cromwell Association (established in 1937 to promote interest in Oliver Cromwell and the period in which he lived, 1599-1658).

Other attractions

One of the best ways to get the low-down on the castle history is to call in at the **Old Bell** (a museum, not a pub) situated in Arthur Street. This was a 17th-century hostelry but ironically it has also been a temperance inn and at one time it was a butcher's shop. The 16th-century building was secured by the Montgomery Civic Society to house a wide range of displays reflecting the history of the town and surrounding area. The displays featuring the castle and the proposed local railway line are particularly fascinating.

WALKING

The main walking opportunities are in relation to **Offa's Dyke Path**. A favourite linear walk is to catch the 71b bus to the Blue Bell at Brompton Bridge and walk back along the national trail to Boardyhall wood, where there's a cross bridleway leading back via Lymore to Montgomery. It is approximately 5 miles so is ideal for an afternoon or morning's walk. The bus also calls at Chirbury and Churchstoke which allow a day's walk in the western fringes of the Shropshire hills before the late afternoon bus back into Montgomery.

There are also a number of local walks, to Town Hill and to Llandyssil (famous for its annual Dragonfest held in mid September), across the rolling hillsides above Montgomery.

CYCLING

There are five cycle routes mapped out from Montgomery all of which are on road and ranging from 4 to 23 miles. The shortest is a lovely little ride down lanes to pass Hen-Domen castle and on to Dolydd Hafren nature reserve on the banks of the Afon Hafren. The five rides are outlined in the *Montgomery Cycle Rides* leaflet – see below.

REFRESHMENT

Cafés and Restaurants

Castle Kitchen: offers locally sourced food and a delicatessen with a delightful courtyard garden. Open daily.

Ivy House Café: has gifts and arts on show as well as offering a good view down Broad Street. Some locally sourced and organic offerings. Open daily.

Pubs

Dragon Hotel: long-time Good Beer Guide entry and it usually lists all of its local suppliers of food.

EXTRAS

Montgomery Cycle Rides, Montgomery Town Council available at local hotels and other venues.

Montgomery Cycle Hire: Tel 0795 974153.

The Old Bell Museum, Arthur street: open April to September Wednesday to Sunday, daily in August.

Moore, J.C. (1933; 147) *The Welsh Marches*, Chapman and Hall.

PUBLIC TRANSPORT

Buses to Montgomery

Welshpool (High Street) to Montgomery (Town Hall). 71B. Monday – Saturday. Only three buses per day but the timings are good for a visit. Travel time 25 minutes.

Note that there is also a direct bus 558 from Shrewsbury to Montgomery on Monday – Saturday.

Operator: Tanat Valley Coaches on behalf of Veolia.

CHURCH STRETTON

The approach to Church Stretton offers exquisite views of the surrounding countryside. To the east (on the left if you are travelling southwards) the impressive hills of The Lawley and Caer Caradoc cannot fail to catch the eye. They were laid down in the Pre-Cambrian era (500-600 million years ago), formed by volcanic lavas with an addition of some schist and a twist of dolerite; millions of years of weathering have merely scratched the surface. These hills have been raggedly contorted into shapes that are an unmistakable, iconic feature of the Marches. To the west lies the Long Mynd, a plateau laid down in very different conditions, a mix of softer sedimentary rocks particularly mudstones and shale. But Church Stretton also happens to sit on a fault line. It is pretty much a rift valley, known as The Stretton Gap, that has at one time been neatly rounded by ice sheets. Flowing in to the broad valley are narrow hollows, called batches, carved out by rushing melt waters when the ice sheets were in retreat. Altogether, this is simply heaven for geologists, but what a landscape for us all to enjoy!

If you come in by train, take a close look at the railway station. It was rebuilt in 1914 to cater for increased visitor numbers. The original station is still more or less *in situ*, to the north of the existing platforms. It can be seen on the right as you arrive from Shrewsbury. The award-winning **station garden** welcomes you to Church Stretton; it is maintained by a group of committed volunteers and their efforts show. The station is equipped with its own rainwater collection facilities, a compost heap and a shrubbery. It happens to be the only station actually located in the Shropshire Hills Area of Outstanding Beauty and you may also note the Walkers Are Welcome sign on the southbound platform. These are all good omens, and you will not be disappointed here.

The Church Stretton Tourism Group has made a gigantic step forward with its sustainable tourism approach. Visitors by train and bus will find that tourism providers in the town (and near countryside) are right behind this new wave in slow travel; they genuinely welcome people arriving by train and bus. The town is doing its best to make walking around town pleasant, and places are well signposted with the addition of interpretation plaques on a number of buildings. In a nutshell, here's a place that really has pulled out the stops in recent years.

Walking around town

The main street is a minute's walk from the station platforms; it is a classic Edwardian street lined on one side with lime trees. It used to be called Station Road. However, the street was re-named to commemorate the initiator of the 19th-century tree planting exercise in town, the Reverend Holland Sandford. To his credit that leafy feel still exists 120 years on.

The walk up Sandford Avenue to The Square brings into focus the diversity of architecture which is a feature of the town. Following a devastating fire in 1593, there was a considerable re-building programme and several of the half-timbered houses dotted around Church Stretton date from this period. There has also been much infilling; thus, some properties are Georgian but most are late Victorian or early Edwardian buildings.

Some of the later dwellings were built when the elder statesmen had aspirations for Stretton to become the big time spa resort of the region, an idea nurtured by the Church Stretton Advancement Association. Their promotion was to good effect, and the Edwardian era witnessed a blossoming of hillside villas still to be seen between the lush tree cover above town. It certainly became fashionable to live here, but the grand expansion plan to become

86

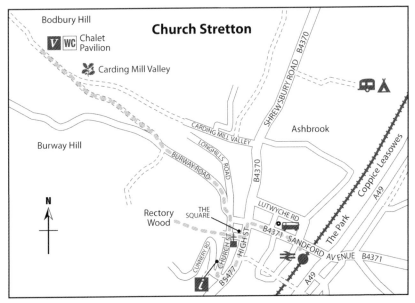

something of a mini Harrogate, was dampened by the economic austerity that followed the First World War. You reach a crossroads at the top of Sandford Avenue where two banks dating from the 1920s stand opposite each other.

Go left along High Street into **The Square**, which has been licensed for markets since 1214. The timber-framed building here was at one time an inn, and this area had several hostelries most of which have gone. There's a good view across to Salt's, the Ironmonger, a Victorian building which really looks the part. There are still a few street stalls on market days but it is small scale. Cut up Church Way to take a closer look at the parish **church of St Laurence** which is on your left. It was built on the site of an earlier Saxon church. Some historians suggest that this might have been the core of the Saxon settlement, expanded by the Normans in a classic rectangular layout. There is also a curious Saxon remnant in the form of a carved female fertility symbol known as *Sheela-na-gig*, to be found by the north door. This is mentioned in a

novel by Victorian author Hesba Stretton; many of her stories were based on this area, where she spent many summers throughout her life. There's also the shell of a stone coffin near to the north door; it is empty – well, hopefully it is. The church nave is of Norman design. The tower, however, is essentially Perpendicular in style and adorned by gargoyles. You can make a detour into Rectory Wood at this point; the entrance to the meadow is just across the road from Church Way (see additional attractions).

Otherwise, continue along Church Street where the visitor information centre is located at the library. On reaching the junction with Cunnery Road, go left. However, there is potential for a little detour. Cunnery Road leads to the **Long Mynd Hotel**, an imposing building which you may have seen from the train if you came from the south. The hotel used to be a hydro, built at the turn of the 20th century as part of the plan to develop the town into a spa. Plans to pump waters from an aquifer near Wentor were not, unfortunately, realised and in a desperate bid to keep the project alive, water was brought in by rail from Llandrindod Wells. This was a stopgap measure and the hydro did not take off. However, the Long Mynd Hotel has served the town well for over a century.

Turn left into Ludlow Road, which leads to the High Street where you turn left and walk back into town. There is a mix of buildings to admire, especially the Buck's Head, which was an old coaching inn built up from an earlier medieval hall.

Main attraction

The main attraction has to be **Carding Mill Valley**, firstly as a great way to access the **Long Mynd** and secondly as a lovely valley in which to spend time. This is a National Trust property managed by a team who are dedicated to conserving one of the most beautiful corners of the Marches. The high ground of the Mynd attracts a fair number of people on walks and rides on clearly defined paths running between heather and bilberries; and there is also a gliding station. There are still several ponies roaming the moorland but numbers have dwindled in recent decades and whilst sheep grazing is permitted, the main use of the land is for recreation.

In the heart of the valley the **Pavilion**, dating from the 1920s, is a much loved

spot. There's a shop, tea room, toilets and information point all located in this building which doubles as a meeting place for talks and walks focusing on different aspects of the ecology of the Mynd. The National Trust is very conscious of the building's environmental impact and is well on the way to meeting targets for a much reduced carbon footprint at this site. The Pavilion is heated by a 50kw log boiler using coppiced wood from Wenlock Edge, a real carbon saver. Most of the food in the café is sourced locally and not much goes to waste. It is highly recommended as a stop-off point when walking on the hills.

The impact of the car on the valley has been a subject of discussion for a long time; records of the debate go back to the 1930s. As yet, there has been no effective solution. The place gets busy with cars on high days and holidays, i.e., mainly sunny Sundays and bank holidays so choose your day to visit bearing this in mind. Needless to say, those of us who walk, cycle or shuttle there are especially welcome.

The main pastimes of those who visit Carding Mill Valley are to walk, to picnic or possibly a combination of both. The principal route up to the Mynd is Mott's Road, named after a well-regarded local doctor in the 19th century. Local people

The Long Mynd above Church Stretton

subscribed to upgrade the path in his honour at that time. It is a bridleway for horses and cyclists too, but for the most part, it is the walker who makes the fairly strenuous trek to the top; some deviate via Light Spout (waterfall) to a point known as the Shooting Box. Otherwise, Mott's Road leads to a crossroads on high, where you join an ancient ridge route, known as the Portway. The latter can be accessed from Plowden to the south and follows through to Pulverbatch in the north-west. There's a really good guide to help you get the best from the area, *Wild Mynd*, which is available at the Pavilion and local bookshops.

Many people simply choose to picnic by the stream that once powered the textile mill near to the Pavilion and watch the world

The Long Mynd shuttle bus climbing the Burway out of Church Stretton (see www.shropshireshuttles.co.uk)

go by. That's not a bad idea, as this is one of the treasured spots of Shropshire. It is even more enjoyable if you are gregarious by nature; it is certainly not the place for a moment of contemplative solitude unless it happens to be pouring down.

Carding Mill Valley is a 15-20 minute walk from the railway station via Sandford Avenue. Go ahead on Burway Road (a climb) to the gate and cattle grid where you peel off right onto a track which becomes a path offering a great view of the valley below as it descends gently towards the Pavilion. There's a flatter route via Beaumont Road, left into Lutwyche Road, right into Shrewsbury Road, and left again into Carding Mill Valley but there's more traffic that way.

Other attractions
It is hard to believe that **Acton Scott Working Farm Museum**, one of the most successful visitor attractions in the Marches, is not served directly by public transport but that is currently the case. There is the 435 bus (Monday – Saturday) which stops at Marshbrook, a little less than a mile away from the village of Acton Scott on a relatively quiet lane. Allow about 20 minutes walking time each way. The bus stop northbound is by the turn for the Station Inn on the main road. The southbound stop is by the Acton Scott turn. Always be very careful on the A49 road, it is a busy trunk road.

The 18th-century home farm provides an insight into life in these parts as it would have been in early part of the 19th century, and has recently been the home base for the BBC 'Victorian Farm' series. The fields are tilled by heavy horses and the skills of the blacksmith, farrier and wheelwright are kept alive in this Victorian agricultural enclave. There are also a couple of waymarked walks through fields belonging to the Acton Scott estate that add to the attraction of the place. One of the most endearing exhibitions enables you to listen to the views of some of the older Shropshire farming community, recorded in 1980, a reflection on life in

SHROPSHIRE HILLS AREA OF OUTSTANDING NATURAL BEAUTY (AONB)

By creating the AONB, the Shropshire Hills have been officially designated one of Britain's finest landscapes. It stretches from the Wrekin in the east to the Clun Forest in the west, the Clee Hills in the south and Long Mynd in the north. These landscapes, in such close proximity, are not only attractive to visitors but are cherished by local people and the AONB continues to seek partnerships in order to conserve them. That includes us! It is committed, for example, to reduce its impact on the environment and has pledged to reduce its own carbon emissions by 10% as part of the 10:10 campaign. It hopes that other organisations and individuals will do the same. Much of the AONB can be reached by train and bus but a large area between Knighton and Bishop's Castle is not that accessible to the slow traveller. That is a cause for concern. See www.shropshirehills.info for more details about the AONB.

the earlier decades of the 20th century. Finally, there's an obligatory stop at the café where homemade food is on sale, situated in the old school house.

Rectory Wood and Field is a mixed site of grassland, wetland and woodland accessed by a lovely walk which follows the Town Brook to the restored Ice House that stands by a pool. A good starting point is to carry on past the church (on the left) at Church Way, then enter the field by a gate. Proceed across the field and up the slope into the wood. The semi-natural mix of oak, beech and some exotic trees such as Scots pine works to good effect; many of the trees date back to the 19th century and some to the 18th century, when the parkland was first laid out as an extension of the grounds of the old rectory. A recent assessment of the landscape suggests that Capability Brown had a hand in the design of the area; at the very least he is known to have advised on setting out the park in the 1770s. Rectory Wood and Field has been the subject of restoration in recent years and was designated by *The Independent* newspaper as the most relaxing spot in England; it is certainly one of them. From the top of Rectory Wood it is possible to turn right and continue ahead into Carding Mill Valley.

The Strettons

The three Strettons were part of a Norman manor (based on an earlier Saxon estate no doubt) known as Stretton-en-le-dale.

The other Strettons are well worth a visit if you fancy a short walk or cycle ride, possibly to one of the hostelries situated in each location. The 435 bus also provides access to both places on Mondays to Saturdays. **All Stretton** lies to the north and there's a fine collection of houses, some of which date back to the 16th century, clustered around the church and the Yew Tree Inn. One of the prominent buildings is Stretton Hall, an 18th-century family home, possibly of earlier origins, which became a hotel that continued until recently. En route you will also pass a mineral water bottling company at Cwm Springs. The spring was first tapped for commercial use in the 1880s.

To the south is **Little Stretton** which is an equally quaint settlement nestled around a small early 20th-century half-timbered church. Buildings of note include The Manor House and Old Hall Farm. The village is ideal as a starting point for a linear walk back to Church Stretton via The Owlets and Cunnery Road or for a harder ramble via Ashes Hollow and Town Brook back to town. Walking in Ashes Hollow is exceptional given the way the path crosses the tumbling waters of the Ash brook as you climb gradually to the moorland. There are two pubs available in the village, the Ragleth and Green Dragon so you will not go thirsty. Between the Ludlow Road and the line of the A49 is the wooded site of Stretton Castle earthworks (no public access) at Brockhurst Hill.

WALKING

Walking still remains the prime outdoor pursuit in and around Church Stretton. The footpaths are well maintained and walked by both locals and visitors. There are several good local walks such as the **Mainwaring Walk** through Rectory Wood, the **Allen Coppice Sculpture Trail** next to Rectory Wood or a stroll through to **Coppice Leasowes**, a local nature reserve situated near to the A49. It is possible to access Coppice Leasowes by way of Essex Road off Sandford Avenue where a public footpath, on the right after the laboratories and by sheltered housing, cuts right to the railway line. Cross with care to enter the nature reserve.

These walks can be enjoyed within an hour or so. For those really into a day's walking or several days walking then Church Stretton is a superb base. A pack of four booklets (a small charge is made) has been designed by the Walkers are Welcome group. This is an ideal taster to the area. They cover some of the best walking in the area, including the climb up to the ancient hillfort, **Caer Caradoc** and to the amazing **Ashes Hollow**. Be warned, however, that walking the Stretton Hills involves some steep climbs.

There are two great linear day walks to Craven Arms (both between 12-14 miles at most): on the **Shropshire Way** (east side) which passes by Acton Scott Working Farm and Wenlock Edge; or up on to the Mynd and the Shropshire Way (west) down the Portway to Plowden, then back over Hopesay Common to Craven Arms. Returning by train or bus is easy. There's another linear day walk through to Pulverbatch via the Portway which offers excellent views across the Severn Plain. There's the shuttle back to Church Stretton on summer weekends or Bus 546 to Shrewsbury from Pulverbatch (Mondays-Saturdays).

CYCLING

As in all of Shropshire, there is a superb network of minor roads around Church Stretton which, although hilly, make cycling a delight. They also mean there is never a need to cycle on the busy A49, a road to be avoided. The **Church Stretton Cycle Rides leaflet** highlights four circular routes out of town. They are graded according to the stamina required to tackle hills and additional mileage. The easiest of the four is a ride through to Wenlock Edge via Acton Scott. A second ride is along the Roman Road to Acton Burnell. Both of these follow quiet back lanes but require a crossing of the A49 so care is needed there. The other two rides feature the Long Mynd; they offer opportunities for off-road sections but require far more stamina.

There's also an increasing interest in off-road riding on the Long Mynd and other bridleways in and out of town. There's a **Long Mynd MTB** map available at the cycle centres (see Extras) and visitor information centre and with half day or day hire available, as well as training courses, it is a good place to get going.

As a great new addition to cycling adventure, Stretton Climate Care launched an **electric bike hire scheme** a couple of years back which encourages visitors to travel around the area on an electric bike. This removes the strain from riding up to some of the hillier parts of the area. An electric bike (or a normal one for that matter) is ideal for visiting All Stretton, where there's a lovely back lane route through to the picturesque village of Picklescott to take lunch at the Jug and Bottle public house. Alternatively, it is possible to cycle to Little Stretton and then loop around to the hamlets of Minton, Hamperley and Marshbrook. Most of these lanes are fairly free of traffic. The good news is that electric bikes can be hired from Plush Hills Cycles in the Square.

REFRESHMENTS

Cafés and Restaurants

Acorn, Sandford Avenue. A firm favourite for those who enjoy good wholefood and with a delightful tea garden. Open daily except Wednesday.

Berry's, High Street, opposite The Square, rightly listed in a number of good food guides, this café/restaurant is a superb outpost of good food. Open daily.

Housmans café bar, High Street, offers refreshment in the day and evening with live music on occasion.

Pubs

By far the best pubs are to be found in the other Strettons, **The Yew Tree** in All Stretton and **The Ragleth** and **Green Dragon** in Little Stretton. If you walk or cycle to Cardington, a stop at **The Royal Oak** is a wonderful place to rest awhile.

Local Produce

There are a small number of shops selling mainly local produce including:

Embreys, Easthope Road: the smell from the open door is very enticing.

Entertaining Elephants, High Street: a wide range of produce is available at this wholefood shop.

Van Deosburg, High Street: deli with an irresistible shop window.

EXTRAS

Plush Hill Cycles, the Square: hire, sales and repairs.

Secret Hills Walking Holidays: guided walks, see breaks-www.secrethillswalking. co.uk.

Shropshire Hills Mountain Bike and Outdoor Pursuit Centre, Marshbrook: sales, hire, repair and courses.

Smith, Leo, Peter Carty and Caroline Uff, (2007) *Wild Mynd*, Southport, Hobby Publications.

Strettons Civic Society (2006) *A Church Stretton Town Trail* available at the Visitor. Information Centre. A small charge is made.

EXCURSIONS FROM CHURCH STRETTON

CRAVEN ARMS AND STOKESAY CASTLE

Ride to Craven Arms

The ride from Church Stretton to Craven Arms is a short one. Craven Arms is the next stop down the line for most southbound trains. The journey takes no more than 10 minutes. There are good views from the train of the southern reaches of the Long Mynd (right), and Ragleth (left) before you breeze through the valley of Marshbrook. This opens up to mixed farming north of Craven Arms itself and expansive views of Wenlock Edge where you should just catch sight of Flounder's Folly, a tower perched on Wenlock Edge, built in the 1830s (see page 94). Just before arriving into Craven Arms, on the right, are the grassy remains of the old Bishop's Castle railway line closed in 1937, part of which has been opened up as a permissive path along a section of the outstandingly beautiful River Onny.

Another option is to catch the 435 bus (Mondays-Saturdays) in the direction of Ludlow from Beaumont Road in Church Stretton. This offers improved views en route as it diverts via a wooded dry valley to Little Stretton. On your left, you will catch sight of the earthwork remnants of **Church Stretton Castle** crowning Brockhurst Hill. The bus rejoins the main A49 and runs through Marshbrook and the hamlet of Felhampton. Sometimes, but not always, the bus leaves the main road again to make its way along the Roman Watling Street passing through the hamlet of Bushmoor and village of **Wistanstow**; the latter is home to the **Wood Brewery** and the Plough Inn brewery tap. The journey time is about 20 minutes.

CRAVEN ARMS

The slow traveller might, on first glance, decide to skip Craven Arms and move on. Admittedly, there is an endless drone of traffic on the A49 and an industrial-looking supermarket that takes centre stage. There are some good reasons, however, for taking time out to walk through this small town. It owes its existence principally to the railway and a sheep market that once stood on the site opposite the Craven Arms Hotel, and these have shaped the place. It has the feel of a railway town even though the engine sheds and sidings have now gone. Perhaps most of all, it has two unusual and very different attractions that are highly recommended. There's also a very fine historic building just down the road. So step off the train or bus and take a look.

Walking around town

From the railway station (southbound platform), go right to cut down the path between the railway fencing and houses. It is not the loveliest of paths but offers a short cut away from the road. This continues past the rear of the super-market to the **Craven Arms Hotel**, named after the land-owning Earls of Craven. This coaching inn dates from the early decades of the 19th century, a little earlier than the railway era. It has a fine porch entrance complete with Doric columns. The buildings adjacent to the hotel were probably the stables associated with the stagecoach services that passed through the town bound for Wales.

Walk around the hotel to the pedestrian crossing and once over the main road, go left and right into Corvedale Road. Take the next right into Market Street where you will see the **Museum of Lost Content**, presumably a reference from Housman's poem *The Shropshire Lad*, in which he refers to the area as 'The land of lost content'. The museum, located in a Victorian market hall along Market Street, is principally there because of the pains-taking work of Stella Mitchell, who has spent much of her life bringing the collection together. It is a collection of artefacts relating to everyday 20th-century life, a celebration of popular culture. There are thousands upon thousands of everyday objects that are no longer familiar in our homes and on our streets. Vintage is now in fashion too. There are a number of vintage style shops opening near the museum; it is a vintage quarter in the making. The odds are against its reaching the heady heights of book town Hay-on-Wye but one never knows.

Continue along Market Street to the **Shropshire Hills Discovery Centre**. Housed in what has been described as a landmark building, mainly because of its eye-catching curves and monumental grass roof, it is an exceptional modern building. The structure reflects that of a hill-fort of which there are many in the central Marches. It is estimated that the roof alone weighs in at about 70 tonnes, but there are many eco features to this building that are not so apparent, such as the underfloor heating. The centre has to be your first stop if you are in the area. It is well stocked with information and has a comfy café, often with art featured on the café walls, so there's food with a view. The core of the Centre is an exhibition which unfolds the making of the Shropshire Hills landscape. It is real polymath stuff with topography, culture and the arts wrapped into a timeline that encourages you to butterfly between displays. The main feature has to be a replica of the Ice Age mammoth from the village of Condover. It is hard to ignore.

Another appealing feature of the Discovery Centre is that the building is adjacent to the **Onny meadows**, some 25 acres of meadow where the rippling waters of the Onny flow beneath tree cover, and by new ponds and woodland. There are several opportunities for relaxing walks. Next door is a community orchard and gardens. In sum, the Discovery Centre is a firm favourite with families and that makes it a lively and pleasant place to be. There are a wide range of events and plenty of hands-on stuff such as an excel-

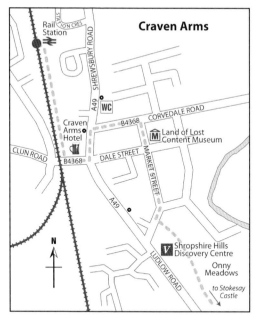

Craven Arms

Rail Station

SHREWSBURY ROAD

A49

WC

B4368

CORVEDALE ROAD

Craven Arms Hotel

M Land of Lost Content Museum

CLUN ROAD

B4368

DALE STREET

MARKET STREET

A49

N

V Shropshire Hills Discovery Centre

Onny Meadows

LUDLOW ROAD

to Stokesay Castle

then first right along a back lane to the castle entrance. It is best to cut through the churchyard as the entrance to the castle is beyond it. The magnificent fortified manor house is a masterpiece.

This area was one known as Stoke and was the manorial seat of the Norman de Say family, hence the name Stokesay. The manor house was later built by the wool merchant Laurence of Ludlow, in the late 13th century, almost certainly as a public exhibition of his wealth. In effect the inner rooms are enclosed, although the manor was clearly not built for military engagement. Only the heavy studded doors and arrow-width windows above the moat suggest that defence was still in the mind of the builders. A devastating blow was avoided in the English Civil War. The brooding forces gath-

lent sustainability trail and some great stuff on geocaching.

Main attraction

On the edge of the Onny Meadows lies **Stokesay Castle**. There's a 10-minute walk from the Discovery Centre across the meadows to a gate (on the right) leading to the A49. Cross with care and go left and

ered for another challenge but, in this case, the incumbents surrendered to a Parliamentarian army on its way to take Ludlow, and thus cheated fate. When you enter, you'll find every aspect of the fortress pleasing to the eye including the remarkable half-timbered gatehouse. This dates from the 17th century, and was funded by the owner in the 1640s, Lord Craven.

Stokesay Castle

It now houses a tea room. The carvings on the building depict men and women, angels and dragons.

Across the courtyard is an enormous 13th-century banqueting hall sandwiched between two fortified towers. The hall is where Laurence would have entertained. The oak timbers that form the supporting roof arches are substantial and a tribute to medieval craftsmanship. But it is hard to imagine how our medieval lordships could have made this place comfortable with large open windows on the side of a prevailing westerly wind and no vent to let out the smoke from a hefty fire grate positioned mid-room. The solar next door offers far more solace and comfort and the 17th-century panelling with floral and figure carvings at the fireplace are remarkable survivors. All this would have been lost had it not been for the life-long ambition of Frances Stackhouse Acton to preserve Stokesay Castle for posterity. There was also the commitment of the Allcroft family to restore the castle with sensitivity in the 19th century. From then onwards, Stokesay Castle was left in the hands of custodians until guardianship was given to the state in 1986. It is now managed by English Heritage.

The church next to the castle is known as a Commonwealth church, mainly built in the wake of the Civil War to put right the damage done by the Parliamentarian army. This included repairing the south door, the only part of the Norman church to survive. The simple interior design, with beautifully crafted woodwork is mainly from the 1650s.

Not far down the road is Stokesay Court (a location in the film *Atonement*), at Onibury. It was completed for John Derby Allcroft in 1892.

WALKING

Although less well-known than Church Stretton, Craven Arms is a great walking centre, with the Discovery Centre a good starting point for many a fine walk. A range of short rambles from the Shropshire Hills Discovery Centre are outlined in a series of leaflets such as the **Three Woods walk** and **Wart Hill Wander** (yes, there's Wart Hill, but the route is a bit more than a wander). There's an even more challenging route onto **Wenlock Edge** via Halmond Hill and Flounder's Folly (a folly funded by Benjamin Flounder in the 1830s).

There are excellent linear walks to Ludlow on the **Shropshire Way**, passing by Stokesay Castle or starting from this point. There is also a good linear walk back to Craven Arms from Clun over **Bury Ditches** but there's now only a bus on Mondays and Fridays to facilitate this. There are also the linear walks from Church Stretton already described as on the Shropshire Way via Ragleth Hill, Acton Scott Working Farm Museum and Wenlock Edge. The walk is ten miles long and will take between 5-6 hours for most people and it is possible to stop off for a break at the café at **Acton Scott Working Farm Museum** (even if not visiting). The walk involves a climb up to Wenlock Edge but this is not steep, and there is one steep descent.

RAIL RAMBLES

Walking from rural railway stations (and sometimes between them) is the main focus of Rail Rambles. The series was first put together by the late Alan Howard in 1989 and the rambles are still as popular 20 years on. They provide a 'rail and walk' experience par excellence. The rambles take place across the Marches and in other parts of Wales. Everyone is welcome to join a walk but you'll need to check out whether you'd prefer an easier or more demanding ramble first! The walks are led by experienced volunteer leaders from a number of Rambler groups with the support of Arriva Trains Wales. They take place on Saturdays (and in addition on some Wednesdays) throughout the year. A programme is available at staffed stations or on line at www.railrambles.com.

It is also possible to make your way to Church Stretton via the Onny Valley to Plowden and then over the Long Mynd, a 12-13 mile walk with some climbs but rewarded with spectacular views.

CYCLING

Clun, Clunton and Clunbury may be three of the quietest places under the sun, as in Housman's eloquent poem, but they are also three of the most difficult to get to. However, all is not lost for the Clun valley and surrounding area offer some interesting cycling opportunities. There are **three cycle routes** designed to encourage use of the quieter roads in and around the Clun valley. The ride from Craven Arms to Clun and back makes for a great day out. **Clun** is a beautiful village lying between the early Saxon settlement, where the church now stands, to the south and **Clun Castle** north of the river. People really like to sit by the riverside next to the late medieval bridge, which has suffered so many 'hits' in recent years that it is a wonder that the ancient structure is still standing. Clun is home to an annual Green Man Festival and has many literary connections. It was the Oniton in Forster's novel *Howard's End*, for example. There are a few tea rooms in addition to two welcoming public houses to reward your effort in getting here. A cycle ride can be tailor-made by catching the train to Hopton Heath (from Church Stretton or Craven Arms) and cycling via Hopton Castle, Three Ashes and Clunton to Clun and back. It is well worth expending that pedal power.

The **Six Castles Cycle Route** passes through Craven Arms with routes to Bishop's Castle and Ludlow. The route to Bishop's Castle involves a climb up Long Lane, for about 2 miles, and that is the acid test as to whether this is for you or not. There are also some slightly scary descents which require control of the bike. The ride to Ludlow has fewer hills and passes by a lovely little pub, the Apple Tree at Onibury and the Ludlow Food Centre (café) en route.

REFRESHMENT

Cafés and Restaurants
Shropshire Hills Discovery Centre café: home made food available.

EXTRAS
Jack Mytton Way: 100-mile route designed for horse riders runs through this area.

Housman, A.E. (2009) *A Shropshire Lad*, Ludlow, Merlin Unwin Books (with photographs by Gareth B. Thomas, an award winning photographer from Ludlow).

KNIGHTON (TREF-Y-CLAWDD) AND PRESTEIGNE (LLANANDRAS)

Ride to Knighton
The little train on the Heart of Wales railway covers the 19.5 miles through to Knighton in 33 minutes. That is remarkably slow so you can relish every bit of the journey across the river Clun and through the temperate Teme valley. There are several halts beyond Craven Arms where the train pulls up, but only if someone on board requests a stop or a potential passenger hails it from a station platform as it trundles down the track. The first halt is Broome which is a 10-minute walk (along a quiet road) to the village of **Aston-on-Clun**, a curious place, for here are two stone round houses and a pub called the Kangaroo Inn. The village is noted for its **Arbor Tree**, decorated annually to commemorate the marriage of a local gent, Squire Marston, to Mary Carter of Sibdon Carwood on 28th May 1786. The couple left a sum of money for the celebrations to continue. Amazingly, the original tree survived until 1995; there's a new one in its place, and the Arbor Day festival is as strong as ever.

Next stop is **Hopton Heath**, the least used station in Shropshire. It is not surprising really, for there's no more than

Hopton Castle

a few houses nestled around the railway station. It is handy halt nevertheless, as it is a little more than a mile to the hamlet of **Hopton Castle**, along a narrow road with incredibly wide verges; it must have been a miry old lane. In plentiful supply are great views of wooded hills and green pastures reaching down to the Hopton Brook. The chances are that you'll fancy a wander along this lane to the castle but there's one factor to take into account before you travel. There are fairly long intervals between some trains, and no shops or inns in Hopton Heath or Hopton Castle. You might need to take a picnic. Perhaps the best idea is to combine the trip with a walk or cycle ride along back lanes to out-of-the-way villages in this quietest of areas (see below). Alternatively, there's a lovely walk through to Clunbury and Broome (railway station) via Aston-on-Clun (see www.slowtraveluk.com for details).

All that remains of the actual **castle** at Hopton is the gaunt-looking keep, dating from the 14th century, surrounded by scant earthworks. The castle is, however, remembered for one particular atrocity carried out in the English Civil War. The Parliamentarians who held the castle came

under siege by a major force of Royalists. Despite the accepted rules of engagement, under which if you chose to defend a place that was deemed indefensible and with no prospect of relief, the attacking force would show no mercy on finally capturing the defences, the Parliamentarians, under the command of a resolute Samuel More, initially refused to surrender. When they eventually capitulated, the Royalists took many prisoners and duly slaughtered them in revenge. Some reports have suggested that the Parliamentarian prisoners were firstly mutilated and then stoned as they tried to escape from what eventually was to become a mass grave. Hopton Castle thus became the byword for treachery in the 17th century.

The castle fell into a serious state of dereliction through the centuries as subsequent landowners seemingly chose to ignore the importance of the site until the late 20th century. Partly through sheer exasperation and partly through visionary insight, a group of local people set up the Hopton Castle Preservation Trust in the 1990s with a view to saving the ruins from total collapse. It won a major grant and the castle has now been secured, thus giving future generations the opportunity to learn more about the turbulent past in the Marches.

The train travels onward to **Bucknell**, a large village sprawling around a medieval cluster and parish church alongside the river Redlake. The village has two pubs and several shops as well as dozens of fine walks so is a good place to stop off. From here onwards, the train progresses through the valley where you catch glimpses of the river Teme to your left and on the right the lovely little church at the isolated hamlet of **Stowe**. You soon arrive at Knighton where there are views of the high hills surrounding this traditional borderland gap town.

KNIGHTON (TREF-Y-CLAWDD)

Knighton is the quintessential border town. The centre of the town stands firmly in Wales but its railway station lies just across the border that runs near to the river Teme so is situated in England. The station buildings are impressive. There's a hint of French Renaissance about the place with its high gables, pitched roof and chimneys. This was not just another small town terminus; it was the HQ of the Craven Arms to Knighton Railway. However, construction of the line was sluggish and the first train arrived on 6th March 1861, some ten years after the opening of Craven Arms railway station in 1851. Passengers now have to make do with a small shelter on either platform although a local group of volunteers do their very best to keep the station cheerful.

One of the pleasant cafés (and in this case also a gallery) near the clock tower

The town of Knighton lies neatly within a gap between hills and this gives it a distinct borderland atmosphere. The wooded slopes are of an Alpine nature and there's a freshness in the air that is invigorating. The town centre is clustered around a small centre at a crossroads. It is crowned with a Victorian clock tower which is an iconic landmark. Rising up from this central spot is a thoroughfare known as **The Narrows**, a part of town that has a potential that has yet to be released. This leads to a network of small streets that are decidedly medieval in layout. Knighton retains its roots as an agrarian market town principally in relation to the sale of sheep that are herded deftly into pens on auction days. Although the street market is now small scale there's also a Farmers Market in town once a month.

The main attraction in the town is the **Offa's Dyke Centre**, as it really does illustrate to good effect the importance of Offa's Dyke in the borderlands and its significance in Welsh-Anglo history. One of the main reasons people come to Knighton is to walk on the surrounding hills, either on Offa's Dyke Path or Glyndwr's Way. A trip down the Heart of Wales line which includes a walk around Knighton makes for an ideal day. Alternatively, it is possible to alight beforehand and walk or cycle from one of the halts en route or from the next stop down the line, Knucklas, into the Teme valley.

Walk around Knighton

The train crews have to exchange a token at Knighton to allow onward working of a single line section. This involves opening up a Dr Who style metal cabinet to key into an ancient piece of equipment that belongs to the steam era. Therefore, there's always a pause here before the single car train tootles off again. From either platform you need to walk up steps (or go via the station entrance) to Station Road, where you turn left for town. Cross the bridge over the river Teme. Continue to walk towards town but then cut first right into Church Road and keep ahead as the road narrows to reach

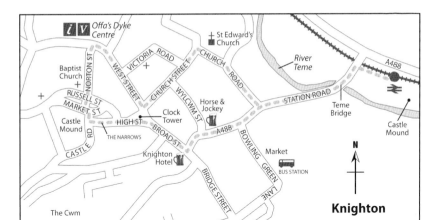

Knighton

the **church of St Edward**. The church, with its small 14th-century turret tower, looks splendid against the backdrop of the wooded hills. The church has been re-built several times. For example, there's Norman workmanship at the base of the tower and yet there's evidence that the remainder has been rebuilt at least twice since. The remainder of the church is an 18th- and 19th-century reconstruction with many examples of Gothic revival on show and stained glass windows which lighten the nave and chancel. From the church, you need to keep ahead along Church Street into West Street where you turn right for Offa's Dyke Visitor Centre.

Main Attraction
The Offa's Dyke Centre offers local tourist information and a number of intriguing displays reflecting the history of Knighton, about the Welsh princes and most of all about that magnificent linear monument that runs through the Marches. Offa's Dyke was instigated by one of the most powerful overlords in Saxon England, King Offa, who ruled with an uncanny level of command over a vast Midland territory from AD757 to AD796. The dyke came into existence for a number of reasons, partly for defence and partly as a means of managing the trade of goods between England and Wales. It was a substan-

tial structure, some 27 metres wide by 8 metres high (from the ditch bottom to the mound tip). It was more or less aban-doned and consigned to history by the 9th century. The displays interpret the histor-ical connections between King Offa and the Welsh princes. The dyke had become an irrelevance to those in power by the late Saxon period, but it has managed to survive on the ground for more than 1,200 years. It has yet to unfold manifold mysteries relating to its existence; it is still a matter of considerable debate amongst archaeologists.

In the 1960s the late Frank Noble set up a movement of like minded people keen to promote a walk along the line of the dyke, a diverse and often wild walking route from the Severn estuary at Sedbury Cliffs to the Irish Sea at Prestatyn. Thus, he gathered support to establish an Offa's Dyke Association in 1969, and the route was designated as a National Trail in 1971. Frank Noble's aim was to ensure that the 177-mile trail remained close to the earthworks wherever possible, though these are largely absent for much of the southern part of the trail; indeed there is dispute as to whether 'Offa's' dyke ever extended further south than Kington. From Kington northwards, however, the path stays largely faithful to the dyke, too faithful in places and there are moves to ease it slightly away from the ancient monument wherever possible, so as to reduce any unintended damage. Other measures in the past decade have been to encourage farmers to reduce erosion and to lessen disturbance from burrowing animals. The Association now manages the Offa's Dyke Centre and has a strong advisory and promotional role in the development of the trail. It is also keen to see more research on the archaeology and history of the dyke. Knighton remains the central point of access to the dyke. For those who'd prefer to make the journey by bus there's no better companion that *On An Offa Bus* by Gareth Wheatley, a description of one man's travel through Offa's Dyke border country.

From the centre, cross the road, turn left and immediately right up Norton Street into the higher end of town. Cross the road by a Baptist church, dating from the 1860s, into Market Street where you go left. Behind the houses stands the remains of a second Norman **castle** built in Knighton. The first was at Bryn y Castell, near the river Teme and a small earthwork still exists there. The castle mound located at this top end of town is located on private property so cannot be seen at close quarters, but glimpses of it can be had between some of the houses on your right. It was, by all accounts, a substantial castle, developed by William de Braose and then subsequently held by the Mortimers. The legendary Welsh prince, Llewelyn the Last, destroyed it and then turned on the town in 1262. Owain Glyndwr repeated the exercise in 1402 before marching on to his substantial victory against Edmund Mortimer at the bloody battle of Pilleth, several miles south of Knighton. It seems that the castle was simply abandoned from the mid 15th century onwards.

Go left into **The Narrows**. This steep and narrow street leads down to High Street, where the Victorian clock tower, dating from 1872, stands tall against the surrounding buildings. Keep right into Broad Street where most of the shops are

located and then turn left into Station Road by the Knighton Hotel, a half-timbered 16th-century coaching inn augmented by a 19th-century hotel, recently refurbished in a contemporary style. The galleried cantilever staircase is a masterpiece. Pass by the Horse and Jockey public house, which is thought to have been a medieval stone house with an open solar. The existing open courtyard structure supports this interpretation and is much loved for al fresco eating in the summer.

It all seems quiet enough in Knighton but the town turns out a good festival or two each year. By far the largest in recent history was a rock concert *A Day out In the Country* organised by three Knighton lads in the 1970s with a little help from the father of British Blues, the late Alexis Korner, who lived nearby. It attracted thousands of rock fans to see the likes of the Move and Killing Floor. There are several musical connections with the town. For example, the late Dick Heckstall-Smith grew up in Knighton

Half-timbered house nestled into The Narrows

and became one of the UK's best known Jazz-Blues saxophonists in the later decades of the 20th century.

If you are going to travel on to Presteigne or into the Teme valley by bus then you need to make your way to Knighton bus station. Turn right into Bowling Green Lane, signposted for the livestock market. There's a lay-by on the left where buses pull up for Kington, Ludlow and Newtown and this is where the town mini-bus pops in and out throughout the day. That's the bus station and unfortunately it is not a credit to the town.

PRESTEIGNE (LLANANDRAS)

If you decide to combine your trip to Knighton with an extension through to Presteigne, it is a 20-minute bus ride through Offa's Dyke country. The bus climbs out of Knighton into the Radnorshire hills and then travels by way of Norton or on some journeys via Whitton. Either way, the trip opens up a splendid set of views. You enter Presteigne by newly created allotments which look luxuriant, at least at the right time of year. Nearby is the **Withybeds nature reserve** and Wentes meadow alongside the wet ground of the river Lugg. When the famous 19th-century writer George Borrow turned up in town, he enquired as to whether Presteigne was really Welsh or English. He was duly informed that it was neither but simply Radnorshire. That's Presteigne, a curious mix of Welsh and English that makes it every bit a border town. Walk over the packhorse bridge at the end of Broad Street, for example, and you have stepped back into England.

There are several places in the Marches where the level of bus service is dire; Presteigne happens to be one of them. Nevertheless, despite the current limited service (Mondays to Saturdays from Knighton), there's just about the right amount of time to explore a town that was once a battleground between the Welsh princes and Norman overlords. **Presteigne Castle** (of which there are scant earthworks at a park called The Warden) and the nearby **Stapleton Castle** (some stonework from a later fortified house exists on private ground) came into the possession of the Mortimers. Their influence in the area was, as you have probably gathered by now, monumental in every sense of the word.

However, Presteigne's claim to fame is more recent. It was almost by chance that Presteigne became the assize court for the county of Radnorshire. This followed the unsavoury murder of a judge in Rhayader which shocked the good and great of mid Wales into action. The seat of the judiciary must be moved, they argued, to somewhere less unruly. Presteigne became that place and by the 17th century it had claimed another prize. Not only was it home to the county's judicial circuit; it was the county town too, thus gaining importance way above its station. In due course, though, these roles were taken from Presteigne by an upstart of a resort, Llandrindod Wells, in the late 19th century.

Walk around town

It is probably best to alight from the bus at the recycling point on Great Western Way as you'll then know where to return to catch the bus after your visit. It also allows you a chance to walk to the innovative **Café Gallery and Electric Bike shop** around the corner, situated on the left side of an industrial estate. This is where much of the *Tour de Presteigne* happens, a zany international electric bike rally packed with people trying out the latest range of electrically powered bikes. This is the future, some argue, and there might be some truth in the assertion as sales of these bikes are booming across the world, and the number one stockist in the Marches happens to be right here. You can try out bikes on the quiet stretch of road adjacent to the shop. To get there, go right from the bus shelter and turn right again. It is a matter of three minutes walk.

Afterwards, retrace your steps to Great Western Way to pass the recycling point and bus stop then go right into Station

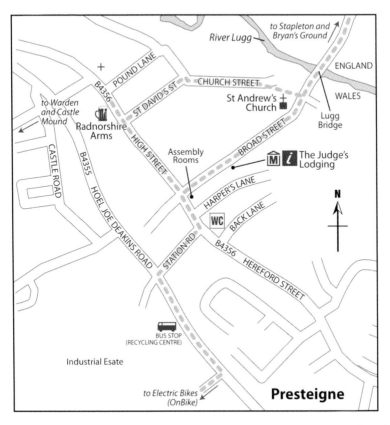

On map:

to Stapleton and Bryan's Ground

River Lugg

ENGLAND

POUND LANE

B4356

CHURCH STREET

ST DAVID'S ST

St Andrew's Church

WALES

to Warden and Castle Mound

Radnorshire Arms

HIGH STREET

BROAD STREET

Lugg Bridge

CASTLE ROAD

B4355

Assembly Rooms

M i The Judge's Lodging

N

HARPER'S LANE

HOEL JOE DEAKINS ROAD

WC

BACK LANE

STATION RD

B4356 HEREFORD STREET

BUS STOP (RECYCLING CENTRE)

Industrial Esate

to Electric Bikes (OnBike)

Presteigne

Road, a reminder that Presteigne once had a rail link, an outpost of the railway empire. It was a short branch from Titley Junction on the Leominster to Kington line, a railway that extended through to New Radnor in its heyday. Station Road descends to Hereford Street where you go left to pass by an unused building in front of Harford House. This was once the home of Sir Harford-Jones-Brydges, one time British ambassador to Persia. There's a vintage petrol pump still *in situ* and a plaque to commemorate the fact that a private girls' school existed here too in the 1860s. Cross the road and stand by the Italianate Assembly Rooms at the top of Broad Street, built in the late 1860s as a market hall and meeting place. It is one of the loveliest corners in the Marches.

Look over at the Radnor Buildings, as from this vantage point you can observe the beautifully coloured and intricate floral plasterwork that renders a softer touch to the place.

At the crossroads leading into High Street, keep ahead to admire the variety of architectural styles along this main shopping street. There are several independent shop fronts, in fact there's hardly a national brand in sight. At the time of writing, Presteigne was still fighting off a supermarket chain seeking to come to town. There's a feeling that this might send the High Street spiralling into decline when at present it is on the up once more. Look out for the carving of the Green Man (Number 47) and Mansion House (both on the left hand side) which was a medieval

The Radnor Buildings in Presteigne. Ornate decoration adds character ...

hall, modified considerably in Georgian times, before you reach the half-timbered **Radnorshire Arms** Hotel dating from the early 17th century. This ancient inn is dripping in history and legend. For example, it is reckoned to have its own priest hole and tunnels underground, although none of these features can be readily seen. The wood-panelled main bar, however, is in full view and looks the part.

Retrace your steps back to the first junction where you go left into St David's Street. It's a step back into the world of old Radnorshire as not much has changed in this street since the late 18th century. On the left is the 17th-century Old Bull Inn which was revitalised in the 1820s. Nearby is the handsome **Manor House**, originally a 16th-century building but restored in the 19th century. It was also a judges' lodgings prior to the establishment of the Shire Hall. At the end, go right into Church Street, which leads to the precincts of **St Andrew's church**. The area leading to the church is known as The Scallions, meaning the environs of the lychgate. Built on a Saxon site, the tower and nave date from the 14th century. The Lady Chapel and the chancel

are of a Perpendicular style, dating from the 15th century. Among the many monuments and artefacts the main treasure is a 16th-century Flemish tapestry.

The most notorious case tried at the court just up the road, was that of Mary Morgan, a young mother found guilty of murdering her newborn child and sentenced to death by hanging. It was a very sorrowful case and her grave lies in the churchyard. There's a curfew bell at the church too. It sounds every night, a practice which started in 1565 to maintain order in the town. No one takes much notice now but it is still rung. Further along Broad Street (to the left of the churchyard) is the Old Bell Inn, a beautiful half-timbered property (now a private dwelling) and the road beyond leads to **Stapleton Castle** and hamlet (about 30 minutes walk each way) or to an enchanting garden at **Bryan's Ground** (30 minutes by turning right at the first junction). If you are not extending your walk out of the town then go right to the Shire Hall, built in 1829 and made all the more formidable by the addition of a grand Tuscan portico. The tourist information centre and the Judge's Lodgings are located here.

... as do the variety of individual shops

Main attraction

The historic connection with the haughty judicial world is the main attraction in town. **The Judge's Lodgings** at the Shire Hall depicts the life of a court in the 1860s. It allows an insight into the privileged world of the judge, and the menial existence of his servants all beneath one roof; there's an associated range of ephemera displayed throughout the lodgings. The judges of Radnorshire were renowned for their desire to dole out harsh punishments even though the area was renowned for its low level of serious criminality. The juries, on the other hand, had gained a reputation for being lenient, possibly because they knew the people before them in the dock, so it was really a matter of balance in this court. You start the tour in the luxuriousness of the judge's living accommodation, before descending to the world of the servants, all the while being bathed in the atmosphere of the gas lighting and with a greater freedom to handle many of the objects in the rooms than is the case in most museums. Then in an area of greater darkness you come to the cells in which those being tried were kept, and from these you emerge into the court room as if you were yourself on trial. There is much for children to enjoy, including dressing up as the judge or felon. What also appeals about this attraction are the numerous other exhibits, for example, one featuring Radnorshire talk, and another one about the world of the rural police force. Add to this a picture about everyday Victorian life in the Marches, all unfolded in a quiet but engaging way.

Make your way back to Hereford Street and then right into Station Road to the Recycling Point. This is the best place to catch the bus as they all call in here. Presteigne is home to Ian Marchant, one of the funniest of contemporary writers on travel, who penned *Parallel Lines* in the 1990s about an epic train journey through Britain. It provides many insights about the trials and joy of travelling by public transport but most of all it brings a smile to your face. As you stand at what is certainly a firm contender for the most downbeat bus stop in the Marches (or possibly the world), keep smiling.

WALKING

Knighton is a major stopping-off point on the **Offa's Dyke Trail**. It is about half way along the trail and people tend to start or finish here if they are not seeking to walk the entire 177 miles. However, if you prefer a taster walk rather than the long distance stuff, then there are leaflets which describe local circular walks which include sections of Offa's Dyke Path.

There's also an opportunity to take the 41 bus up to Whitepool plantation near Hawthorn Hill, where the monument to a local Victorian notable can be seen. This monument recognises the good work done by Sir Richard Price-Green to improve the health of poor people in the area. From here you can walk back into Knighton; it takes approximately 2 hours.

Knighton is also the starting point of **Glyndwr's Way**, a National Trail that covers 135 miles of very isolated countryside in Powys. It is dedicated to the Welsh warrior, Owain Glyndwr, as this would have been his territory and from these isolated hills he waged war on the Norman-English overlords. One possible sampler on this trail could be to walk between the railway halt at Llangunllo and Knighton, about 6 miles. On alighting at Llangunllo station (the railway refers to it as Llangynllo), turn left once on the road towards the village of Llangunllo. On reaching the railway bridge over the road, you join Glyndwr's Way. Follow the waymarks to Llangunllo, about half a mile away. This village lost its pub in 2006 when the long standing landlord died. The villagers were devastated and soon afterwards they lost their regular bus too. In desperation they decided to put furniture into the bus shelter and made it their very own social club for use on summer evenings. The good news is that the Greyhound public house is now up and running again so the shelter social club is less in demand. Glyndwr's Way is waymarked through to Knighton and offers great walking. A tougher ramble would be a linear walk from Felindre (Bus 41 from Knighton) over the Black Mountain to Llangunllo, approximately 9 miles and then possibly to continue into Knighton, making it 15 miles altogether.

There are other opportunities to use the line for linear walks – ask for the leaflet *Four Railway Walks from Knighton* at the Offa's Dyke Centre. One favourite, for example, is to walk to Bucknell via Stowe (or vice versa), about 7 miles, and catch the train for the outward or return leg. Another is a walk back from Knucklas halt into Knighton. Most of the walks in the area involve climbs; some of them are fairly severe so be prepared.

Presteigne has some great local walks including a lovely circular walk to Lingen via Willey Hall and Harley's Mountain returning via Noisy Hall (see www.slowtraveluk.com). There are also local walks to Nash Wood.

CYCLING

The Teme valley is ideal for exploration by bike. The Heart of Wales train carries two bikes and there are a number of places you might consider for a ride. As mentioned previously, there's a ride from Hopton Heath station to Hopton Castle. This could easily be extended through to **Bedstone** and **Bucknell** (there are two pubs, shops and a railway station). Alternatively, you can go ahead on the B4367 to Abcott so as to call into the famous **Rocke Cottage Tea Room,** a 17th-century half-timbered building that was at one time an inn. It is also possible to visit nearby **Clungunford**, once described by *Guardian* newspaper correspondent Justine Hawkins as a dinky hushed hamlet in south Shropshire. The 14th-century church of St Cuthberts is surrounded by houses of note, including the timbered framed Abcott Manor and 19th-century Clungunford House (both private dwellings). A return can be made on the back road from the Rocke Cottage to Three Ashes. Make a left there and then a right (manoeuvre with care here) to Hopton Castle, where two left turns get you back to Hopton Heath Station. All in all, this is about 5-6 miles or 9-10 if you decide to ride on to Bucknell or through to Knighton.

The upper part of the Teme valley is pretty good leisure cycling territory too. It is slightly off the tourist radar but the section between Knucklas and Beguildy has a Radnorshire beauty about it. Take your bike on the train to **Knucklas** for a ride into the valley to see for yourself. There's an imposing viaduct at Knucklas, some 190 yards long, and supported by thirteen grand arches. It was built in the early 1880s to replace an earlier structure and embellished with battlemented turrets so as to complement the non-existent battlements of **Knucklas Castle**. The earth ramparts are high on the wooded hill above.

The community actually owns the site of Knucklas Castle now; the people's revolution, in this instance, has taken centuries to come about. According to a local historian the castle was built between 1215 and 1230 to remind the Welsh inhabitants that the Normans were here to stay. Ralph Mortimer, however, married the daughter of the Welsh prince Llewelyn the Great, and the castle evidently did not figure strongly in borderland military campaigns. One hundred years later it was most probably in disrepair and that is why there's not that much to see 800 years on. There's a strong sense of community here. As well as looking after the castle, it has established a Community Land Project, a transition scheme which has laid out a community orchard, allotments and a village green.

From Knucklas it is possible to cycle up the valley, either on the quiet B4355 or via Llanfair Waterdine on the back road through to the village of **Beguildy** where the church stands on a circular raised churchyard. The Radnorshire Arms is at hand to provide refreshment. There are a group of Bronze Age monuments near to the road as well as tumuli on Beacon Hill.

An alternative outing is to ride out as far as Lloyney and then turn right for Monaughty and Skyborry back to Knighton railway station; this adds up to no more than 12-13 miles of cycling but there are some hills. The **Radnor Forest Ride** is a 70 mile trail designed for horse riders using remote bridleways and lanes. It is also suitable for cyclists and walkers. It starts above **Llanfair Waterdine** (where it joins The Jack Mytton Way trail into Shropshire, also designed for horse riders) and finishes at the Brecon Beacons National Park centre south of Brecon.

There's also an East Radnor Cycle guide available at the visitor information centre at the Judge's Lodgings, Presteigne. This highlights six local cycle rides, and in the Presteigne area a good ride is along the Radnor Ring route between Presteigne and Knighton. There's also a Cycle Breaks Pack for Knighton and Presteigne highlighting five local rides, so cycling is definitely becoming better promoted locally. Traffic is low but there's still the challenge of the hills to factor in before you set out on any adventure.

REFRESHMENT

Clungunford
Rocke Cottage Tea Rooms, Clungunford: traditional tea rooms laid out in the style of the 1920s and '30s including the music. The owner produces fabulous homemade food from local ingredients. Walkers and cyclists very welcome here.

SLOW ENTERTAINMENT

At the centre of the village of Knucklas lies a homely pub, the Castle Inn. This pub, in addition to other village pubs down the track, hosts a slow travel music evening once a month. The germ of the idea began when Graham Lambert of Myriad Organics in Ludlow, together with the landlady of the Castle Inn and the landlady from the Sitwell Arms at nearby Bucknell agreed to join forces with local musicians to make it happen. Under the banner of *Folk down the Track* the evening outings have flourished. The key organisers, Myriad Organics and Ludlow 21, welcome visitors and locals on board for a slow trip down the Heart of Wales line to a pub where musicians play on your arrival. There's often impromptu music on the return train. For a current programme contact www.ludlow21.org.uk.

Knighton

Clock Tower Tea Shop: homemade cakes including bread and butter pudding baked in Prince and Pugh's rayburn within the store.

Tower House Gallery: offers locally sourced food in a gallery on Broad Street.

Knucklas and Beguildy

Castle Inn, Knucklas: see www.castleinn.org.uk.

Radnorshire Arms, Beguildy: Good Beer Guide entry in recent years.

Presteigne

Gallery Café Bar, Industrial Estate, Presteigne: lovely homemade cakes.

The Hat Shop Restaurant, Presteigne: long-standing restaurant in the town renowned for its good food.

Mistletoe House at Combe (about 1.5 miles out of town so a 493/4 bus or cycle ride) has a tea room serving lovely homemade produce plus a gallery and garden, see www.mistletoehouse.co.uk.

Local Produce

Leon's Deli, High Street, Presteigne: much welcomed newcomer with wholesome bread and combination of food from the Marches and Spain.

Extras

Gaia's Garden, The Narrows, Knighton: see www.gaias-garden.co.uk.

Eco cabin, Obley: excellent low footprint ecocabin four miles from Bucknell railway station. Great for cyclists and walkers.

Knighton Farmers Market: Community Centre, 2nd and 4th Saturday of the month.

Knucklas projects: see www.knucklascastle.org.uk.

Marchant, Ian (2003) *Parallel Lines,* Bloomsbury.

Presteigne Farmers Market, Radnorshire Arms Hotel: first Saturday in the month.

Radnorshire Wildlife Trust manages the **Withybeds** nature reserve – see www.radnorshirewildlifetrust.org.uk.

Wheatley, Gareth (2009) *On An Offa Bus*, Bridge Books.

PUBLIC TRANSPORT

Trains

Knighton is served, daily and directly by trains from Church Stretton on the Heart of Wales line, which also provides a service up from Swansea via Llandrindod Wells. Travel time: 33 minute journey from Church Stretton.

Buses to Knighton

There is a bus from Ludlow (Assembly Rooms) to Knighton Bus Station. 738/740. Monday – Saturday. Four trips per day. The 740 bus also serves Clungunford and Hopton Heath. Travel time: 50 minutes. Operator: Arriva.

Buses from Knighton to Presteigne

Presteigne is served by bus from Knighton Bus Station. 41. Monday – Saturday. Three trips per day. Travel time: 15-20 minutes. The 41 bus also serves Knucklas and Beguildy. Travel time: 25 minutes. Operator: Veolia Transport Cymru.

Presteigne is also served by the 493/4 bus from Leominster Bus Station. Monday – Saturday. Three trips per day. Travel time: 35-44 minutes. Operator: Lugg Valley.

LUDLOW

Travel writers have served up just about every superlative in the book to describe Ludlow and, of course, it is more or less true. Ludlow still earns its title as 'the capital of the Marches' but more than one author has alluded to the fact that there's a balance to be struck. Writing in the early 1930s, a travel guide writer, J.C. Moore commented:

> 'All men kill the thing they love', wrote Oscar Wilde; and perhaps it may be argued that I am one of the potential murderers of Ludlow, since I am writing about it and trying to persuade crowds of people to visit it.

It is good to report, some 80 years after these words were penned, that tourism is alive and well in Ludlow. But so is everyday life; that is what makes the place so enjoyable. Ludlow became the first Cittàslow town in the UK in 2003; there are over 140 such towns across the world. The idea of Cittàslow (meaning slow town) was nurtured by the Mayor of Orvieto in Italy. He was concerned to improve the quality of life for his residents by holding on to good traditions, respecting the locality, encouraging local food production and nurturing distinctiveness. From this start, the movement spread, firstly to other Italian towns and now across the world. The approach seems to work well in Ludlow, although there are few or no mechanisms to resist the influx of national chains that do not compete on a level playing field with local businesses.

The historic core of the town sits neatly on a flattened ridge within a horseshoe of the river Teme, which flows through a gap created by meltwaters at the end of the last Ice Age. Ludlow may have been settled in the earliest of times by prehistoric tribes and there was a Bronze Age tomb ascribed to 'Luda' located beneath St Laurence's church. However, it is essentially a Norman town and one that is beautifully compact. Ludlow developed as one small part of the wider manorial seat of Stanton, held by the influential de Lacy family. Their choice of defensive site could not have been better.

Two medieval structures can be seen from miles around. These have remained constant for the best part of 600 years.

Looking over Ludlow from Whitcliffe Common, with the castle in the foreground and the tower of St Laurence's church to the right

Of the two, the tall tower of St Laurence's church holds greater prominence on the skyline and you may have seen it from the train. Built in the mid 15th century, it is testimony to the wealth of the wool merchants and clothiers of the town who chose to invest some of their surplus in this grand church. However, the battlements of the Marches' finest Norman castle, located on a woodland promontory, are also clearly discernible. By far the best views of the castle are gained from the west when walking into town on the Shropshire Way from Bromfield or on the Mortimer Trail across Whitcliffe Common.

Between these two buildings lies a grid street plan belonging to a 12th-century settlement. To the south of the ridge are parallel streets running down to the river, an architectural mélange reflecting changing tastes throughout the centuries. The collection of dwellings is so intact (and with minimal contemporary infill) that it has impressed historians and literary giants down the ages, including Sir John Betjeman who described it as 'the perfect historic town'. Without doubt Ludlow's handsome town houses are to be admired, but equally the alleys leading to secret gardens, the plant pots by doorways and colourful hanging baskets give a warm feel to the town. To the west and north of the castle there is a steeper descent to the valley floor. The narrow lanes and paths drop

down to riverside meadows, a narrow strip at the Dinham Millennium Green and the recreational area off the Linney, all within a few minutes walk from Castle Square. As you wander round the town, keep your eyes open for the variety of carvings on the outside of many buildings, not just the well known ones such as The Reader's House and The Feathers Hotel; see if you spot the one known to some as Busty Bertha, a modern carving that 'complements' a more modest 17th-century carving on the same building (hint: look in Raven Lane).

Getting to Ludlow by train is as easy from Shrewsbury, the North West and North Wales as it is from Hereford, Cardiff and South Wales. There are connections from London at Shrewsbury, Hereford and Newport and trains operate from early morning to late at night. It is also reasonably well served by buses from Hereford, Kidderminster (for Birmingham) and Shrewsbury. Beyond these main routes there are only a few other bus services, principally one to Knighton and a twice weekly run through to Builth and Llandrindod Wells and another twice weekly service to Bishop's Castle. Other inter-town routes have been withdrawn in recent years; this renders trips to Bridgnorth and Tenbury Wells, both ideal places to visit from Ludlow, virtually impossible to reach by public transport.

Walking around town

Ludlow is a place best explored on foot. While some footways are narrow, others provide ample space to linger and browse. Ludlow residents have a reputation for taking advantage of the full width of the highway; the pace is relaxed. Cycling is more of an adventure as a means of navigating around Ludlow, partly because of the hilly terrain and partly because of a one-way system that is shared with faster moving vehicles. You have to be on your mettle in some places. Nevertheless, Ludlow is becoming more popular with cyclists and there's nothing better than cycling from the railway station along the fairly quiet street called the Linney to

Whilst Ludlow is often remembered because of the richness of its timber-framed buildings, there is Georgian elegance too

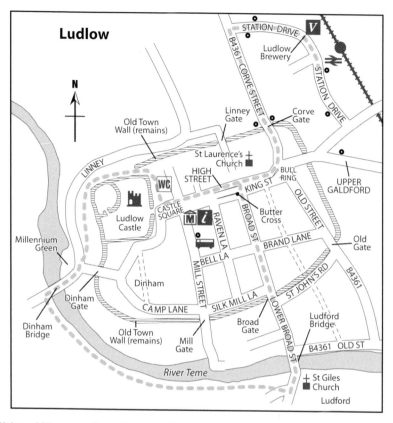

Dinham Millennium Green for a meal or coffee and cake while watching the Teme flow over one of the many town weirs.

The main attraction is the town itself with almost 500 listed buildings and an eclectic mix of independent shops and restaurants, market stalls, cultural events and old-world pubs. This makes the place vibrant throughout most of the year. As you wander around you'll notice blue plaques which provide an insight into the history of each site as you pass by.

Go right from the station entrance along Station Drive to Corve Street. The first few minutes of the walk is mundane, although there's **Ludlow Brewery** to your right (beyond the Aldi supermarket) and also on the right an attractive shop which sources its flowers from nearby Stokesay

Court at Onibury. At the traffic lights go left into Corve Street. Cross over to walk by **Myriad Organics**. There's often an array of fine herb plant pots displayed and you are welcome to step inside to look at a display featuring organic food production in the Shropshire Hills.

The lower end of Corve Street is characterised by Georgian houses, but as you make your way up the road widens then narrows to become the Bull Ring (where bulls used to be traded by local farmers). As you climb up the hill, the **Bull Hotel**, on the right, is one of the earliest hostelries in the town. Take a look through the stable gateway at the 15th-century timber framing and extensive jetty (projecting storey). Across the road is the much photographed **Feathers Hotel**, an iconic feature of Ludlow because of its elaborate wood-work and fine balconies, dating from the 17th century.

At the Bull Ring, go right into King Street, where the Bull Ring Tavern and adjacent shop exhibit another splendid timber-framed frontage. Walk ahead to the 18th-century **Butter Cross**. The pavement is narrow but people simply spill out into the road here, an early version of traffic calming that has seemingly stood the test of time. To the right, just by the Butter Cross, is a path leading to St Laurence's church (see below) and ahead there's the narrow Church Street through to Castle Square. This is a much frequented part of Ludlow, a meeting place of narrow streets by the Church Inn, thoroughfares originally made for carts and carriages only. Look out for the old conduit used to supply drinking water in previous centuries. Further along on the right is the gateway to the 15th-century courtyard of the Rose and Crown public house, at one time a coaching inn which stabled a dozen or so horses.

There's a choice of routes at the Church Inn. You can simply wander around this part of town, which is on the level and

with lovely cosy corners to get lost in, like **Quality Square**. Each and every one begs exploration. On the other hand you can make a short circular walk (with one climb), which shows Ludlow's strategic position and the importance of the river in powering several early town mills. If you've plumped for the latter, go left into **Broad Street** with its fine range of half-timbered buildings to be seen on the left. The renowned De Greys café comes into sight first and then look out for the former Angel Hotel, identi-fied by its oriel bay windows. This former inn is now lost to Ludlovians, a matter that is much lamented by the older drinking cohort.

Broad Street has many handsome Georgian townhouses, so many that the symmetry and simplicity of it all demands every ounce of attention. Pevsner and Newnham described it as 'one of the most memorable streets in England'. People love to stroll down the wide raised pave-ments of Broad Street to pick out their favourite dwelling, before reaching the only remaining **gateway** in the old town wall. Your way is through this gateway and down Lower Broad Street which leads to

One of Ludlow's many independent shops

A line of walkers crosses Ludford Bridge, possibly heading for the Charlton Arms on the left, and onwards to Whitcliffe Common and Mortimer Forest

the medieval **Ludford Bridge**. Take a look back at the battlements of the 19th-century gatehouse standing above the gateway. It really is a treasure. Cross the bridge to the Charlton Arms, an inn that has balconies overlooking the flowing waters of the Teme, a place to be on a summer's evening.

You are now in **Ludford**, with its own ancient **church of St Giles**, which has a splendid 13th-century nave and many fine examples of stained glass windows. The lane by the church offers a quiet back-water where there are many architectural features of note, especially the 17th-century timbered Old Bell House which has long since ceased to be a hostelry, and by the river is the old Ludford Mill. Ludford House offers another superb collection of build-ings enclosed by a walled garden which, however, are not open to the public.

If you are not making a detour into Ludford, turn right out of the Charlton Arms and right again along Whitcliffe Lane (leading to Whitcliffe Common) where there's an outcrop of world fame on the corner, known as the **Ludlow Bone Bed**.

This is a thin strata of sedimentary rock laid down 419 million years ago. Geologists have noted that it contains the remains of early fish but also particles from forest fires which offer evidence of early plantlife on terra firma (rather than just a sea bed as previously thought). There's an excellent display in the Charlton Arms.

A few paces beyond, go right once more onto a path known as the **Breadwalk**, a lovely town walk favoured by the Victorians. It is surfaced but there are also steps on bare rock so neat footwork is required. Along this stretch you can see how the Teme cuts a path over the bedrock, some-what relentlessly and only impeded by one of the many weirs built since medieval times to harness water power for local mills. The preservation of the weirs and associated industrial heritage has been the focus of the Teme Weirs Trust. In recent years the Ludlow Community Hydro Group has been looking at ways to develop hydro power using the river. It will not be the first time that the river has been used to generate power for the town.

The Breadwalk rejoins a road at **Dinham Bridge**, dating from 1823 and looking as good as ever despite its age. You'll need to walk over it, unless you intend to make your way on the Mortimer Trail path up to **Whitcliffe Common** in which case follow the Mortimer Trail signs, to the left before the bridge, which guide you up the hillside to the grassy area at the top of the climb. This is a much loved piece of countryside in Ludlow, with a set-piece of a view of the town that is splendid whatever the weather. It has inspired artists throughout the ages, including the romantic landscape painter J.M.W. Turner. The common is managed by Shropshire Wildlife Trust and the Friends of Whitcliffe Common so as to maintain that essential balance between informal recreation and conservation. Once across Dinham Bridge, turn left by **Dinham Millennium Green** (see below).

Just before Mr Underhills (a famous restaurant and accommodation) join a path on the right which rises quite steeply and circles round beneath the castle ramparts. A second right-hand turn brings you round to the entrance to Ludlow Castle (see below). From here you can see Castle Square and across the road the neo-classical **Assembly Rooms** dating from the late 1830s and now an arts and community centre. It is hard to believe that there was once a town hall located on the very spot where the market stalls now stand. It was demolished in 1986 and opinion about whether this should have happened or not has raged ever since. However, it is really pleasant to have that open space in the very centre of town. If you'd like to take a look at the old town hall then buy or rent the re-issued *Blott on the Landscape* DVD which features Ludlow throughout. It is said that Tom Sharpe, who adored the area, wrote the book (from which the series was derived) partly to vent his frustration at the proposals to build a bypass around Ludlow. It was published in 1975 and the road came to fruition a couple of years later. The Butter Cross is a hundred paces or so beyond Castle Square.

Other attractions

There are several attractions around town; here's a rundown of five of them.

The Ludlow historian, the late David Lloyd, concluded that **Ludlow Castle** must have been built sometime between 1085 and 1095. The early stage of building was under the patronage of William fitz Osbern but taken forward by Walter de Lacy. The Normans had a clear-cut view of castle building. They invariably built earthworks and a wooden palisade in a first stage of development. If this structure became superfluous to their ongoing subjugation of the Welsh they tended to simply abandon the site after a few decades. Alternatively, if they rated a site as strategic in the long run, they invested heavily with stonework, buildings and walls built out from an inner core. Ludlow Castle fell into the latter category and a substantial inner bailey was secured in a second stage of development. Subsequently an outer bailey and town walls were progressed as successive stewards took control of

The keep – and original gateway – of Ludlow Castle

the fortification. The rich and complicated history of the castle is a detailed one and offers an intriguing insight into the Norman approach to ownership and control. The story of the castle is told in *Ludlow Castle, its History & Buildings* (see Extras), a good read for those into medieval life and power struggles.

One crucial event in the long history of Ludlow Castle was the marriage of Joan de Geneville to Roger Mortimer in 1307. This led to one of the most powerful dynasties in the medieval period being based in Ludlow, a period that lasted for well over a century. The Mortimer family had by this time gained a stronghold at Wigmore Castle, and the addition of Ludlow brought more power and wealth than most of us can imagine. The Mortimers ruled the mid-Marches with an iron rod and were extremely influential, even in relation to the destiny of the monarch. The castle has played host to many famous historic figures, including 'the princes in the Tower', Edward IV's sons Richard and Edward. They spent their childhood here before being murdered in the Tower of London in 1483.

On the payment of an entrance fee you can look around the expansive castle site which still retains substantial curtain walls and several towers, including the early keep (look out for the shadow of the original blocked gateway at ground-floor level) and later residential quarters. One very distinctive building in the inner bailey is the unusual round chapel with its wealth of Romanesque sculptural detailing, albeit somewhat eroded as the building has been roofless since probably the end of the 1700s. As the Marches became more peaceful, successive owners of the castle set to upgrading the rooms and facilities of the inner bailey, everything from the kitchens to the solar block. Edward, son of Richard Plantagenet, Duke of York, who had married the Mortimer heiress, brought the castle into the hands of the Crown when he became King Edward IV in 1461. It was used as a palatial residence within the monarchy and flourished even more

when it became the seat of the Council in the Marches (which essentially governed Wales) until its abolition in 1689. However, from then onwards until the 19th century the castle fell into disrepair. It came under the influence of the Powis estate in the 1770s; full ownership came in 1811. In the latter part of the 19th century more extensive repairs were undertaken and it has continued to be in the possession of the Earls of Powis ever since.

The church of St Laurence is one of only 25 churches in England belonging to the group of 'Greater Churches' because of their grand proportions and Grade 1 listed status. It is a large structure, dating principally from the Perpendicular period in the mid 15th century but including significant older structures. It is hemmed in on two sides by buildings, including the timber-framed Reader's House, a half-timbered building with some parts dating back to the 13th century. The limited space of the church precinct was well illustrated when the historic church bells were taken away for restoration in 2009; it was something of a feat to get them back *in situ* down such narrow passages. However, the presence of the church in the confines of this essentially medieval quarter that renders it all the more interesting.

There is an unusual hexagonal porch; beautifully crafted stained glass windows depicting not just religious scenes but also telling the story of the local Palmers' Guild showing a number of the various lords of Ludlow Castle, some of which are medieval in origin; many magnificent

The tomb of Lady Mary Eure in St Laurence's church

Looking down the choir to the east end of St Laurence's

misericords (found under some of the seats in the choir) and pietas date from the 15th century as does the chancel with its fabulous ceiling. Take a walk to the north

ARTHUR
PRINCE OF WALES
DIED AT LUDLOW CASTLE
2nd APRIL 1502
AGED 15 YEARS 7 MONTHS
His Heart was buried near this place

The plaque marking the spot near which Prince Arthur's heart was buried

side of the church, where on the wall is a commemoration to the poet and scholar A.E. Housman. Also see if you can find where the heart of Prince Arthur, the older brother of King Henry VIII, is buried.

You can cut back to the Butter Cross by turning left into College Street by **Hosyers almshouses** dating from 1758; the building displays the old Ludlow Coat of Arms above the main entrance.

The **Dinham Millennium Green** project is a testimony to the sheer determination of local residents to hold on to Ludlow's heritage, despite continuous demands for development. That is very much the story of the mill and adjacent land during the past ten years or so. Situated on the north side of Dinham Bridge the green has been restored as a lovely riverside recreational spot for everyone to enjoy. Part of the old Dinham Mill complex is home to the Green Café, offering some of the tastiest, locally sourced organic food in town, and next door is a clock repairer. In between these two is a working water wheel that generates electricity for the complex. Interpretation panels tell about the changing uses of the site through the centuries including its contrasting roles as a former iron foundry and swimming baths.

Ludlow Museum's collection was first put together in 1833 and is now to be found next to the visitor information centre. The main exhibitions focus on the archaeology and history of Ludlow but also feature a fascinating collection of fossils endowed to the museum by two local citizens living here in the 19th century who had a passion for geology and natural history. The 19th-century geologist Sir Roderick Murchison made the Ludlow Bone Beds internationally famous by establishing them as a bench-mark for the Silurian geological period; the Museum explains all.

When the **Ludlow Brewing Company** set up in 2006 there was a great cheer from the town's drinking fraternity. After a gap of 70 years, the brewing tradition had returned and the beers are very drinkable. They also sell locally-made Mahorall Cider from a farm situated on the slopes of Clee Hill. The Ludlow Brewery was originally in an old malthouse but has moved a hundred yards or so away to the old railway goods shed, dating from the 1850s, just 2 minutes from Ludlow Railway Station. A brewery tap dressed with memorabilia is open to the public and there are guided tours available.

LUDLOW FESTIVALS

Ludlow's tourism has become increasingly based on festivals and events. The long standing arts festival, known as the Ludlow Festival, occurs in late June/early July and the centre-piece is an open air production of one of Shakespeare's plays in the inner bailey of the castle; it is an experience not to be missed. It is now in its 50th year although there was a precedent as early as 1634, when Milton's *Comus* was performed within the castle walls, and no doubt many a poet, musician and storyteller has stood within the castle precincts before an audience over the centuries.

There's also a Ludlow and Marches Food & Drink Festival held in May and September. The spring festival combines a celebration of beers, ciders and perry from the Marches, and the late summer festival places an emphasis on food from the Marches. In both cases the festival activities spill out into the town with foodie trails galore to whet the appetites of lovers of good local food. There's also the mini and magnalonga food and drink walks (in June and August) which attract hundreds of guests to follow a food and beverage trail on foot.

A relative newcomer is the Green Festival, organised by the environmental group, Ludlow 21, which is held on the weekend of August Bank Holiday. This brings together dozens of exhibitors, mainly from the Marches, offering green services, products and advice as well as demonstrations of traditional crafts, helped along by local food and music.

WALKING

Ludlow makes a useful centre for walking and there are numerous leaflets and books pointing out local circular and linear walks, for example, around the nearby **Mortimer Forest**, where you will also find several waymarked routes and a fossil trail. For more information see *Mortimer Country Bus Walks*.

The **Mortimer Trail** starts right by Ludlow Castle and is ideal for a day walk (or the full two day monty to Kington, some 30 miles). The trail follows a ridge for more or less the entire route, passing by the magnificent **Croft Ambrey Iron Age Fort** and by another **Iron Age camp at Wapley Hill**. It also drops down into the Aymestrey Gap where the river Lugg flows peacefully by the Riverside Inn, noted for its food and real ale and then follows another ridge to Titley where the foodie paradise Stagg Inn is located, so the two days could easily become a walking and gourmet tour.

The **Shropshire Way** also passes through Ludlow, and there are three linear walks from the Way in the Ludlow area (see *Mortimer Country Bus Walks* in Extras).

CYCLING

The Six Castles route passes near to Ludlow and can be picked up just beyond Dinham Bridge. This section of the route leads through to Leominster and is fairly hilly, especially the outbound section through Mortimer Forest and the strenuous climb between Elton and Orleton Common, which requires stamina and tenacity.

The **Ludlow Cycle Rides leaflet** highlights four really good rides, an 8 mile short run out to Stanton Lacy, a ride through orchards to Tenbury Wells, a run through Mortimer Forest to Leintwardine (8, 16 or 23 miles) and a ride out to the medieval lost villages near the Clee Hills (18 miles).

REFRESHMENTS

Ludlow was at one time the UK headquarters of the Slow Food Movement (now in London!) but still has an active local group which encourages food that tastes good, is ecologically sound (in terms of respecting the environment, animal welfare, and human well-being) as well as offering a fair return for producers and workers. That's a tall order but the movement is growing in numbers and influence. Another group with similar aims has emerged in recent years, Taste Real Food, which has its headquarters in Ludlow. Finally, the 'Local to Ludlow' campaign of Ludlow 21 has done sterling work to encourage the sourcing of local foods in shops, restaurants and hotels – see the websites listed below. Local does not always mean good but it usually encourages diversity and quality; local and organic is even better.

Cafés and Restaurants

Ludlow has a good number of restaurants and cafés for such a small town. Many seek out local produce wherever possible and some go out of their way to source organic foodstuff.

The place that comes top of the list is the **Green Café** at the Mill on the Green, Dinham Bridge. The food and beverages taste good and the menu tells you exactly where everything is sourced. People sit outside to watch the river flow by, even in winter, when staff will supply a hot water bottle if you need one!

The cafés in Quality Square are also appealing, in particular the **Courtyard** and **Aragons** which adhere to the Local to Ludlow principles of sourcing food.

Other places include the **Olive Branch** on the corner of Old Street at the Bull Ring, a wholefood restaurant and café which sources local ingredients whenever possible. Just around the corner at the top of Pepper Lane is the **Working Together café** which offers lovely homemade cakes. The café at the Assembly Rooms on Corve Street also prepare home made dishes from local produce. **Koo**, near to the bottom of Old Street, is an award-winning Japanese restaurant.

Pubs

Ludlow has retained a number of traditional pubs, most of which are in fine historic buildings. In the central area there are a few to look out for. **The Church Inn** on Church Street is a deservedly popular haunt much frequented by locals and welcoming to visitors. It has occasional music sessions and outside is the meeting point for Ghost walks on Friday nights. There are many local beers on tap. Just along from the Church Inn is the **Rose and Crown**, which is a friendly pub serving pub food using ingredients bought from the local butcher and baker; the landlord prides himself on serving ale in good condition.

The Queens in Lower Galdeford (pronounced jail-ford) is also a good pub for those seeking out local real ales and has a homely restaurant. The chef sources local produce where possible. South of the river Teme is the **Charlton Arms** at Ludford Bridge which has superb balconies overlooking the river. The Charlton is home to the Riverside Club often featuring blues and jazz events. The bar in the Feathers Hotel also hosts jazz on Sunday lunchtimes.

Local Produce

There are several local butchers and bakers in addition to two fruit and vegetable shops, two delis (Broad Bean, Broad Street and **The Deli** on The Square) all of which sell local and seasonal products in line with the ethics of Local to Ludlow campaign.

As well as this, two shops of note are: **Myriad Organics**, Corve Street: a centre for organic and eco products where there's a remarkable range on offer including many from local suppliers such as The Dairy House, Weobley and Clun Valley Organic Meats. **The Mousetrap**, High Street: is the place for cheese including tasty Little Hereford made to an old recipe at Monkland Dairy.

EXTRAS

Cittàslow Ludlow: places emphasis on quality of life so that Ludlow remains a great place for residents and visitors alike. See www.cittaslow/ludlow.org.uk.

Produce Market, Castle Square: 2nd and 4th Thursday of the month.

Guided walking tours: these depart from the cannon outside Ludlow Castle on Saturdays and Sundays from April to October at 2.30pm. A small charge is made.

Ludlow Ecolog Cabins: delightful eco cabin ideal for those seeking a low carbon footprint break. Located near Caynham which is good for cyclists but there's no bus to the village.

Ludlow 21: promotes sustainable living in Ludlow and organises monthly Green Drinks meeting in a local pub – visitors are more than welcome. See www.ludlow21. org.uk.

Lloyd, David & Karen Johnson (2009), *Festival Ludlow*, Logaston Press.

Lloyd, David, Margaret Clark & Chris Potter (2010) *St Laurence's Church, Ludlow; The parish church and people, 1199-2009*, Logaston Press.

Moore, J.C. (1933) *The Welsh Marches*, Chapman and Hall.

Mortimer Country Bus Walks, a leaflet outlining three local walks which can be downloaded from www.simonholtmarketing.com.

Shoesmith, Ron & Andy Johnson (eds) (2000) *Ludlow Castle, its history and building*s, Logaston Press

Pearce Cycle hire: cycle hire, sales and repairs. Located one mile from Ludlow town centre on the Fishmore Road.

Wheely Wonderful Cycling: cycle hire and holidays from Ludlow (bikes can be delivered to holiday accommodation) www. wheelywonderfulcycling.co.uk.

Taste Real Food: campaign to encourage the production and consumption of real food and drink and in the process to improve biodiversity and local cultures. The HQ is in Ludlow. See www. tasterealfood.com.

Visitor Information Centre: Castle Street. Tel: 01584 875053.

PUBLIC TRANSPORT

Trains

Ludlow is served daily and directly by trains from Cardiff, Manchester, Shrewsbury and north Wales. It is a 27-29 minute journey from Shrewsbury.

Buses

Ludlow is served by bus from:

Shrewsbury. 435. Monday–Saturday, approximately every 2 hours, Operator Minsterley Motors. Hourly. Travel time 1 hour 20 minutes.

Hereford, 492, daily, duration approximately 1 hour 15 minutes, Operators, Lugg Valley, First Midland Red. Approximately every 2 hours. Travel time 1 hour 10 minutes.

Kidderminster, 292, Approximately every 2 hours. Operators: First Midland Red and Central Connect. Travel time 1 hour 5 minutes.

There is also a bus to Knighton (738-740) and a park and ride service (buses 702-704) from the Eco-Park just off the A49 (Monday – Saturday and when there's a major event on).

EXCURSIONS FROM LUDLOW

CLEE HILL AND CLEOBURY MORTIMER

Ride from Ludlow

The 30 minute bus ride to Cleobury Mortimer runs through the outskirts of Ludlow to Rocks Green, passing the Nelson Inn, a traditional pub and long-standing Good Beer Guide entry, where impromptu music events are common. It then sweeps past Henley Hall and the climbing begins in earnest. The bus begins to crawl up Angel Bank (alight here for a great 7 mile walk back to Ludlow via Caynham – see below). The road continues to rise through **Clee Hill village**, a mining and quarrying settlement, where the residents understand the meaning of the words 'extreme weather'; it can get very cold in winter.

The bus leaves the village over a cattle grid and across moorland to Doddington. Make sure you sit on the right-hand side as the views across the Teme valley to the Malvern Hills are stunning. There's a scary descent to **Hopton Wafers** where you see the outline of the 19th-century church and, in the background, the classical style Hopton Court dating from the 18th century and then it is onward between arable fields to Cleobury Mortimer.

CLEOBURY MORTIMER

John Betjeman is alleged to have said that 'few small towns can boast a High Street like Cleobury Mortimer', whereas Pevsner was a little less enthusiastic. He suggested that the town was little more than 'one long continuous street'. The pleasure of strolling along this street has improved immeasurably in recent years. There's been a sensitive re-modelling of the pavements to very good effect, so when you step off the bus (the stops are in the centre of town opposite London House) the immediate impression is of a pride about the place. The pollarded lime trees bring a special character to the town and the parked cars alongside the fairly busy main road act as cost-free traffic calming.

Walking around town

Cleobury's High Street contains several small reminders of times past, such as a small marble fountain by the bus stop, dedicated to W.H. Trow, a son of Cleobury Mortimer who died in South Africa in 1900. Go right to pass by the Talbot Hotel, a Victorian pastiche of a Tudor building that actually looks the part. In front of the hotel is the base of a preaching or trading cross dating from medieval times.

Main attraction

Cleobury's pride and joy is the sandstone parish **church of St Mary**. This is a restored medieval church with the nave, chancel and south aisle all dating from the 13th century. There is also a 13th-century chapel sponsored by Roger Mortimer (he who deposed Edward II and lived with his queen). The church has an unmistakably twisted spire, contorted over the years since its erection in the 14th century and best admired from Church Street. It also has several fascinating stained glass windows including one depicting the Vision of Piers Plowman (dating from 1875) which reflects the poem of William Langland, a 14th-century writer who is said to have hailed from Cleobury Mortimer (and Ledbury too!). Next door stands the old **Assembly Rooms** and market, now refurbished and managed by the social enterprise company, Cleobury Country; it includes a visitor information centre.

To the east of the church, a little further along the main street on the right, are the Wells, restored town wells with a clear running stream alongside. That is what is so engaging about Cleobury Mortimer. There are several reminders of bygone days which crop up between fine terraces, Georgian and Victorian town houses and tempting roadside inns such as the Fountain Inn and King's Arms, a 17th-century half-

St Mary's church, Cleobury Mortimer, with its twisted spire

timbered property best appreciated from the rear of the building. The **King's Arms** is the **Hobson's brewery tap**; the brewery is located at New House Farm on the edge of town. Hobson's is one of the most environmentally conscious breweries in the Marches. It has a refreshing policy (in more ways than one) of sourcing local Maris Otter barley for malting and Teme Valley hops for the dry hopping in the brewing process. In sum, the brewery pursues, almost relentlessly, ways to reduce energy and waste even down to its local supply network; that is a real bonus, and the beer is good too. However, the brewery is not open to the public except for group bookings, but you'll be able to sample its excellent brews around the town.

THE CLEE HILLS

The Clee Hills are a feature on the skyline in all seasons. The southern of the two summits that can be seen for miles around is known as Titterstone Clee Hill, that to the north, Brown Clee Hill. Both are brooding masses of considerable character which dominate the landscape of south Shropshire. Titterstone Clee is the more prominent with its western scarp forming the impression of a lion's head, and is festooned with radar aerials tracking flight paths across the Midlands. It is best accessed from the settlement of Clee Hill village (see the walking section below). Brown Clee lies several miles to the north and actually has two summits, Abdon Burf and Clee Burf.

The area to the east of Ludlow is less frequented than the other parts of south Shropshire. The pastures and woodlands that characterise these foothills rise up to the Clee summits. They offer great scope for walking around the villages of Hope Bagot, Coreley, Hopton Wafers and Neen Sollars. The fittest among us might possibly think about cycling down these back lanes to enjoy glimpses of these hamlets, but you'll need to tackle the hilly terrain. These parishes are now part of a destination area based on Cleobury Mortimer and referred to as Cleobury Country.

Clee Hill

At first glance, there's no reason to alight at this windswept place as industrial quarrying still plays a major part in the life of the area. However, there are three reasons why you should. Firstly, Clee Hill is a key point for walks to Titterstone Clee, which is the only British hill shown on the medieval map, Mappa Mundi (now housed at Hereford Cathedral). Secondly, Clee Hill has one of the finest bakeries in the Marches. Richard G. Swift produces speciality breads that southern Europeans, let alone us, would die for. Finally, it has the Kremlin pub, with its unique name that is part of local history, wonderful panoramic views, plus great beer.

There are many prehistoric earthworks on the hills, but the main features clearly discernible are the scars of mining and quarrying on the landscape. There are also many dwellings associated with past mining times at the edge of common to the north and east of the village; these would have been squatters' cottages in past times. One of the best ways to discover this rich industrial heritage is to walk along the line of the old mineral railway from a point below the Kremlin pub to Titterstone Clee Road. Turn right here and follow the road to the site of the old quarry at Titterstone Clee Incline.

There's also a longer, more strenuous walk from Wheathill to Clee Hill which climbs Titterstone Clee on the Shropshire Way (see below). The Titterstone Clee Heritage Trust arranges guided walks and events for those interested in getting to know more about the area (also see below).

WALKING

Cleobury Mortimer is a 'Walkers are Welcome' town and is a good base to discover the footpaths and countryside of this part of south Shropshire. There are several interesting day walks from the town. In fact, there are over 30 illustrated on the Cleobury Mortimer Footpaths Association website (see below). It is also possible to walk between Clee Hill village and Cleobury Mortimer on the **Shropshire Way**. This skirts the edge of **Catherton Common**, where linnets and meadow pipits, skylarks and yellowhammers can be readily seen. The common is one of the largest nature reserves in the Marches, now owned and managed by Shropshire Wildlife Trust. It is wild and relatively untouched.

There's also an extension of the Shropshire Way from Cleobury Mortimer to the **Severn Valley Railway** near Arley. This makes for a good day out, firstly by walking the route, then by catching a steam

Titterstone Clee

train on the Severn Valley Railway from Arley (or Highley) to Bewdley and finally catching a direct bus back from Bewdley to Cleobury or Ludlow. Another good walk is Simon Evans Way, an 18 mile walk to commemorate a writer who adopted Cleobury Mortimer as his home in the 1930s. He has been dubbed the postman poet as much of his writing reflected rural life in and around the area. Unfortunately, damage to his lungs from being gassed in the First World War destined him to an early grave in 1940.

CYCLING

Four cycle routes have been designed to encourage visitors to enjoy the country lanes through the villages and hamlets surrounding Cleobury Mortimer. They are the **Rea Valley route** (16 miles), the **Milson and Mamble ride** (13 miles), a trip to the edge of Wyre Forest (19 miles) and finally the **Clee Challenge**, which is 24 miles in length. They include some hills and require some stamina, but the rider is rewarded with some great views and timeless rural villages. The real joy is that the areas through which they pass have changed little over the years so nostalgia comes to the fore.

REFRESHMENT

Clee Hill Village

Cafés

Craven Place café and tea rooms is on the eastern edge of the village (in the direction of Cleobury Mortimer) and reckons on having one of the best viewpoints in Shropshire.

Swift's Bakery, open Mondays to Saturdays for sales of bread and cakes, has a small café adjacent.

Pubs

The Kremlin and **Golden Cross** welcome walkers and cyclists.

Cleobury Mortimer

Cafés

Cleobury café uses products baked at Ashley's bakery in Mortimer Gardens.

Crusty Cob, Church Street: uses Swift's bread and cakes in its tea room.

Pubs

There are several public houses on the main street all of which have character.

The Fountain Inn sources local food wherever possible.

The King's Arms (open from 10am for breakfast) makes a point of buying local; its bread comes from Ashley's bakery, meats from one of the local butchers and free range eggs from a farm just off the Bayton road. Needless to say, the beer is fresh from Hobsons brewery, less than half a beer mile down the Tenbury Road.

Local Produce

Bowketts and Hems, Church Street: make their own sausages and pies.

EXTRAS

Cleobury Mortimer Country: provides visitor information, www.cleoburycountry.com.

Cleobury Mortimer Footpaths Association: a group which has done so much to open up paths for residents and visitors. See www.cmfa.co.uk for routes.

Mahorall Farm Cider is located at Nash near Cleobury Mortimer.

Titterstone Clee Heritage Trust: offer occasional guided walks with local historian Alf Jenkins and organise events to publicise the conservation of the heritage, flora and fauna of the area. See www.thecleehilltrust.co.uk.

PUBLIC TRANSPORT

Buses

Cleobury Mortimer is served by bus from Ludlow (Corve Street). Bus 292. Daily. Approximately 2 hourly. Travel time 30 minutes. Operator: First Midland Red on Monday – Saturday; Central Connect on Sunday.

LEINTWARDINE AND MORTIMER COUNTRY

Ride to Leintwardine

The bus ride to Leintwardine takes about 25 minutes. It runs through Bromfield, where there's a stop for the Ludlow Food Centre (a subway aids the crossing of the busy A49). The bus then climbs through gentle countryside with views over to Mortimer Forest. The finale is a winding section of road at Fiddler's Elbow and Mocktree. There's then a descent through woodland, where there are recently restored limekilns to your right and glimpses over the Teme valley to the Radnorshire hills ahead. You then enter the large village of Leintwardine, a northern tip of Mortimer Country. The best place to alight is at Rosemary Lane opposite the Lion Hotel.

LEINTWARDINE

The unusual name Leintwardine is a mixture of Celtic, the word 'lent' meaning torrent, and Old English, 'wardine' meaning enclosure. This perhaps seems a little odd given that the place owes its existence mainly to the Romans. They decided to build a sizeable settlement, called *Bravonium*, on the Roman road between Chester and Caerleon known to this day as Watling Street West. The line of the old road more or less runs along High Street, a town street almost parallel to the main road. The Roman road continued south through the low-lying land of Wigmore Lake to Wigmore and onward to Aymestrey and Kenchester in Herefordshire. The Roman occupation began to take hold locally in about AD70 and excavations of the site show continuous development throughout several periods. The settlement was maintained by the Romans until AD196 when the garrison fell into disuse after a more or less complete withdrawal of the Roman army.

The settlement's main function was to supply the cohorts of soldiers billeted at other nearby forts, thus providing support for the onslaught against the tribes of the

Walking in Mortimer Forest,
accessed by way of the Mortimer Trail from Ludlow

borderland. There is another dimension to Roman Leintwardine. According to some historians, it was built as much for pleasure as warfare for there was a bath-house, temple and mansion located within the perimeter of the fort. The enclosure was rectangular and this has more or less been the shape of the village through to the 21st century. Subsequent development has simply followed the Roman street pattern. There are no remaining earth-works that can be easily explored; they are beneath the new build of different centuries. However, over the years pottery, coins and other artefacts have been found.

The Saxons settled in Leintwardine at some stage after the Roman departure and an early church was established during this period. However, the large parish **church of St Mary Magdalene**, located in the very centre of the village, dates principally from the 12th and 13th centuries, though only the Norman doorway in the west wall of the nave highlights the Norman presence. It is said that King Edward III was associated with the church; he came to worship at a statue of the Virgin Mary, evidently more than once. Lesser figures than sovereigns, but still of great import, were the Mortimers of Wigmore. They were major benefactors of the church, especially during the 14th century when the Mortimer Chapel (now Lady Chapel) was added. The endowment included a payment for nine chaplains to pray on a daily basis for Roger Mortimer's soul, no doubt much needed as this was the Roger Mortimer (amongst many of that name) who had a very public affair with Queen Isabella after imprisoning and quite possibly ordering the murder of her husband, Edward II.

There are also several misericords in the chancel stalls (believed to have come from Wigmore Abbey) dating from the 15th century, and also a 19th-century memorial (in the vestry) commemorating the life of Banastre Tarleton who spent the latter years of his life in the village until his death in 1833. Tarleton made his career in the British army and gained a particular notoriety during the American War of Independence, where he earned the reputation among North Americans as being 'The Butcher' on account of his brutal approach to warfare. Press coverage in the UK was kinder; he came back a hero. After becoming an MP for Liverpool, in which role he supported the continuation of the Slave Trade against the campaign waged by William Wilberforce, he retired to live in the village. Like many churches it was given a major makeover in the 19th century and it is now an important venue for many classical and medieval music performances throughout the year as well as a place of worship.

The river Teme marks the southern end of the village; there was a fording point confluence with the river Clun. In medieval times a bridge replaced this earlier upstream crossing; the bridge that exists now is a strengthened version of an earlier structure. Nearby they used to launch coracles in the waters of the Teme and these were used for fishing. The river flows into a flat-bottomed valley known as Wigmore Lake, where the abbey once stood on the edge of the lush alluvial valley floor. This was gouged out by melting ice waters which eventually forced a route east through Downton Gorge.

Main attraction

The main attraction in Leintwardine is **The Sun Inn**, a parlour pub dating from the 1860s owned by local entrepreneur, Gary Seymour, in partnership with Nick Davis, Head Brewer at Hobson's Brewery. They took it on following the death of the long-standing landlady, Flossie Lane, in 2009. Her death prompted obituaries in several of the national quality daily newspapers, most of which delivered a fascinating insight into the life of an ale wife. Her service to the community has been commemorated by a newly carved misericord located in the parish church. It depicts her by a cask, two regulars supping ale and the emblem of the local fly fishing club. The greatest tribute to Flossie Lane, however, was that a loyal group of regulars continued to run the Sun Inn as she became less able to do so. At the age of 94, she was, in fact, the oldest landlady in the country. But the regulars have since committed themselves more deeply to this fine hostelry. They wanted to keep the parlour pub going for future generations. We are fortunate that they have stuck to their guns for this is no ordinary pub to be left to the vagaries of a fickle market; it is an institution. If you have not seen a genuine parlour pub this is the place to spend a while.

The Sun has been home to several groups over the years, such as the local fly fishing club, and continues to spawn new ones such as the 'On Yer Bike Sun' cycling club. It also attracts people from all walks of life who call in for a good chat over a glass or two. Each year there's a late summer beer festival and this marks the inauguration of a new 'informal' mayor. There have been seventeen to date, sixteen humans and one dog, appropriately named Hobson, after the fine ales sold here. Evidently, he did very well.

The beer is dispensed by gravity, directly from the cask, into a jug or glass; this has been a tradition at the Sun for the best part of 150 years. There are currently two rooms, a sitting room (the parlour) and the Red Brick bar, where locals and visitors readily mingle. Under the stewardship of its new owners, the existing front of house layout remains intact (it is listed) but is augmented by a new garden room and bar, at the rear of the premises. The repair work and new build incorporated a range of energy saving measures to make the pub carbon neutral.

The Sun Inn may well be right there in CAMRA's top ten list of heritage pubs but this is not a place for tourism trophy hunters. It is a homely pub much loved by its community, so relax and enjoy your time at this unspoilt rural hostelry. There are not many about.

Wigmore

Wigmore is not an easy place to get to by bus. In fact, it is well nigh impossible. The few that pass through on market days do not offer a suitable return trip into Ludlow or Leominster, for that matter. However, it is possible to cycle to Wigmore from Ludlow or alternatively from Hopton Heath railway station via Leintwardine. It is good cycling territory as the country lanes are quiet and there are few main roads to cross. The village of Wigmore has its own community stores which sources local products and it also has two hostelries. It is a welcoming place in the heart of this northern part of Herefordshire. This area is now known in tourism speak as Mortimer Country – bounded, more or less, by the towns of Leominster, Ludlow and Presteigne.

Wigmore Castle is situated on high ground above the village amid bramble and bush. It is a wild place and it is hard to grasp the scale of this medieval fortress which served the Mortimer family well for centuries. It was one of many castles commissioned by William fitz Osbern, Earl of Hereford, but when his son rebelled against William the Conqueror it was passed to Ralph Mortimer. From then onwards, the castle remained in the Mortimer family until the mid 15th century, even though one of their number was besieged in the castle by Henry II and

Wigmore Castle

another was responsible for the death of Edward II; it was their true home even during periods of aggrandisement at Ludlow and elsewhere.

However formidable these castles may appear, the Norman occupation of the Marches was always a tenuous one. It took over two centuries to bring about a more peaceful regime and then only through a combination of social coercion, military force and legal measures to crush the population into an existence of penury. In fairness, castles were good for the local economy; they required skilled stonemasons, supplies for banquets and all manner of trades that worked through a tightly-knit patronage system. Wigmore was no exception; the castle enjoyed a considerable upgrade in the 14th century which generated much work. No longer was the castle a solitary fortress; it became a place to live in comfort and style, relatively speaking. This investment lasted for at least 100 years, until the castle became Crown property on the accession of Edward IV, the Mortimer heir, in 1461. It was subsequently used as a prison and then decayed into a ruinous state after being partly dismantled by the Harley family of Brampton Bryan in 1643.

There's a lovely short walk to the castle from the centre of the village, passing by Wigmore parish church, which also sits on high ground with the Wigmore Rolls (the nearby hills) seen to good advantage. The influence of Wigmore Abbey remains to this day as this is the **church of St James**, one of nine still within Wigmore Abbey parish. There are many fine medieval features inside the church including an early Norman nave and a rare piscina mounted on the south wall. Outside, you can see herringbone stonework in the style of the Saxons which denotes that there was perhaps an early church on the site.

WALKING

Leintwardine is an ideal location for walking in the Clun and Teme valleys. There's a pleasant and easy walk (4-5 miles) near the Teme to Brampton Bryan on the **Herefordshire Trail**. **Brampton Bryan** is an attractive cluster of houses nestled around a crossroads a few miles up the road from Leintwardine. The remains of a castle lie within the grounds of Brampton Bryan Hall (not open to the public). They are associated with a fascinating history of the Puritan Harley family. Lady Brilliana Harley, a Parliamentarian through and through, defended the castle in 1643 from a Royalist siege, alongside her loyal tenants and children. Failure to take it was a major blow to the Royalists at the time. Unfortunately she succumbed to something akin to the flu and died soon after, and the castle was eventually sacked by the Royalists. The church is located next to the grounds of the hall and is said to be one of the few Commonwealth churches built during the period of Cromwell's Parliament. **Aardvark Books** is to be found at the edge of the village on the Lingen Road; it has a wide range of books shelved in an old converted barn with a nice café too. You'll be strong-willed to resist a whiff of the coffee and the irresistible homemade cakes. The downside is that there's only one bus back to Leintwardine or Ludlow directly from the village of a late afternoon, so timing is of the essence although it is easy enough to walk back to Leintwardine.

There's a much longer walk to Ludlow (12-13 miles) from Leintwardine via Downton and Bromfield which makes for an ideal day ramble, i.e., catch the bus out and walk back. You might find *A Teme Valley Walk* useful for this one (see Extras). There are also several local circular walks from Leintwardine to **Downton Castle estate** (again on the Herefordshire Trail), a hamlet associated with Downton Castle, built for Richard Payne Knight in the late 18th century. The trail leads to Castle Bridge and onward to Burrington where you cut right to return to Leintwardine. The gorge and the walks that were so loved by the Picturesque movement are not open to the public. However, get hold of a superb booklet, *Notes on Bringewood Forge and The Downton Walks*, to unravel the fascinating history of the estate surrounding the gorge. There are other short walks from Leintwardine village to Church Hill and Haregrove Wood that offer deliciously tempting views across to Wales.

CYCLING

A great way to explore the Leintwardine/ North Mortimer Country area is by cycle, following the route outlined in the **Ludlow Cycle Rides leaflet**; look up Route 3. This is a 23 mile circuit with climbs out of Ludlow and on the return ride climbs up to Mary Knoll. The recompense for the effort is beautiful scenery and a chance to discover some unusual spots such as the secluded church of Burrington and the beautiful river Teme at Burrington Bridge. Nearby is the site of **Wigmore Abbey** at the Grange Farm (private property); it is not easy to see any of the remains from the road. The Augustinian abbey was founded by Hugh Mortimer in the 12th century. It is, however, easy to make an extension to Route 3 in order to visit the village of Wigmore by turning right at Leinthall Earls on the return leg from Leintwardine and then retracing your route afterwards (extra 2 miles).

Another cycling option is to take the train to Hopton Heath railway station on the Heart of Wales railway line then ride to Leintwardine via the B4367 in the direction of Bedstone, passing by the 17th-century Heath House. Take the next turning left, Jay Lane, and follow this through the water meadows of the river Clun to Leintwardine. It is then possible to extend the ride to Wigmore. This is good cycling country and it is possible to create a number of cycle days from a base in the area or to buy into a lightly packed tour provided by Wheely Wonderful Cycling.

REFRESHMENT

Cafés

Aardvark Books, Manor Farm: café serving homemade cafes and coffee, see www.aardvark-books.com.

Ludlow Food Centre: Conservatory Barn café, see www.ludlowfoodcentre. co.uk.

Walford Court Tea Room: homemade food par excellence, see www.romantic-break.com.

Pubs

Sun Inn, Rosemary Lane, Leintwardine, see suninn-leintwardine.co.uk.

Local Produce

Mortimer Country Stores, Wigmore: community shop selling local produce.

EXTRAS

CAMRA (Campaign for Real Ale) *Good Beer Guide 2011*, St Albans, CAMRA. Herefordshire CAMRA has been an ardent supporter of rural pubs and has resisted attempts to close village pubs which are so important not only for the villagers but for tourism. It produces an encyclopaedic guide to pubs in Herefordshire which is available at local bookshops as well as a free quarterly magazine, *Hopvine*, available in pubs.

Milton, David (2002) *A Teme Valley Walk*, Oldbury, Meridian.

Mocktree Holidays, near Leintwardine: superb self catering cottages. Recently received a Gold award for being a Green Tourism Business and the friendly owners really do know the best walking and cycling outings in the area.

Rolfe-Smith, B. (2009) *Notes on Bringewood Forge and The Downton Walks*. Leintwardine History Society. Available from local bookshops in Ludlow.

Wheely Wonderful Cycling: see www. wheelywonderfulcycling.co.uk

PUBLIC TRANSPORT

Buses

Leintwardine is served by bus from Ludlow and Knighton. 738/740. Monday – Saturday only. Travel time from Ludlow 23 minutes. Four buses per day. Operator: Arriva.

LEOMINSTER

Ride from Ludlow

There's a regular daily train service between Ludlow and Leominster (pronounced Lemster). It usually takes 8 minutes so there's barely time to get settled down. On departure from Ludlow station there's a moment of darkness then a view on the right across to Mortimer Forest, and near to, lovely south-facing trackside gardens. The train makes its ways through rich farmland to the parish of Orleton. You will probably spot the tall radio transmittters; they were erected in the Second World War to boost overseas transmissions; this is BBC Wooferton. After going under the next bridge, look out for a tree-lined remnant of the Kington, Leominster and Stourport canal (on the right). Construction work began in the 1790s but only half of the 31 miles were completed as financial difficulties brought operations to an abrupt end. It was officially closed and drained in 1859 when the railway acquired it. Despite this early demise, there are several places where the canal structure can still be seen some 150 years later.

The bus ride between Ludlow and Leominster (Bus 492) takes the traveller into the ancient settlements of Richard's Castle and Orleton. These villages mark the eastern border of Mortimer Country and offer access to the fringes of Mortimer Forest, which is ideal for woodland walking and gives opportunities for off-road cycling too. The bus dips into the edge of the hamlet of Bircher, where it is possible to walk to **Croft Castle** (about 1.5 miles – see below) by way of the village of Yarpole, or alternatively across the medieval Bircher Common, still grazed by the commoners' livestock. The **church of St Leonard** at **Yarpole**, with a rare 12th-century detached tower, is a charming building. This simple 14th-century church has a much restored interior, and is now partly given over to a community shop run by the residents.

LEOMINSTER

Leominster is a compact market town which owed much of its prosperity in former times to a monastery founded in the 7th century, and subsequently a dependent of Reading Abbey. It specialised in the rearing of sheep on the surrounding monastery granges. The sheep were the Ryeland breed, known for the quality of their wool, which brought much wealth in the late medieval period, resulting in investment in building. The wool was so profitable it was referred to as Lemster ore.

The centre of Leominster has around 200 listed buildings, though many medieval timber frames are often hidden behind Georgian façades. If you look above first-floor level, you can sometimes see carved bargeboards or other artistic details. With its mix of narrow streets and alleys, and parkland around the Grange and Priory, there's a laid-back atmosphere about the place. It makes for a pleasant day or part day excursion.

Walking around town

Leominster railway station is on the edge of town. From the station entrance, go right

The detached bell tower near the church and castle at Richard's Castle

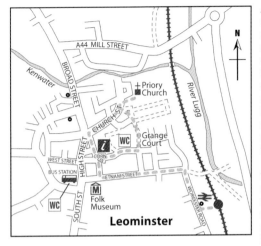

Leominster

Almost opposite the museum, cut right along one of Leominster's medieval thoroughfares. This is School Lane and has a cobbler, a cheese shop and a half-timbered inn nestled on the corner as you enter Corn Square, where barley corn was once traded. The square has lost some of its vibrancy in recent years; it is now a car park except on Fridays when it comes to life with the town market.

You'll find the visitor information centre in an old shop, on the corner of **Draper's Lane**. This medieval street retains considerable character, with a couple of narrow passages leading off it including one called Cordwainers Lane, referring back to the shoe trade. It is easy to imagine how these streets thronged with local traders in past centuries, as the scale is very human with some overhanging jetties in places. More recently it was in Draper's Lane that the retailers dreamed up a loyalty card scheme to encourage shopping locally rather than at out-of-town supermarkets.

and follow the main road around to the left. This is Etnam Street, tree-lined and with a fine collection of Georgian and Victorian buildings which lead up to the Leominster **Folk Museum**. This houses an eclectic mix of artefacts collected from Leominster's past, from Bronze Age burial remains to a traditional cider mill. Cider mills were at one time very common in Herefordshire.

The Three Horseshoes in Corn Square, Leominster

Examples of the carving on Grange Court

Fortunately there's still a good spread of shops.

From the top of Drapers Lane head back across Corn Square and proceed between Lloyds bank and the Merchant's House tea room to **The Grange**, a splendid piece of open ground adorned with a sculpture of a giant green person pushing a roller. The Pavilion, a community-run café in an old Victorian pavilion, sits beneath tall Wellingtonia trees. It is a quiet spot where you can watch the world go by. Across from the green stands **Grange Court**, built in 1633 by John Abel, a Herefordshire craftsman revered for his carpentry, including by the king. It is a beautiful half-timbered building with unusually well preserved wooden carvings, heads and torsos and a Latin inscription, one of the tell-tale hallmarks of Abel's work. The inscription can be roughly translated as: 'Live thou receptive to God, dead to the world, free from crime, prepared to pass away. Live that you may live; quick enough, well enough. The just will enjoy eternal remembrance.'

In previous centuries The Grange was actually located in the town centre; it was the main market hall and at one time even doubled up as the town hall. Over two centuries later, in 1856, it was saved by a local man and moved to its more leafy posi-

tion near to the priory church. The Grange is currently subject to a major refurbishment so that it can become a centre for local community groups and charities. The Victorian and Civic Societies have been campaigning hard to save the rich Victorian interior in the proposed refurbishment; let's hope that good repair work pays off.

Main attraction

Walk through the grounds to the **priory church**. Built in the early decades of the 12th century, it stands on the site of a much earlier ecclesiastical building dating from the 7th century and associated with the monk, St Edfrith, who brought Christianity to the area. It suffered considerable damage from Welsh and Danish raids over subsequent centuries and by the time of the Norman Conquest it stood in ruins. Not that all was lost. A second priory was established on the same site as part of the Benedictine order of Reading Abbey, which enjoyed royal patronage. It became a very wealthy ecclesiastical outpost for centuries.

The priory, however, was disbanded during the Dissolution and the eastern part of the priory church and most of the monastic buildings were destroyed; the youth hostel is based in some of those which survived (located behind the church

The Norman west door to Leominster priory church, with examples of Herefordshire School of Romanesque Sculpture on the capitals

from the direction you've approached it). The priory church, however, survived. It has an unusual shape in that, on first glance, there appear to be three naves. But, before you enter to unravel the mystery, take a look at the workmanship of the Herefordshire School of Romanesque Sculpture in the west doorway. There are intricate carvings of birds, lions, serpents, palm shoots, foliage and doves above the columns surrounding the door. These craftsmen were not, however, responsible for the later decoration of the south side of the church where there are an amazing number of ballflowers (three petals enclosing a ball) decorating the stained glass windows.

Step inside to take a look at the Norman nave (the northernmost of the three), with a number of rounded arches and some unusual tablets and monuments on the north wall. These include a Wheel of Life, in the form of the remains of a 13th-century mural which depicts happiness, loss, suffering and hope. There's also a most unusual artefact to find in a church, a ducking stool, last used to torture a

poor woman in Leominster in 1806. The poster next to it describes it as a cucking stool, tumbrel or cumstole, and explains its purpose as being: 'the ancient and universal punishment for common scolds, and for butchers, bakers, brewers, apothecaries and all who give short measure or vended adulterated articles of food'.

The central nave, built in the 13th century for the residents of the town, the original nave being preserved for the abbey's monks, is Perpendicular in style, and there's a 45-foot tall west window, added in the 15th century, with stained glass depicting St Peter and St Paul. The third nave is actually the south aisle, built in the 14th century, and with windows in the Decorated style. It also houses the Lady Chapel, dating from the same period and with three stone seats separated with columns embellished with ballflower decorations.

The priory church was damaged by a fire in 1699 and it took the citizens of Leominster over five years to repair it. Amazingly the church bells were saved, and in the mid 18th century transported by boat down the Lugg and Wye rivers from Leominster to Chepstow to be re-cast. The church was modified again in the 19th century.

The way back into town is along Church Street, where there's a cluster of handsome Georgian dwellings and on the right is the Forbury chapel dating from the 13th century. On reaching Broad Street you can turn left into Draper's Lane to return to Corn Square. Alternatively, you might like to browse in the antique shops for which the town is well known. These are located principally in **Broad Street** (on your right), which has a fine collection of buildings, including the Lion Gallery and courtyard; look up to see the lion sitting majestically at the top. Behind is the Georgian-style **Lion Ballroom**, a restored building dating from the 1840s, and now used for arts events. At the bottom of Broad Street, there's an unusual retailer, the Barometer Shop, just across the road in New Street.

You may choose to retrace your steps into High Street, a narrow street laid out originally for the horse and cart. Here there's a surprisingly rich grouping of traditional shop fronts characterised by old fashioned lettering and recessed doors, especially No. 41. Keep right at the Talbot Hotel to walk along West Street where you'll find the **Blue Note Café and Bar**, one of the most unusual café-cum-bars to be found in the Marches. It is the venue for live jazz in Leominster and hosts musical events at the weekend.

RIDE TO KINGSLAND, EARDISLAND AND PEMBRIDGE

Leominster is the gateway to some of the half-timbered villages on the Black and White Village Trail. Buses 493-7 provide a service to one or more of these north Herefordshire villages. The bus calls firstly at **Kingsland** (10-minute ride; ask for The Angel inn), a long linear village with a mix of Georgian and half-timbered dwellings set back from the road behind extensive gardens. There's a short walk to the impressive 13th-century **church of St Michael and The Angels** which sits at a crossroads of village paths. From here you can just make out the earthworks of a motte and bailey castle in the adjacent field to the west of the church.

As with many churches in this part of the Marches, the Mortimers were key benefactors for almost two centuries; the churches are architecturally richer for their patronage. One interesting feature is the ornate north porch where you'll find the little Volka chapel where prayers are still said at Candlemas for the 4,000 soldiers who fell at the bloody **Battle of Mortimer's Cross**, just to the north-west of Kingsland, on a cold day in 1461.

There's also a dusty roadside monument at the top end of the village to commemorate the battle, which was a decisive engagement between the Yorkists and Lancastrians that ended in defeat for the latter. It eventually led to a Mortimer descendant acceding to the throne, young King Edward IV. It is chronicled that an omen appeared in the sky before the battle that Candlemas day in 1461, a phenomenon known as a sun dog or parhelion. These can occur in cold weather when the sun reflects on ice-crystals falling through the air, giving an effect of a halo of light, and sometimes an added impression that there is more than one sun in the sky. It must have been an eerie sight on that cold, dark day. There are two public houses in Kingsland (the Angel and Corners Inns) and two tea rooms offering refreshment, so this is a good place to stop especially if you are cycling or walking the Black and White Village Trail.

After Kingsland the bus calls at a very English village, **Eardisland** (about 10 minutes down the road), where half-timbered houses and red brick cottages nestle about a lush riverside green. The

Examples of the buildings clustered around the centre of Eardisland, where the river Arrow meanders by

One of the two inns in Eardisland, the Cross, with one of the village's idiosyncrasies – an old AA telephone box

slow flowing waters of the river Arrow make it a ducks' paradise and there's a popular spot on the other side of the bridge to spend a lazy half hour or so. The village is a veritable storehouse of historical interest. Several of the buildings are particularly striking, such as the Staick House (private), a yeoman's dwelling which became a mote court for the purpose of settling minor legal matters. You can see it on the right on the way into the village just before the bridge. There's also the Manor House (private) with its 17th-century **dovecote**, sitting neatly by the Arrow Bridge.

This dovecote, which happens to be the only one in the country that houses a community village store, is a good place to start your exploration. There are interpretation leaflets available and up the stairs on the first floor is a small exhibition mainly focusing on the golden age of motoring and also on Eardisland in the Second World War. The main story, however, is how this brick tower dovecote, with its four gabled roof and pigeon loft, survived a hundred years of slow deterioration before being brought back to life as a community shop in 1999. It is now going from strength to strength.

Across the road is the old school complete with a whipping post (no comment!). The **church of St Mary the Virgin** is away from the main road. There's a footpath signposted between buildings from the car park to the churchyard nearby. The church provides a good example of 13th-century architecture in this area but has been much altered through the centuries. Of particular interest is the 14th-century sedilia and piscina in the sanctuary. Adjacent to the churchyard is a wood-covered motte thought to date from Saxon times.

Pembridge, rather like Eardisland, enjoyed substantial prosperity in medieval times amid a sea of rural poverty. This is reflected in the rich architectural endowment from this period, with many fine examples of half-timbered dwellings along the main street. It certainly has the feeling of a small town; in medieval times it supported flourishing trades and markets to match the likes of Kington and Leominster. But Pembridge peaked in the 15th century and its destiny has since been that of a large village serving its rural hinterland.

The **market hall**, behind the New Inn, dates from the 16th century; it originally had two storeys and has always served as a market place. Recently it has been restored, and a coin found in the process offers a clue as to the last refurbishment. The date was 1806; needless to say there's another new coin in place waiting for the next major

Pembridge: examples of timber-framed houses, and looking through the market hall to the steps leading to the church

refurbishment, perhaps in a century or two. Just down from it stands the magnificent **New Inn**, dating from the second decade of the 13th century, after the old New Inn had burned down in 1311. Some historians say that it is possible that an important treaty was signed at this very inn, over a mug of ale, by the Yorkists and Lancastrians following the Battle of Mortimer's Cross. Most of what you see now dates from the 17th century when this handsome building would have been a flourishing coaching inn on the Aberystwyth run. Step inside the public bar where there's a very long settle,

CROFT CASTLE

Croft Castle is a 14th-century fortification which has been modified in later centuries. It has been in the hands of the Croft family for over 1,000 years, with only a brief interrup-

tion, and is now managed by the National Trust. The family chapel is also open to the public, as is the parkland, which is full of veteran trees, including a mature row of Spanish chestnuts.

There are lovely walks throughout the grounds especially through woodland and by old fish pools to the Iron Age hill-fort at Croft Ambrey, where the views are exquisite. **Croft Ambrey** was established as a hillfort in 550 BC. There is evidence of a succession of tribal communities rebuilding the site over the centuries until AD 50. This was not merely a fort, but a trading post for this part of the Marches.

If you are walking from the bus stop at Bircher you'll need to allow 30 minutes each way and at least 2 hours to enjoy what is on offer at this property. See www.slowtraveluk.com for details.

accompanied by old chairs and tables and a fireplace fit for any storyteller to sit by.

The **church of St Mary** stands in a quiet spot behind houses and beyond one of the finest detached towers in the country, let alone Herefordshire. This 14th-century, three-storey **bell-house** is styled in a Scandinavian manner, part stone and part wood. The effect is stunning. The bells and clock mechanisms stored inside are intact and in good working order. You'll know when they chime on the quarter! The church is Norman but little remains from the earlier centuries although there's a 13th-century font and a Jacobean pulpit. You can drop down steps by Ye Olde Steppes shop to the main street. It's a short walk to the river Arrow along Bridge Street, which leaves the High Street almost opposite Ye Olde Steppes, passing Duppa's almshouses on the corner, founded by Bishop Duppa of Winchester Cathedral in the 17th century. Across the bridge, there is a small **park** by the river, ideal on a summer's afternoon for an even slower pace. Sit quietly and you could see dippers and kingfishers skimming the rippling waters of the river.

WALKING

Leominster has two main walking routes. The first is the **Herefordshire Trail**, with walks into the undulating country-side nearby, en route to Bromyard or to Richard's Castle. The second route is the **Black and White Walking Trail**, with day walks and loops from some of the half-timbered villages of north Herefordshire. In both cases the walking is pleasant, mainly across a landscape characterised by mixed farming, quiet lanes, and with some tree cover, but it is not spectacular. The main appeal of these trails lies in the hamlets and villages through which they pass; many are untouched by modern develop-ment. For those who enjoy riverside walks, David Milton's tale of his journey to the source of the river Lugg from Leominster, just over 41 miles through the quietest of parts to Llangunllo (railway station) will be appealing (see Extras).

Herefordshire Council has produced a bus walks leaflet *Bus Walks in Mortimer Country* in conjunction with Ludlow 21, which sets out three easy to moderate walks around the 492 bus route between Ludlow and Leominster. There are very few climbs and the walking routes are between villages (or their pubs) and are timed to fit with the pattern of the daily bus service.

There's a useful leaflet published by Leominster Town Council highlighting a more local riverside walk in the town which is available from the visitor information centre. There are also plenty of local walks in the Black and White villages. These include a lovely and well-signed path between Pembridge and Eardisland across water meadows, near to the Arrow from the Arrow Bridge in Pembridge. Be aware that flooding does occur from time to time.

CYCLING

Leominster is on the Sustrans **Six Castles cycle route** offering a route between Ludlow and Leominster via Croft Castle. The section between Ludlow and the Goggin via Killhorse Lane is a hard climb but admittedly the scenery is delightful. From Orleton onwards the riding gets easier although there are more traffic hazards as you come near to Leominster.

Another good ride is *The Herefordshire Cider Cycling Route*. This presents a back road experience through the northern Black and White villages. The 19-mile route, written up in a leaflet (see below), points out several attractions such as **Dunkerton's Cider Mill** and a half-timbered dovecote at Luntley which can be readily seen from the road. However, you will need to access the Cider Route from Leominster. The suggested outward and return leg would be via Ivington and Venmore Bridge to pick up the Cider Route at Dilwyn. This adds an extra 11 miles to the trip making it a 30-mile day outing through orchards and by pastures on lanes with only light traffic.

REFRESHMENT

Leominster

Cafés and restaurants
Blue Note café, West Street: a café cum bar with a difference.
Pavilion Community café, The Grange: community run tea rooms.

Pubs
The Grape Vaults public house, Broad Street: traditional pub serving locally produced beers.

Local Produce
Manuel and Barber, Victoria Street: deli and café offering wide range of local products.
Mousetrap Cheese Shop, Old School Lane: cheese from Monkland dairy and other products.
Nitty Gritty Wholefoods, West Street, local and organic produce sold here.

In the Villages

Cafés and restaurants
Eardisland Tea Room and Gift Shop: home baking plus books and gifts.
Sally's Pantry, Pembridge: locally sourced and homemade food.
The Garden Tea Room, Kingsland: tea room and café – home made food, a selection of scrummy bites.
Village Green Stores, Kingsland: café, tea garden, store and post office. Sources local ingredients wherever possible.

Pubs
The New Inn, Pembridge: old fashioned inn of character.

Extras

Gorvett, David, and Les Lumsdon (1991) *The Black and White Village Trail, A Walkers Guide*, Cromford, Scarthin Books.
Farmers Market, Corn Square: 2nd Saturday in the month.

Herefordshire Cider Cycling Routes – Pembridge: www.ciderroute.co.uk. Small charge made for paper copy.
Herefordshire Trail: Guide book available in local bookshops or see www.herefordshiretrail.com.
Milton, David (2005) *An Upper Lugg Valley Walk*, Arty Publications: available at Leominster Tourist Information office.
Phil Prothero Cycles, Etnam Street, Leominster.
Visitor Information Centre, Corn Square: Tel (01568) 616460.

PUBLIC TRANSPORT

Trains
Leominster is served, daily and directly by trains from Cardiff, Manchester, Shrewsbury and Hereford in addition to North Wales. It is an 8 minute journey from Ludlow and 40 minutes from Hereford.

Buses
Leominster is served by bus from:
Ludlow. 492. Daily, approximately 2 hourly. Operator Lugg Valley, First Midland Red. Travel time: 30 minutes.
Hereford, 492, Daily, approximately every hour. Operators, Lugg Valley, First Midland Red. Travel time: 42 minutes.

The Black and White villages of Kingsland, Eardisland and Pembridge are served by bus from Leominster (en route to either Kington 495-497 or Presteigne 493/4). Approximately two hourly Monday – Saturday. Travel time: 10-22 minutes.

LLANDRINDOD WELLS

Once the British public had become interested in spas, Llandrindod Wells was to develop into the most important inland spa town of Wales. By the second half of the 19th century it was thriving. This popularity lasted through to the Edwardian era, when it possibly peaked, and only came to an end with the Second World War. By 1911, for example, it was estimated that the population of the town (no more than 2,800) increased at least threefold each summer. Visitors came by train to taste the waters, socialise and promenade around the town. The local paper reported the names of notables and celebrities who were staying each week, amongst them Lloyd George.

The fashion of taking the waters at Llandrindod Wells has long since gone but the historic legacy remains. The town is now the principal seat of government in the extensive and sparsely populated county of Powys. The county council buildings, set in wooded grounds, are a creditable modern addition to the town. The splendid restoration work of many of the town's substantial buildings, dating mainly from the spa era, is inspiring. This has been achieved in recent years as part of a townscape heritage project; the town's wide streets and pavements now abut restored Victorian and Edwardian façades that are much to be admired. Llandrindod Wells also has a number of parks dotted about the place, which are at their best on a warm summer's day.

Whether you arrive by train or bus, your stop is Llandrindod railway station, which is something of an interchange. Buses leave from the front of the station, either beneath the small awning or on the main highway, Station Crescent. Evidently, larger vehicles have difficulty squeezing into the forecourt when there are parked cars *in situ* so stop on the main road. There are no set rules; buses come and go from either place, so be vigilant.

Llandrindod Wells rightly prides itself on its Victorian era architecture

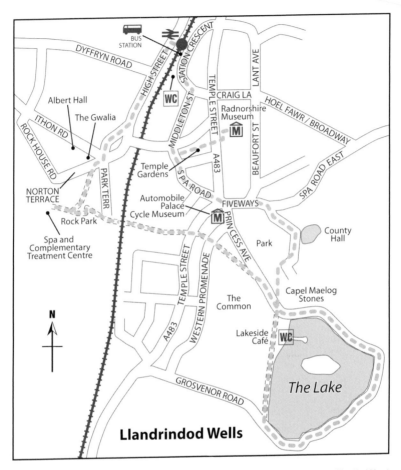

Llandrindod Wells

Walking around town

One way to enjoy a stroll around Llandrindod Wells is to follow the **Heritage trail**, which is mapped out between interpretation boards, each one unfolding a piece of the story about the resort and its rise to fame throughout the decades. There is a board at the railway station beneath the footbridge (number 3) which lets you know about the trail and specifically about the heritage of the railway station. However, if you prefer, what follows is an abridged route; either way you get to know the town a little better.

Cross the footbridge over the railway but slowly does it, as on the southbound platform is an old London North Western Railway signal box from Llandrindod crossing. It is now a small **museum** focusing on the life on this railway, previously known as the Central Wales Line. On the right is a canopy spanning part of the platform, but this does not originate from the railway. It used to adorn the demolished Pump House Hotel mentioned later in the walk.

Once on the other side, go left to walk along High Street to pass Heart of Wales bikes and the Radnorshire Wildlife Trust offices and shop. Cross Ithon Road and pass by the Gwalia building. Across the road is a beautifully restored Edwardian

Crescent known as The Towers. Enter **Rock Park**, previously known as Blacksmith's Dingle. Descend to a footbridge beneath a canopy of tall trees, many of which were planted in the 1860s. Before you continue over the bridge go left to look at the Four Kings, four hardwood seats designed by a local student and crafted by local artists. These overlook a small waterfall on the Arial brook that flows through the park to the river Ithon near Lovers Leap. You may like to pause by the marble drinking fountain that has spouted out chalybeate waters since 1879. It is drinkable but perhaps best described as an acquired taste and needs to be drunk as soon as you've collected it.

Take a look over to the **Rock Park Spa**, a complementary treatment centre and conference facility located in the old pump house, pavilion and treatment buildings. The buildings date from the turn of the 20th century and fell into disrepair in the 1970s. Some restoration work was undertaken in the 1980s but the complex is in need of more work to restore the building to its former glory. The Llandrindod Wells Spa Town Trust, a community group working to enhance the environment of the town, is leading on the project.

Go left up steps to meet another path where you go left again, passing by several sculptures. The paths have been upgraded thanks to the work of the Friends of Rock Park, who aim to maintain the character of the park as it would have been in Victorian days. This paths climbs to a footbridge, which you cross then go right beneath the railway and keep ahead until you reach Temple Street. Cross over to walk up a side street, crossing Western Promenade and onward to Princes Avenue. Turn right and right again to walk by the boathouse and café.

Main attraction

The lake is the main attraction. It was dug out of a swampy peat bog in the 1870s and modelled into a lake designed for rowing and promenading. If you look at the photographs of the 1890s (in the Radnorshire Museum – see below) the area looks distinctly urban, open and lined with traditional clinker-built rowing boats tied up to short jetties. Walk the entire perimeter of the lake and it becomes abundantly apparent that this is no longer the case. It has recently been designated as a Local Nature Reserve. You can see why. The mature oaks give way to wetter ground,

The serpent in the lake

colonised by marsh marigold and valerian, a positive sign that nature is thriving here. Sensitive restoration of the banks, as part of a Lake Restoration project, and the encouragement of reed beds, will bring great benefits in years to come. The lakeside offers a welcome in all seasons, but especially in summer and autumn when you enter a different world of tree canopies and subtle colour combinations that are soft in the afternoon light.

Follow the path alongside the road and you begin to make your way back to the boathouse. The centrepiece is *The Fabulous Water Beast,* a serpentine-like sea dragon sculpture, some 40 metres long from the leaping fish to the dragon's tail. It functions as a fountain. This was the first **Arcady project**, spearheaded by coppersmith sculptor, Richard Taylor, which seeks to encourage creative public art as a part of the regeneration process. The sculpture involved the community, with over a thousand volunteers inscribing their initials or a message on the dragon's scales. There are several other sculptures around the lake featuring mythical figures known as Llandoddies, based on a book by outdoor writer David Bellamy writing under a pseudonym.

Cross over the highway here, apparently closed for several nights in March as thousands of frogs, newts and toads take to the road for the mating season. They make their way to the lakeside edge and are most vulnerable to being squashed by cars at nightfall. Peel off to the right across the grass to the scant remains of **Capel Maelog**, a medieval chapel moved from another part of town to conserve it for future generations. Join a more prominent path and turn right again to follow this to the county council buildings, located on the site of the 18th-century Pump House Hotel; all that survives is the old boiler house incorporated into the modern complex. You might note the sculpture of a red kite on the roof of the building.

Go to the left to walk by the sculpture *Gaia* by a local sculptor, Edward Folkard,

One of Llandrindod's individual shops, many of which are clustered in Middleton Street

who has also made various other local sculptures, such as that of a drover at Newbridge-on-Wye and Henry VII at the old Market Hall, Hay-on-Wye. You also pass by Coleg Powys, a magnificent Victorian red brick building which was originally Ye Wells Hotel. On reaching Five Ways, cross the road into Temple Street to admire the late art deco styling of the **Automobile Palace** (see National Cycle Collection below). Turn left into Spa Road which leads to **Temple Gardens**, another fine example of open space in the town. Walk through here to Temple Street. Cross the road and this leads into the smaller Memorial Gardens where you will find the **Radnorshire Museum** (see below). From the museum, cross Temple Street again, and then walk along South Crescent. Take a right turn into Middleton Street where there has been much work done to restore the Victorian shop windows. It really is impressive. At the end of the street, turn left into Station Crescent. The post office and garage stand across Station Crescent; the building is another fine example of a late art deco style of architecture.

Other attractions

Housed in the Automobile Palace, **the National Cycle Collection** offers a resonating reminder that fashions change. There are over 250 cycles on view and many reflect the design and values of UK society throughout the ages. The one-time owner of the building, Tom Norton, also had a penchant for collecting bicycles and used to hang them from the showroom ceiling. Some of these have been retained as part of the collection.

The Radnorshire Museum, located in the Carnegie Library in the Memorial Gardens, is a must for explorers of geology. The Rock of Radnorshire display includes unusual fossils collected by geological expert Dr Botting, publicising research on local geological systems, referred to as the Builth-Llandrindod Wells inlier. There are several other unusual displays including the review of Llandrindod as a spa town and a medieval boat dating from 1200, evidently fished out of the river Ithon. The Kilvert Society has granted permission for its collection to be displayed here too and it is a must for those interested in the Reverend Kilvert's diary notes illustrating life in the Wye valley in the 1860/70s.

WALKING

Llandrindod Wells is a Walkers are Welcome town and there are a number of superb local walks through to Cross Gates or Pen-y-bont via Shakey Bridge. Many local walks are available on the Leaping Stiles website (www.leapingstiles.co.uk).

CYCLING

Llandrindod Wells is a great place to cycle as the traffic levels are low and most streets are wide. **NCN Route 25**, the Radnor Ring, passes through Llandrindod Wells. It offers an 86-mile circular ride to Rhayader and Knighton. It is possible to cycle to Knighton via Kington and catch the train back to Llandrindod Wells with cycle. This is, for most people, a two day ride stopping off for one night.

REFRESHMENTS
There are a number of cafés in town. Most are located on or near Station Crescent but there's a café at the Lakeside Pavilion.

Cafés and Restaurants
The Herb Garden Café: it is located off Station Crescent at the Spa Centre, next to the Co-operative supermarket. It makes for an excellent choice as it serves local organic food wherever possible and vegetarian dishes are a speciality.

Pubs
There are few to choose from in Llandrindod Wells. The nearest to the railway station, however, is the **Llanerch Inn**.

Local Produce
Vans Wholefoods, Middleton Street: long-standing wholefood shop.

EXTRAS

Heart of Wales Bikes, High Street: sales, repairs and bike hire.
Heart of Wales Travellers Association: campaigns for improvements to services-see www.howlta.ruralwales.org.
Radnorshire Wildlife Trust, High Street: office and shop.
Rent and ride Cycle Hire, Leisure Centre; bike hire available.

PUBLIC TRANSPORT

Trains
Llandrindod is served, daily, by direct trains from Shrewsbury and Swansea. It is a 1.5 hour journey from Shrewsbury.

Buses
Llandrindod Wells is served by buses from:
Brecon. 704 TrawsCambria service. Monday – Saturday. Two hourly. Travel duration is 1 hour. Operator: Stagecoach in South Wales.
Hereford. 461-3. Monday – Saturday. Two hourly. Travel duration is 1 hr 48-55 minutes. Operator: Sargeants Motors.
There are also weekday services to Rhayader and Newtown.

EXCURSIONS FROM LLANDRINDOD WELLS

BUILTH WELLS (LLANFAIR-YM-MUALLT)

Ride to Builth Wells

The 25-minute bus ride between the two Wells is usually by way of the village of Howey and beneath the high ground of Carneddau, home to several prehistoric tribes. It then runs alongside the quarry scars of Llanelwedd on the approach to Builth Wells. Sit on the right-hand side of the bus as the views over to the Cambrian Mountains are superb. A few buses follow a different route through Newbridge-on-Wye, across the river Ithon to Builth Road, reversing at the Cambrian Arms, once the tea rooms at the Cambrian Railway's low level station. Coming from either direction, the bus soon passes the Royal Welsh showground to cross the Wye Bridge into Builth. Some may prefer the train, which is only a short trip of 10 minutes between two stations, but the walk or cycle ride from Builth Road station is not pleasant. They involve stretches of the A470 and buses are sparse on this route.

BUILTH WELLS

Builth Wells grew up in the last century as a tourist resort, nestled between two rivers, and amid low hills. It is now principally a market town servicing the surrounding district although there remains a small tourism base. It is one of the few places, rather like Kington, that is relatively untouched by visitors coming into town. They are welcome of course and there are several accommodation providers in the locality, but everyday life rules in this modest little Welsh town. The entire place changes dramatically, however, during the Royal Welsh show in July. There are even extra trains and buses put on for this event; the town is bursting at the seams.

The farming community from the whole of Wales and beyond descends on the show to celebrate the success of prizewinners, to eye up new machinery and to lament the loss of traditional skills no longer practised on a day to day basis. Builth Wells is not a place that will immediately enthral you but it does have good access to nearby countryside, especially the Wye Valley Walk.

Walking around town

All buses stop at The Groe, where there's a statue of a Welsh Black Bull, all 1.5 tonnes of it. It was commissioned from sculptor Gavin Fifield, who has an affinity with the area. You can walk along the beautiful river Wye from this point, making your way upstream of the six-arched Wye Bridge. Beyond the toilet block you soon reach a row of trees known as Abram's Folly as, when they were planted, everyone thought that the benefactor was daft. Now the trees are mature, residents and visitors alike admire their beauty. As you walk along look out for a wooden sculpture of salmon leaping. At the end of the avenue of trees, go left to follow the river Irfon upstream. A tributary of the Irfon is the Nant-yr-Arian stream which in Welsh means money brook. The name is said to come from the Great Plague when country folk brought food for the dying townspeople and in return money was thrown into the brook to cleanse it before it exchanged hands. You go next left opposite the suspension bridge into Love Lane and ahead along Broadway.

On reaching Park Road, cross over and go right and then left into Garth Road. Much of this part of town was rebuilt in Victorian times; it gave Builth a new lease of life as a spa town. The Reverend Francis Kilvert

The Wye at Builth, with the Wyeside Arts Centre in the background to the right

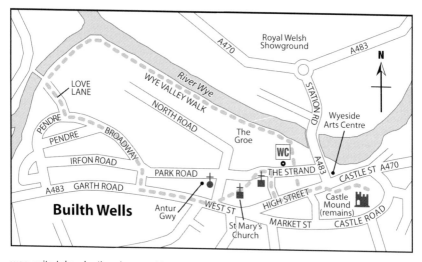

Builth Wells

was quite taken by the place on his perambulation. The pioneering growth came in the 1830s, but it was slow, and the town enjoyed its major tourism boost with the arrival of the railways in the 1860s. There were two principal spas, Park Wells (saline) and Glanne Wells (sulphur), both located out of town in the direction of Cilmeri. The houses along the Garth Road reflect this period; a time when the word 'wells' was added to the original anglicised name of the town, Builth.

On reaching West Street, you will see **St Mary's church** which is for the most part a Victorian rebuild on the site of an earlier church. The tower is of 14th-century origin and there is an effigy of a knight in the porch that is breathtaking. Take a walk through the churchyard to exit into The Strand. Go right into Strand Street to walk by the Strand Hall, an assembly rooms dating from the 1860s. Opposite is the old post office where there's a small plaque indicating that this was the only office to be designated in the time of Edward VIII, the uncrowned king that abdicated in 1936.

Turn left into Builth's main shopping area, High Street. The town was a place where drovers stopped off in earlier centuries and the Drover's Rest (at one time an old inn) commemorates this fact. Ruth

Lane, cutting off here, is also a reminder of the late medieval town passages. Continue ahead into Broad Street and just past the Café Fontana, there's a passageway on the right with a marker for the castle. This is your route, along a surfaced way grown over with vegetation. There's a stile to cross then the route becomes a narrow path festooned with a collection of litter and discarded metal. Don't be put off. This soon leads up to the magnificent earthworks of Builth Castle. Whilst the paths are not entirely clear on the ground, the thistle, knapweed and thorn attract all manner of butterflies and birds. This historic location doubles as a nature refuge.

Main attraction

The main attraction has to be the castle. There's no stonework but the foundations of **Builth Castle** are substantial; they indicate that this was a major player in the medieval borderland battleground. The site was first developed as a Norman stronghold by Philip de Braose in the 12th century, probably on the site of a previous fortification, but there is no firm evidence to support this. From the very start, there was severe resistance by the Welsh princes of Powys. It is not surprising then that the castle was to be occupied by the Welsh then regained by Normans and so on, a see-saw existence which continued for the best part of one hundred years. However, in 1277, King Edward I decided to rebuild the castle on a far grander scale than hitherto, to subdue Welsh uprisings once and for all. In addition, it came into the possession of the Mortimers who were equally determined to hold back any gains by the native population.

The great Prince Llywelyn ap Gruffyd rode from Aberedw to Builth Castle in 1282 to seek support for his uprising, but his efforts were to no avail. That is not surprising as in 1260 he had burnt the castle and surrounds to the ground. The Norman English forces were hot on his heels and he had to beat a hasty retreat. It is chronicled that he was mortally wounded (another interpretation is that he was murdered) at nearby Cilmeri. There's a granite monument and plaque located there to mark the deed and to commemorate his role as the last prince in this part of Powys. It is a short bus ride (Bus 48) and Cilmeri is also a halt on the Heart of Wales line.

Another Welsh legendary figure, Owain Glyndwr, travelled to Builth to gather support for a revolt against the Norman overlords in 1409. However, he decided to topple the castle and proceeded to wage an immense attack, but this failed to overcome the besieged English force. He had to flee from the gathering forces but lived to tell the tale. From this period onwards, or at least until the late 1600s, Builth Castle enjoyed a period of relative peace and thus lost its rationale for existence; it fell slowly into disrepair. A devastating fire consumed the town in the 1690s and historians infer that the castle was systematically dismantled, including the Great Keep, the inner and outer walls and six towers, in order to re-build several properties in the town. That is a worthwhile legacy.

Make your way back to Broad Street where you can see across to the **Wyeside Arts Centre**, housed in an Italianate hall, dating from the 1870s. This was the Market House or Hall and there are some interesting terracotta roundels of Shakespeare, Mozart and Haydn on the exterior walls. It is on a busy corner by the Wye Bridge.

WALKING

The main walking route, waymarked throughout, is the **Wye Valley Walk** and it lends itself to several superb linear rambles based on Builth. It is, of course, possible to simply wander upstream to the rapids on the Wye at Pen ddol rocks, about a mile to the west of the town (about 20-30 minutes each way). Otherwise, a good outing is to catch the bus to Newbridge-on-Wye from Llandrindod Wells (47 Mon – Sat) then walk back to Builth, some 5-6 miles on paths that mainly hug the river. If you prefer a longer walk it is possible to start at Llandrindod Wells and walk via Disserth to Newbridge-on-Wye (4-5 miles) on local footpaths and lanes – see the *Leaping Stiles in Mid Wales* website. You can then continue along the Wye Valley walk. Newbridge-on-Wye was the place to cross the river in earlier times and became the stop for drovers in need of refreshment and rest. There's a statue in the village centre to a lone drover, reflecting this intriguing aspect of history in the Marches.

Alternatively, catch the bus to Erwood Bridge (704 Mon – Sat). Across the bridge is the **Erwood Station craft centre** based at the old Erwood railway station, once on the Moat Lane Junction to Three Cocks Junction railway line, closed in 1962. There's a café here and a chance to see some very lovely craft products. The walk back is some 6 miles over high ground, away from the river, so requires more energy than the Newbridge walk.

CYCLING

National Cycle Network route 8, Lôn Las Cymru offers opportunities for cycle rides in the Wye valley down to Hay-on-Wye. It is mainly a river route with only a few climbs on back lanes and offering a chance to visit Glasbury. There is also a hillier section through to Rhayader. This is becoming an increasing popular route and cyclists often use the cycle racks at The Groe while they rest awhile.

REFRESHMENT

There are several cafés and public houses in town but none that stand out especially.

Erwood Station craft centre and gallery: home made food available.

EXTRAS

Bicycle Beano, based at Erwood, is a long-standing cycle tour operator with a tremendous reputation for cycle tours in Wales.

Leaping Stiles website highlights dozens of walks in Mid-Wales: see www.leapingstiles.co.uk

Tretricket Mill, Erwood: camping barn which offers genuine vegetarian food.

PUBLIC TRANSPORT

Trains

Builth Road is a good 2 miles out of town but is served, daily, by trains from Llandrindod Wells, Shrewsbury and Swansea as well as some of the trains from north Wales. It is an 8 minute journey from Llandrindod Wells.

Buses

There are buses from Llandrindod Wells (Railway Station) to Builth (The Groe). Buses 47 and 704. Mondays to Saturdays only. Hourly. Travel time: 20 minutes. Operator: Stagecoach in South Wales and Veolia Transport Cymru.

Bus 704 (TrawsCambria) extends to Brecon and offers opportunities to explore the Wye valley between Builth Wells and Llyswen.

KINGTON AND NEW RADNOR

Ride to Kington

The bus ride to New Radnor and Kington is one of the best in the Marches for it offers panoramic scenic views across Radnor Forest. On reaching the village of Pen-y-bont it then climbs up to a summit before Fforest Inn. The bus descends from here into the Radnor valley to New Radnor. It stops opposite the Old Town Hall in the direction of Kington and there's a shelter on the other side of the road for buses back to Llandrindod Wells. There's an equally attractive onward run through to Kington. The bus passes between Old Radnor and Bradnor Hills into the valley of the Back Brook. It climbs into Kington over a small ridge where the parish church is sited. This is the stop for Hergest Court – see below.

KINGTON

Kington is a resilient border market town still wedded to its tightly-knit agricultural economy. It is not given over too much to tourism and that adds to its appeal, but visitors are made very welcome, as walkers on Offa's Dyke Path or Mortimer Trail will testify. The town has an interesting range of events throughout the year, including the Kington Show, which really does stick to its agricultural roots, together with more off-beat offerings such as the annual wheelbarrow race in June, which is great fun. The town also has an emerging and progressive approach to the environment (see below). There are two key attractions or maybe three if you happen to be a historic pub aficionado: Hergest Croft gardens, the Small Breeds Farm Park and Owl Centre and the Olde Tavern.

All buses drop off and pick up at a terminus at Mill Street Car Park. Just across the road is the **Kington Museum** (open Tues – Sat, April to September) displaying all manner of local artefacts and photographs and there's a tourist information centre opposite. Adjacent is the old

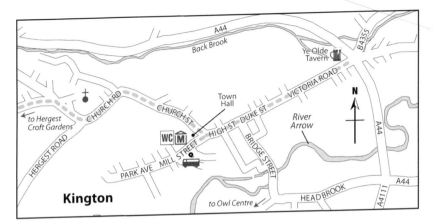

Kington

market hall where there are a few stalls on market day, Tuesday, as well as toilets. There are plaques throughout the town (referred to as 'Kington Past') that indicate historic points of interest.

Walking around town

The centre of the town is focused on High Street which runs east from the **Town Hall**. This red brick building, dating from 1885, replaced an earlier building designed by the very capable John Abel. The one you see now has been described by the architectural historian, Pevsner, as ugly. This seems a little unkind, but take a look yourself and cast your vote accordingly. The tower was built in 1897 and has a bust of Queen Victoria to mark the occasion of her Golden Jubilee in that year. Opposite the Town Hall is the Burton Hotel, a fine example of an old coaching inn complete with a superb porch entrance across the pavement.

The town has a fair share of modest Georgian and Victorian buildings but collectively they give the place its atmosphere as they sit alongside the vestiges of old mills and warehouses. Head along Duke Street to the third attraction, **Ye Olde Tavern**, an historic pub par excellence. It was located near to the old Kington to New Radnor railway line and had the name of The Railway for some time. The two rooms in the public house have not been changed

much over the decades; they are packed with old seats and curios which catch your attention as you settle down over a drink. The locals are rightly proud of this characterful corner of Kington.

Main attraction

The main attraction in Kington is **Hergest Croft gardens**, about half a mile out of town. Leave by Church Street, a street that has seen better days. Pass the Swan Inn in The Square and walk up to the parish **church of St Mary** which dates from the 12th century but with many refurbishments in the Victorian era. The font is Norman and there are several fascinating monuments, including effigies of local notable Thomas Vaughan and his wife. Kington Castle was situated on this high ground too but there are only scant earthworks remaining.

For Hergest Croft gardens go left into Ridgebourne Lane (as waymarked re Offa's Dyke National Trail) and the hall and garden entrance are soon to be found on the left. If you are keen to walk onto Hergest Ridge first, then continue ahead to the end of the lane and follow the green track as it rises relentlessly to **Hergest Ridge** where superb views are on offer. This is also part of the larger Hergest Estate and is associated with tales of haunting by the Black Dog of Hergest; it is said that this legend stimulated Arthur Conan Doyle to write *The Hound of the Baskervilles*.

Hergest Croft was built in 1895 and the gardens created one year later. It has been in the good hands of the Banks family for four generations and some of the trees planted in the early days are fine specimens now. The garden has a number of highlights, including its azalea borders and the exceptional maple grove. There's also a delightful kitchen garden and tearooms (for garden visitors only). Above all else it is the location of the gardens that counts for much. The views across Herefordshire to the Black Mountains are superb. There is a public footpath that you can take through part of the arboretum and then down the valley beyond and on through a wood in the centre of which is a combe planted with rhododendrons.

Other attractions

The second key attraction, the **Small Breeds Farm Park and Owl Centre**, is also out of town. This is a wonderful place. Not only are there all manner of rare breeds of pigs and goats to see, but there is also a collection of all of the native British owls. Evidently, owls are not as wise as the Greek legends made them out to be; ravens and crows are much smarter, so the experts say. Nevertheless, humans love owls and that might be something to do with those piercing eyes at the front of their heads and all of those fluffy feathers. If you would like to know more about these birds and their habitats then beat a path to the Owl Centre. It is about a 30-minute walk along a relatively quiet lane. Firstly, walk out of town via Bridge Street and once across the bridge over the River Arrow take the first right by the old toll house along Kingswood Road. Climb up this lane until you reach an entrance to the Owl Centre by way of a car park.

En route to Kington from Llandrindod Wells is **New Radnor** in the Radnor valley. It is more of a shallow bowl, drained by the Summergil and Hindwell brooks which flow through a gap at Nash into the Lugg valley, just to the east of Presteigne. This is rich Welsh farming country surrounded by the high hills of **Radnor Forest**, the

Kington is full of little lanes and alleyways, which also give a good chance to see an unusual aspect of the town: its varied roofs and chimney stacks

Houses near Kington's church

'forest' element of the name denoting that it was once a royal hunting ground as opposed to be being covered in trees.

The sleepy village of New Radnor stands on the gentle slopes beneath Knowle Hill. Beyond is the mighty Whimble, the highest point of the eastern ranges of the Radnor Forest. New Radnor was at one time a place of far greater significance. Walk up its High Street from the Radnor Arms and you cannot fail to be impressed by the formidable size of the **castle earthwork** towering above the houses. It suffered siege after siege between legendary giants in borderland history, such as Llewelyn the Great and Roger Mortimer (the grandfather of the infamous Roger Mortimer who deposed Edward II). Owain Glyndwr sealed its fate in 1401 when the castle was ransacked and this brought the demise of an entire garrison of defenders. Standing near to the castle is another Norman legacy, the large **church of St Mary**, but little early work remains following a wholesale rebuild in the 19th century. There are two

Part of the monument to George Cornewall Lewis at New Radnor

frayed effigies of a knight and a woman in the church porch.

The street pattern of New Radnor betrays the town's medieval origins and it retained its importance into the 16th century as the county town of Radnor. In the centre of the village stands the Radnor Arms and across the road the village shop. From the Radnor Arms turn right to walk down the street until you reach a masterpiece of a monument designated to George Cornewall Lewis. It is currently surrounded by security fencing which dampens the initial appeal of this 77-feet-tall Gothic-style tribute to an aristocrat and politician who wielded much power locally in the 19th century.

New Radnor has never been a hotspot for tourism, although the Wordsworths came to stay on more than one occasion at Harpton Court, which is no longer standing. The railway company did not bring with it visitors in their hundreds. This was essentially an extension of the branch line from Leominster to Kington to the quarries at Burlington and Dolyhir. It eventually arrived at the outskirts of New Radnor in 1875 much to the surprise of the local population. Its trade was based around agricultural produce. There were only three passenger trains per day which brought little more than a trickle of passengers in or out of the valley on most days. Ironically, the railway terminus is now a caravan site and the old goods shed remains. It can be seen on the right as the bus leaves New Radnor in the direction of Kington.

It is possible to drop off at the Crown Inn at Walton, a recently renovated public house which stands at a crossroads in the hamlet. From the entrance to the Crown, go right to walk up the lane for a 15 minute climb up to the village of **Old Radnor**. As you approach the village, peel off left to climb a grassy path to a high point. Here sin and salvation stand warily before you on either side of a small green. The ancient hostelry, the Harp, is set in a timeless location. It is very much a rural pub as well as a place to stay or eat. On the right stands the **church of St Stephen**

and some suggest that it sits on the earthworks of a Bronze Age settlement. It is a church of some antiquity, probably dating back to the 8th century but having been much altered in the late middle ages. Amongst other points of interest, there is a rough-looking font carved from a glacial erratic, some medieval tiles and a 16th-century nave ceiling with carved bosses. There's a great viewpoint here and two information plates that name every high point in sight. The view over the Radnor valley is one of the best in the borderland. This was once a war zone, first calmed by the Romans. They had a settlement at Hindwell Farm. It is difficult to imagine that each and every settlement across the panorama possesses earthworks associated with a Norman stronghold, but that is the case.

WALKING

Kington is a great place to enjoy some of the best of walking in the Marches. The local footpath group has done much over the years to clear and waymark paths throughout the entire area. The area is known as the Centre for Walking and is a 'Walkers are Welcome' town. It is a crossroads for a number of long distance or local walking routes including the **Black and White Village Walking Trail**, **Herefordshire Trail**, **Mortimer Trail** and **Offa's Dyke National Trail**. There are several superb walks to be sampled. Catch the 41 bus (Mon – Sat) to Titley and walk back along Mortimer's Trail or take the 462 bus to Eardisley (Mon – Sat) and walk the 9 miles back to Kington. There's a lovely linear 5 mile walk along Hergest Ridge from Gladestry following Offa's Dyke path. Catch the Tuesdays only market day bus (Bus 464) out of Kington to start the walk.

There are also many fine walks from New Radnor, for example to or from the Fforest Inn on the many bridleways in this area including high ground walks via Harley's Dingle and Davy Morgan's Dingle and Water-break-its-neck waterfall.

CYCLING

An alternative way is to cycle on the **Radnor Ring** to Kington from Llandrindod Wells. This is an under-rated route which offers a great introduction to this part of the Marches. Traffic levels are low and there are some stretches off-road so you'll need a hybrid or mountain bike.

REFRESHMENT

The town has several cafés and shops offering light refreshments including the **Chocolate Box** (which is also a chocolatier).

Cafés

Jane's Parlour, High Street: homemade food available.

Loafers Patisserie, Bridge Street: offers home cooked food.

Pubs

Lovers of real ale will enjoy Kington as it has many pubs, most of which offer beers from local breweries.

Old Wine Vaults, High Street: down to earth single bar which brews its own 'Arrow' beer.

Oxford Arms, Duke Street: where the beer is always sourced from local breweries and kept in superb condition.

Penrhos Court Hotel, near Lyonshall on Bus 461 five minutes from Kington: quality organic food, home of green cuisine.

Ye Olde Tavern, Victoria Street: atmospheric and chatty local pub with good range of beers.

Local produce

Glyn Slade Jones, High Street: a butcher's that has achieved much in the Flavours of Herefordshire scheme.

EXTRAS

Kington Tourist Information Centre: Mill Street Tel (01544) 230778.

PUBLIC TRANSPORT

Buses
Kington and New Radnor are served by bus from Llandrindod Railway Station. 461-463. Monday – Saturday. Travel time: 38 minutes. Operator: Sargeants Motors.

Kington is also served on weekdays by buses from Hereford and Leominster.

HEREFORD

The medieval walls of Hereford mark the boundary of the oldest part of the city, a line also largely chosen by highway engineers for the inner ring road some years back. The inner central core covers a little over 75 acres and thus makes it an ideal place for a foray on foot. Hereford is a city that displays a diversity of historic buildings which reveal its many associations with the past. By far the most impressive of these is Hereford Cathedral but other churches, such as All Saints and St Peters, sit beautifully in their urban surroundings. Medieval Hereford is represented in The Old House and pockets of half-timbered buildings restored and sandwiched between modern facades. Wide thoroughfares such as Broad Street and St Owen's Street still hold their presence with a number of fine Georgian and Victorian buildings (or sometimes simply façades behind which lurk remnants of timber-framed buildings) that make a wander worthwhile.

The southern border of this heritage quarter is the river Wye, one of the purest rivers in the country. The riverside has remained surprisingly undeveloped and offers a breath of fresh air for those who need an hour or so away from it all. The river, of course, is one of the main reasons for Hereford's very existence; it has been a fording and bridging point from the earliest times. The Wye is much loved by Hereford's citizens, except on the occasions when it floods. It then brings chaos to nearby dwellings and sometimes to the roads south of the city. Hereford has often been described as a county town but it is more than that; it is a major administrative and service centre for the mid-Marches and thus attracts people from outlying areas, especially on Wednesdays, the principal market day of the week.

However, there's a downside. The sprawl of housing over the past two decades has led to untold traffic conges-

tion. There's also a major controversy over the development of part of town where the cattle market was located until recently (it has moved to an out of town site), with plans for a further stretch of inner relief road that would pass directly in front of Hereford's railway station. That is a pity for it means more traffic whereas the city should be a walking and cycling paradise. Instead, many of its streets have simply been rendered unpleasant through unbridled traffic and unfortunately that is the first impression gained on a 10 minute walk into town from the railway station, a grand-looking building dating from the 1850s. It is one of the small transport hubs sited around town. Buses leave the railway station for different parts of the county and into Wales, and that is a real bonus for the slow traveller. Before you move on, however, take a look at Hereford's charming inner quarter.

Walking around town

Your way into town from the main station forecourt is signposted left along Station Avenue and then right into Commercial Road, which is the main drag into town. The first part of your walk is fairly pedestrian-unfriendly. Photographs of Commercial Road from the early decades of the 20th century, show it to be a *gran via*, a street for people to promenade beneath the shade of tall trees. One hundred years on there's a stark contrast. It is currently a heavily trafficked street, overly populated with pub chains, fast food frontages and few trees. There are, however, one or two sanctuaries en route such as the Merton Hotel, handy for both the railway station and the country bus station.

Once you make it to the pedestrian zone by the Kerry Arms, located near the site of Bye Gate, one of the main gateways through the old town wall, things begin to look up. There's a traffic-free street ahead, Commercial Street, and this

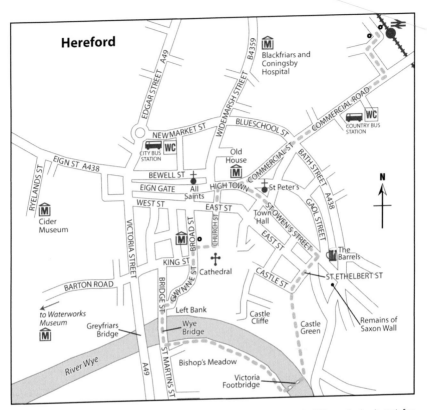

Hereford

leads into **High Town**. You can now start to relax more. High Town is the central point of the city and there are street cafés and children's amusements located here. That might be too much clutter for some people; the place seems to work best when the market stalls are set out and people are browsing.

Many of the buildings around are several centuries old but you'll need to look above the retail fascias, for example above River Island and W.H. Smith, to appreciate their architectural merit. Unfortunately, some were damaged in a fire in 2010. Further along in High Street, there's a half-timbered masterpiece to note. The building was wheeled out, restored and wheeled back in the 1960s during a tricky operation when it was squeezed in between two modern slabs (to the right of Marks and Spencer).

There are two buildings to look out for while you wander a little. The first is the **Old House**, a half-timbered masterpiece which has housed both butcher and banker in the past. Built in the early 17th century, as part of Butchers' Row, it stands defiantly amidst a barrage of modern retail premises. It is now a museum providing fascinating insights into Hereford life throughout the 18th century. There are also snippets about famous people associated with the city, such as David Garrick of theatrical fame and Nell Gwynne, actress and companion to King Charles II, and there's a chair used by the late 19th-century photographer-author, Alfred Watkins. The museum features mainly items of furniture, some of which are most unusual, such as the Quarter Jacks which stood either side of the elaborate timber market hall that stood proudly in High Town in the late medieval period. There's much to learn in the museum, including information about the use of different woods as some exhibits were carved from pear, others from oak and walnut.

The second building to look out for is less obvious but is probably the more loved of the two. It is the **Buttermarket**.

Above: part of the main entrance to the Buttermarket
Left: the restored half-timbered frontage repositioned and sandwiched between new buildings in the 1960s

The pedestrianised High Town in Hereford, with the Old House in the background and the spire of St Peter's church beyond

This building is a true reflection of Hereford, especially in the eyes of older Herefordians, who say it has not changed much since they were children. The entrance lies beneath a striking clock tower on the right-hand side of High Town as you look west. Built in 1860, this market hall is home to many traditional traders, offering local produce and goods. A recent survey of residents gave the thumbs up for a sympathetic refurbishment of the Buttermarket, one that holds true to the market hall tradition. We'll have to see what transpires. Take a look inside before you move on.

From here, you might like to cut left along a narrow medieval passage known as Capuchin Lane. This is severed by East Street, between the Moka café and Grapes Tavern (and which marks the northern edge of the Saxon town), so watch out for traffic coming by from the right. Continue ahead along **Church Street**, a mix of unusual shops, cosy cafés/restaurants and a traditional pub, the Lichfield Vaults, mid-way along. There has been some careful restoration work in this street, including the old shoe menders at 14 Church Street, now being brought to life by the Pippen Trust,

The cathedral tower as seen when entering Cathedral Close from the end of Church Street

a building charity looking to restore historic buildings for long term sustainable use.

Church Street gives out into one of Hereford's loveliest quarters, the Cathedral Close, which has been subject to a revamp in recent years. Around it stands a range of fine buildings: the Bishop's House, the Cathedral Barn (dating from 1253), Cathedral School and in one corner, the statue of composer, Edward Elgar, leaning on his bike. These surroundings make it an engaging place and mark the boundary between the civil society of Hereford and the sanctuary of the cathedral. In recent years it has been a spot for young people to while away the time, but is currently undergoing a major facelift.

Main attraction

Nevertheless, **the cathedral** remains the main attraction and attracts visitors from across the world. Pevsner, in his meticulous discussion of the buildings of Hereford, noted that the cathedral 'dominates unchallenged'. His words remain true five decades on, in part because local planners have dictated that no building in Hereford should be taller than the cathedral; a visit is as obligatory as stepping inside the Buttermarket. It was first built in the late 7th century and was subsequently dedicated to the martyr, King Ethelbert, in the late 8th century. It was almost completely re-built in the early 11th century only to be ransacked by a Welsh invading army in 1055. That was an enormous blow to the Christian enclave of that time.

The Normans, however, invested time and time again to provide outstandingly high quality architecture in the cathedral, for example, as evidenced by the magnificent nave, a Norman design with later modifications. The 14th-century tower is also a fine feature, adorned with ballflowers, and there are regular tower tours for those able to climb the steps and stomach the heights. Throughout the building you cannot fail to notice the light shimmering through the wide range of stained glass windows. Some of them are of medieval origin but most date from later centuries, notably the recent glass by Tom Denny in the Audley Chapel depicting the visions of **Thomas Traherne**. You can take a guided tour of the cathedral or make your way around at your own pace in order to admire the abundance of wood and stone carvings, effigies and monuments. Each provides an insight into the hierarchical world of Hereford throughout the past twelve centuries. A point of particular interest is the beautifully restored **shrine of St Thomas Cantilupe**, bishop of Hereford from 1275 to 1282. An advisor to Edward I, he was a firm upholder of the rights of the see, even administering the rod to the back of Lord Clifford for assaulting some of the bishop's tenants. His determination led to an argument with the archbishop of Canterbury who excommunicated him. To plead his case he sought out the papal court in Italy, where he died before his case was fully heard. His bones were brought back for burial in a shrine at Hereford Cathedral where they became the focus of a pilgrimage cult and the source of many supposed miraculous cures. Rome was urged to canonize him, not least because he always wore a hairshirt and refused to kiss even his sister. He was duly made a saint in 1320.

The cathedral is also home to the world-famous **Mappa Mundi**, an ancient map of international repute. It is one of the few surviving medieval maps of the world, superbly sketched on parchment made of calf skin. In a form of cartography prevalent in the 12th and 13th centuries, it is a pictorial representation of the main elements of the world. Perhaps more to the point, it exhibits a rich tapestry of medieval mind-mapping, a reflection of how the scholars who put this together drew on the legend, lore and learning of the time. There are drawings of over 400 towns and cities on the Mappa Mundi as well as illustrating some of the cherished sites of the time, for example, the Tower of Babel, Jerusalem and Paris, and animals from different continents such as the crocodile and elephant. Encased in an air controlled cabinet, the map is well protected from the thousands of visitors breathing over it at close quarters.

The Mappa Mundi is housed in a unique **chained library**, said to be the largest in the world. The cathedral now also houses the chained library originally held by All Saints church, just up the road, which happened to be the *second* largest chained library in the world. Originally, hundreds of books were chained down in the cathedral in the 17th century so that the reader had to peruse the work *in situ*, hence the name. The books were, at one time, spread far and wide in the cloisters, but were collected together as their precious worth began to be appreciated, given that some books dated from the 8th century. There are also several extremely rare medieval manuscripts on theology and the law. In 1996, a new purpose-built library was constructed to conserve the books and the Mappa Mundi. The entrance is by way of the cathedral café.

The cathedral café makes use of part of the old cloisters and the recently formed Chapter House Garden, made around

The old entrance to All Saints church

All Saints church – as seen from near the counter of the café which the church now also houses

the ruins of the old chapter house, where sometimes free recitals and concerts take place.

On leaving Cathedral Close the Discover Herefordshire Centre is on the corner of Broad Street and King Street. Walk down Gwynne Street on the left, where there is a plaque to commemorate actress Nell Gwynne and her time in Hereford. This leads to one of the few developments allowed on the river in recent decades, The Left Bank, unfortunately recently closed. From here cross the Old Wye Bridge (1490) and cut left by the Saracen's Head public house to walk alongside the river into the **Bishop's Meadows**, a long-standing recreational area where residents and visitors picnic and play. The tree-lined walkway (shared with cyclists) leads to the Victoria Bridge, suspended across the river in 1898.

Cross over and cut left into the **Castle Green**, a place known to residents of the city but often missed by visitors. This area represents a relatively untouched corner of Hereford, which is ironic given that you

stand amid the remnants of a castle built for the pugnacious Earl of Hereford, William fitz Osbern, on a previous Saxon site. The castle was substantial and witnessed a fair amount of bloodshed in the ebb and flow of localised warfare. It seems to have been more or less dismantled in the mid 17th century and certainly helped the building programme elsewhere in the city. The Nelson Column on the Green is a marvel. This early 19th-century monument was erected by the loyal inland citizenship of Hereford to commemorate the viscount's illustrious career until his demise at the Battle of Trafalgar in 1805. There's also a bowling green. What is it about castle sites that attract bowling greens? The one remaining building of the castle, a stone-built house on the river bank that is now a private residence, was originally the watergate, and then served for a while as a Bridewell (prison). From here you can branch right to the Castle Pool (part of the old moat), by an elegant 19th-century house, The Fosse, and into Castle Street where you turn right by St Ethelbert's Hospital then left into St Ethelbert Street and Cantilupe Street. All of these are in close succession; you end up in one of the least altered parts of Hereford, St Owen's Street.

Turn right if you are need of refreshment. The Barrels is a welcoming pub, legendary amongst Herefordshire's imbibers, and what a brewery tap it is for the Wye Valley Brewery! It is a bohemian sort of place which is busy at most times of the day. Five minutes beyond is the Victory with its unusual wooden galleon bar; it is the Hereford Brewery tap (formerly called Spinning Dog Brewery).

Between the two lies the only excavated part of **Saxon town defences** on view in the UK. To find it, go through the brick archway of St Owen's Court (just by the traffic lights), walk up to the remains of the medieval town walls just ahead, and then turn right along the path in front of them. Whilst the Saxon stone wall is original, and part of the ditch has been cleared out, the wooden palisade on the top of the wall is fairly obviously a reconstruction to show how the whole structure would have appeared. An interpretation panel is nearby.

Otherwise, if not taking a pit stop, go left into this very Georgian street to walk back towards High Town via St Peter's Square where the terracotta Town Hall (with a marvellous interior so it is worth having a peep) stands on the left and the classical stone Shire Hall, with its impressive Doric columns, is to the right. In addition, the **church of St Peter** lies ahead. The superb awnings by the church were once used as bus stops. That's how bus shelters should be. Return to the Old House in High Town and from here you can turn right to retrace your steps to the railway station.

Other attractions

Blackfriars Monastery and the **Coningsby Almshouses** lie along Widemarsh Street, about a quarter of mile beyond the ring road, and are well worth the stroll. The black friars, or Dominicans, came to Hereford in the early 13th century and after a dispute with the cathedral's clergy were finally given a site to the north of the city walls in the early 14th century. Founded before 1246 and dissolved 1538, in 1352, the community consisted of a prior and eleven brethren. At the Dissolution in 1538 the numbers had reduced by a third. The surviving buildings are from the western range and a rare style of preaching cross – so rare that it is the only one of its type left in the country. To the south, north and east were enclosed gardens. Parts of the adjoining Coningsby Hospital and Museum date from the 13th century, the almshouses themselves having been founded by Sir Thomas Coningsby of Hampton Court, near Leominster, in 1614.

The Museum is open for a guided tour all year Wednesday and Saturday 11am – 3pm, but you need to book advance: 01432 274903 (group tours) or 07807 564520 (casual visits), or email: JWallin07@aol.com.

The **Cider Museum** is a little way out of the centre. It is located near to Sainsbury's on the site of the old Bulmer cider works (somewhere between Number One and Two sheds) on Ryelands Street. Percy Bulmer was the first in a long line of the Bulmer family to bring cider to a wider market in the 19th and 20th centuries The museum charts not only the production process but the major marketing successes which led to the company being swallowed up by the global giant, Heineken NV, a company interested in merchandising mass-produced products across the world. The museum, however, also champions the revival of traditional cider as produced by a small but increasing number of craft cidermakers located across Herefordshire. The climax of the year is the cidermaking weekend at the museum in October.

Hereford's main **museum** is situated at the Library and Museum in Broad Street and could be visited after looking at the cathedral. The way up to the museum is via steps, just before the suitably old-fashioned gothic entrance to the public library, dating from 1874. There is a mosaic on the

The entrance to the library, museum and art gallery

wall on the stairwell from the Roman fort of Kenchester, a tremendous archaeological find in the county. There are a wide range of displays in the museum extending from geology to folklore and there are plenty of hands-on educational items of interest for children. The museum also houses an art gallery with displays often featuring local artists.

HEREFORD FESTIVALS

The most endearing and for that matter enduring of them all is the Three Choirs Festival, an annual event since the 18th century, held on a rotating basis between three cathedral cities (Gloucester and Worcester being the other two). There are great choral works in the cathedral as well as other musical events throughout the city. The festival is held in early August. Two other events are the Cider Festival at the Cider Museum and the Flavours of Herefordshire Food Festival held at the Racecourse. Both happen in October of each year. In the county there are a range of events including a Walking Festival in late June, a Sustainable Herefordshire Week called h.Energy held in October and h.Art, when a wide range of Herefordshire artists open to the public in September each year. In addition there is the Hereford Photography Festival which has now been running for 10 years and brings the work of international photographers to display in a variety of sites, from the cathedral to galleries to public arenas around the city. For details check www.photofest.org.

WALKING

Hereford lies on the **Wye Valley Walk**. If you'd like a taster walk then there's an opportunity to catch the 453 bus to Mordiford (from the County Bus Station or St Peter's Square) and follow the walk back into town by way of the hamlet of Hampton Bishop, an easy 5-6 mile walk. There are also local circular walks from Hereford to **Breinton** to see the old camp earthworks and St Michael's church at Breinton Springs. The

path runs along the riverside to the west of the city but can get very muddy in the winter season. Otherwise, pathways out of town are not that attractive as any walk involves trudging through areas of modern housing.

The real benefit of using Hereford as a centre for walking is that it is a major transport hub and you can catch buses to many different villages across the county which offer a diversity of walking environments, for example, to the Woolhope Dome or Weobley, for the Black and White Villages.

CYCLING

Cycling around Hereford is possible if you know the back roads that link up the traffic-free paths. The principal route to the south side of the river is the **Great Western Way** which can be accessed from Whitecross Road. There are also good routes across the Bishop's Meadow to Putson and into the countryside. Unfortunately, the network is currently too disjointed to make sense for the visitor but if you have your bike and want to know how to escape into the near countryside then there's a useful map of facilities at www.herefordshire.gov. uk/community_and_living/25712.asp.

There is an exciting proposal in the pipeline to develop a greenway from the centre of Hereford to Rotherwas industrial estate, in the south of the city, which will allow access to a network of quieter lanes to the lovely hamlets of Ballingham, Carey and Hoarwithy. That will be a real boon for the visitor when it happens. If you are thinking about cycling in the county then pick up the Cycling in Herefordshire booklet (small charge made); it highlights six different cycle routes in the county.

REFRESHMENTS

Hereford has a wide range of cafés and pubs; here are some favourites:
Cafés and Restaurants
Café Ascari, West Street: one of Hereford's longest standing cafés which stays open early evening.

Café at All Saints, Eign Gate: a fascinating café in All Saints church and offering good food and plenty of vegetarian choices to boot.

Flying Monkeys, Aubrey Street: café which focuses on vegetarian cooking.

Green café, St Owen's Street: pleasant café and restaurant but not always open in the evening. Offers good food some of which is organic and local wherever possible.

Nutters, Capuchin Yard, off Church Street: a well respected wholefood coffee shop and licensed café in a lovely setting.

The Stewing Pot, Church Street: restaurant serving great food, sourced locally and with a policy re sustainable fish too.

Pubs

Two pubs serving local beverages nearest to the centre are: **The Barrels**, St Owen Street: This used to be the Lamb Hotel until it became the brewery tap for the Wye Valley Brewery over three decades ago. It has since then provided the citizens of Hereford with a genial, lively community pub which welcomes young and old alike to sample the full range of Wye Valley Beers; and **The Victory,** St Owen Street: Brewery tap for the Hereford Brewery. Open all day.

Try also the **Merton Hotel**, Commercial Road and **The Lichfield Vaults** in Church Lane, as well as **The Volunteer** in Harold Street. The latter is slightly away from the centre (to the east) but has a range of real ales and does a good variety of food at lunchtimes with lots to offer vegetarians. It has a pleasant, local, atmosphere.

Local Produce

Fodder Wholefoods, Church Lane: good all round organic food specialist which also sells local produce.

Hereford Deli, The Mews, off St Owen Street: has many locally sourced products.

Mousetrap, Church Lane: cheese purveyor par excellence including their own from Monkland Dairy cheese.

EXTRAS

Farmers' Market, High Town: 1st Saturday and 3rd Thursday in the month.

Rail For Herefordshire: a pressure group campaigning for better public transport in the county meet on a monthly basis at All Saints church and welcome visitors: see www.railforherefordshire.org.

The Courtyard Centre for the Arts, Edgar Street: a venue for live events and films with a lively café bar for morning coffee, lunch or pre-theatre supper.

PUBLIC TRANSPORT

Trains

Hereford is served, daily and directly by trains from Cardiff, Manchester, Shrewsbury, London and the Midlands as well as trains from north Wales.

Buses

Hereford city is very well served by buses. There are also direct buses on weekdays (and for some on Sundays – marked +) to the following towns:

Abergavenny	Ledbury+
Brecon+	Leominster+
Bromyard+	Llandrindod Wells
Hay-on-Wye+	Ludlow+
Kington	Ross-on-Wye+

There are two main points for country buses:

Hereford Railway Station
Hereford Country Bus Station
Neither will pick up an award for being the most attractive bus interchanges but these are the best places to be sure to catch your bus. The information provision at bus stops is good.

As well as these, there are three other places where buses can be boarded:
Broad Street for buses to the south of Herefordshire and to south Wales
City Bus Station (Tesco) is where most city buses depart
Shire Hall for buses to the east and north of Hereford.

EXCURSIONS FROM HEREFORD

BLACK AND WHITE VILLAGES

The Black and White villages are, as the name suggests, places where there are many half-timbered buildings on show. There are, of course, many half-timbered buildings across the Marches but they are especially numerous in the western reaches of Herefordshire, notably between the market towns of Kington and Leominster and south towards the river Wye. 'Black and White' buildings have been built using oak frames with panels of mud, plaster lime and woven sticks. The effect is very distinctive especially where there are clusters of houses built in this manner. The colours refer to the timbers, tarred black, and panels of wattle and daub or lime plaster painted white. Whilst this style of architecture is associated with the 15th to 17th centuries some of the older cruck houses, using a simple whalebone structure, date from even earlier. There are also newer houses built in a similar manner. For example, there is now a return to the use of oak timbers in modern houses. These are left to weather naturally rather than adopting the Victorian fashion of coating them in tar.

The villages were promoted to good effect in the late 1980s with the advent of a Black and White Villages Trail, an idea dreamed up by David Gorvett, who lived in Eardisley at the time. He also brought together villagers to offer Country Village Weekends, a short break package with a difference; people were invited to stay in villagers' homes and to join in with community activities for a couple of days. The breaks no longer exist but the villages still invite visitors to enjoy this pocket of gentle borderland countryside and heritage.

The ride to the villages

The ride out to the villages from Hereford is by way of the undulating landscape of the Wye valley. There are two principal bus routes to two of the finest Black and White villages. The bus directly to Eardisley (Bus 446) passes through **Kenchester**, famous for its Roman town known as *Magnis*, although the scant earthworks are not open to the public. It then continues by way of Byford, where the orchard blossom is a joy to be seen in April and May. The bus diverts into the village of Staunton-on-Wye and then through Letton to Eardisley; some journeys extend to the nearby village of Almeley.

The bus to Weobley (Bus 461 which runs through to Kington and Llandrindod Wells) does not call at Eardisley, but makes its way to **Credenhill** where there's an extensive Iron Age earthwork on the wooded crown above the village, currently managed by the Woodland Trust. It then continues to Moorhampton, offering great views across the Black Mountains as it runs through orchards beneath the wooded slopes of Foxley. On the way it diverts through the pretty village of **Mansel Lacy** with its Norman church and nearby Mansel Lacy House entered by a restored half-timbered gatehouse.

However, for those willing to plan ahead it is feasible to combine a visit to both villages using the one and only morning bus (Bus 462) that diverts to Eardisley. There's a return journey early afternoon from Eardisley to Weobley. It is also possible to travel on from Weobley to Kington and then onwards to Pembridge, Eardisland and Leominster (495-7) if you want to make a circular trip. The possible options are outlined in the *Black and White villages by bus* leaflet.

WEOBLEY

To the good residents of Weobley (pronounced webb-ly), the buildings that line the streets of this ancient borough are not necessarily remarkable. It is their home village. But to the visitor, Weobley has to be one of the finest villages in the land. It even has a wooden bus shelter to die for; functional perspex stuff is not good enough for Weobley. The bus drops you in the very centre of the village, Broad Street, where there are many superb examples of half-timbered buildings that give the place its reputation as being the quintessential English half-timbered village.

Weobley has a traditional interest in folklore, as chronicled in a classic work by past resident Ella Mary Leather in 1912. It is also a place that attracts artists; there's an annual arts festival and trail. Some of these themes are relayed in a small **museum** at the old police station on Back Lane. There are displays, for example, featuring the craft of half-timbered buildings. In addition, there are tea shops nearby if you want to rest awhile. The legacy of its manufacturing past is barely noticeable but Weobley was into tanning, and making gloves, nails and above all else beer. These trades were lost in the 19th century but there has been a revival of brewing in the recent past when Wilds Brewery came to the village in the first decade of the 21st century (now closed). Weobley is still known for its organic dairy products (such as those supplied by the Dairy House).

Walking around the village

Walk ahead to a corner where the Red Lion Inn illustrates the fine workmanship of Weobley builders of old. The lower floor is of sandstone whilst the upper floor is half-timbered and with a fine jetty, an overhanging piece which offered early incumbents more interior room. There's even a plaster red lion, from a later date, attached to the building that adds to the appeal. To the rear of the Red Lion is a good example of a cruck structure relating to an earlier building.

From here, there's a short walk to the **church of St Peter and St Paul** along Church Road. The church is a landmark for miles around as it has the second tallest spire in Herefordshire (only Hereford Cathedral tower is taller). The church enjoyed a major benefactor in the form of the de Lacy family and there are several fine Norman features to admire, including the south doorway, although much of the church is Perpendicular in style. There are also several monuments to wealthy notables from the past, including Sir William Devereux, the Marbury family and Colonel Birch, a staunch Parliamentarian during the Civil War who was responsible for the third and final capture of Hereford for the Parliamentary cause. In due course

Looking down to the Red Lion and the church in Weobley

162

he supported the return of the monarchy and King Charles II, and subsequently the handing of the Crown to William of Orange at the expense of James II. These monuments provide insights to the hierarchical layering of society at Weobley over time.

Weobley's importance in years gone by is evidenced by the fact that it used to elect two Members of Parliament despite its small population. By the mid 18th century the candidates were mainly the absentee lords of the manor, the Thynne family who resided at Longleat, or their adherents. This was achieved by drafting in loyal tenants to live in village houses which otherwise lay empty during the run up to an election so as to swell voting support on an election day. This age old practice, referred to as 'the pocket borough', ceased with the 1832 Reform Act.

Retrace your steps up Portland Street, i.e. the other side to Broad Street. The central strip between the two, now a communal rose-garden, was at one time a row of half-timbered houses; they suffered

The start of the path that leads to Weobley's castle site

A buzzard soars around Weobley's church tower

the brunt of a major fire in 1943 and were demolished *en bloc*. The appropriate black-and-white sculpture was made by local sculptor Walenty Pytel. Intermingled with the half-timbered dwellings are cottages and fine Georgian houses which seem to blend in so well with the earlier buildings. On reaching the top of the street go left into High Street.

On the right, next to a red telephone kiosk, is an access gate to a public footpath that leads through **Weobley Castle**. The name Weobley is thought to be derived in part from a 6th-century Saxon lord who almost certainly built some form of basic fortress on the site of Weobley Castle. The earthworks that remain mark the Norman de Lacy fortification of the 12th century, which suffered a battering in the struggles between King Stephen and the Empress Matilda for the crown. Stephen won possession of the castle and also retained his title following the struggle. Needless to say, the castle was allowed to become ruinous. Further along High Street into

Hereford Street is **The Throne**, a Grade II listed dwelling, named as such after a stay there by the peripatetic King Charles I in 1645 when it was a coaching inn. There's also the old Grammar School at this end of the village, a Jacobean building of some standing.

Once back at the telephone kiosk, you can undertake a short walk out to **The Ley**, a magnificent timber-framed house built around 1590 on an H plan. Turn left on the road by the kiosk and walk down past the Salutation Inn, to turn left again at the next junction. Up the rise, turn right onto a lane and this will lead you to The Ley. You can return to Weobley across the fields by taking the path waymarked from by the side of the pond in front of the house.

EARDISLEY

Eardisley is a linear settlement on the main road from Hereford through to Kington and is a little dustier than Weobley thanks to the passing traffic. Throughout the village there are half-timbered properties from different ages which are very appealing to the eye. The central point is **Tram Square** and there are two inns to celebrate this, The Tram Inn and The New Strand. The latter is also a café and bookshop. The old horse-drawn tramway from Brecon, dating from 1818, terminated nearby and horses were stabled here; there's a piece of track to commemorate the fact. This early tramway was superseded by the railway link between Eardisley and Titley Junction railway, and there are fine railway station buildings remaining in the villages of Almeley and Lyonshall. The old Eardisley station buildings were removed in the 1960s to be rebuilt as the terminus of the Llanfair and Welshpool railway at Welshpool.

Walking around the village

One of the oldest buildings in the village is the **Cruck House** (private dwelling) situated on the road to Woodseaves that peels off to the left by the Tram Inn, and this is the way to the **Great Oak**, probably

One of the many reasons why the Black and White trail is so named

900 years old and the single remnant of an ancient forest. It is about a 20-minute walk along the back lane. However, you may choose to head down the main street to the **church of St Mary Magdalene**, principally dating from the 12th century and illustrating Romanesque architecture to good effect. Of note is the font dating from the mid 12th century attributed to the Herefordshire School of Sculpture. The ornate depiction on the font is of the Harrowing of Hell where a sinner, wrapped in knots, is saved from the Devil, represented in this case as a large lion. The two knights depicted fighting might well refer to benefactor Ralph de Baskerville, who killed his father-in-law in a dispute over land.

Near to the church are the earthworks of **Eardisley Castle**, once home to a branch of the Baskerville family, ransacked by the Welsh in the late 13th century and finally destroyed in the English Civil War. The site is now occupied by a farmhouse. Also near to the church is Eardisley's **community orchard**, an ideal place for a picnic with a walk between old fruit trees. There is also an option to travel on to the village of Almeley by bus and walk back into Eardisley via New House Farm, an organic farm which supplies the milk for September Dairy icecream. Check out the leaflet *Black and White Villages by bus* for details.

WALKING

The main walking route between Weobley and Eardisley is the **Black and White Walking Trail**, a distance of approximately 10 miles. The route is not waymarked but is written up in a walkers' guide (see below). There are several local walks around both Eardisley and Weobley as well as the linear walk from Almeley to Eardisley included in the *Black and White Trail by Bus*. The **Herefordshire Trail** passes through Eardisley and there's a 7 mile walk through to Kington where a regular bus returns to Weobley and Hereford.

CYCLING

The lanes around the Black and White villages are attractive to cyclists for they are quiet. It is possible to cycle via Almeley and Broxwood through to Pembridge and return via Weobley, some 20 miles and ideal for a day's cycling. A network of routes and additional ideas for cycling tours between The Black and White Villages is outlined in the *Cycling for Pleasure Pack* (see Cycling section in the Introduction for details).

REFRESHMENT

Eardisley

Cafés
Cottage Shop Café: friendly café offering homemade food.

Pubs
The New Strand: pub cum café/restaurant which also houses a bookshop.
Tram Inn: old fashioned pub in half-timbered building which sources local food for its menu.

Weobley

Cafés
Old Forge Tea Rooms, Back Lane: homemade food.
The Gables Tea Room, Broad Street: traditional tea rooms in half-timbered building.

Pubs
Salutation Inn: sources local beers and uses local ingredients wherever feasible.

Restaurant
Jules, Portland street: a wide menu using many local ingredients and with several vegetarian options, popular with locals.

Local Produce
Green Bean Deli, Portland Street: offers local and some organic produce.

EXTRAS

Black and White villages by bus leaflet is available at www.simonholtmarketing.com

---

PUBLIC TRANSPORT

Buses
Weobley is served by bus service from Hereford. 461 and 462. Monday – Saturday. Travel time: 40 minutes. Operator: Sargeants Bros.

Eardisley is served by bus 462 via Weobley. Monday – Saturday. Travel duration is 57 minutes. However, there is only one 462 bus each way (10am outward and a return at 1pm) allowing two hours in Eardisley with a stop off at Weobley on the route back into town. Operator: Sargeants Bros.

Alternatively use bus 446. Monday – Saturday. Four buses per day only. Travel time: 46 minutes. Operator: Yeomans Canyon Travel.

LEDBURY

Ride to Ledbury

There's a regular daily bus and train service between Hereford and Ledbury so it is an easy place to get to by public transport. The train rattles along through Herefordshire's green and pleasant land and it takes about 15-20 minutes. By bus travel time is just over 30 minutes. The run, in either case, offers good views across the Frome Valley to the wooded slopes of the Woolhope Dome. Ever present are the magnificent Malvern Hills, a backbone of pre Cambrian rocks that forms the boundary between the rolling hills of Herefordshire and the shallow Severn Plain.

This part of Herefordshire is known as hop country; here you'll see the last vestiges of a farming sector that once attracted thousands of migrant workers each autumn, brought in to harvest the hops. The crop was dried to use in brewing or medicinal products. Whilst the cultivation of the hop has declined dramatically, it has not been entirely lost. In fact, there has been something of a small scale revival as the Wye Valley Brewery, based somewhat ironically in the old Symond's Cidery at Stoke Lacy, procures its supply mainly from local farmers. It buys in Fuggles from Weston Beggard and Goldings from Ashperton, all of which can be spotted on the bus. You will see the poles and tall wires that are features of the hop fields otherwise known as hop yards. In the summer, these are festooned with hop bines reaching out for the sky.

En route you should also see the old oast houses, at one time an integral part of the hop farm. These were built to dry the freshly hand-picked hops using a charcoal fired kiln. Most are of red brick and are a rectangular shape but some are white-washed and round. They are noticeable, even those converted into dwellings, as they have a steep pitched roof with a cowl or cap on top used to vent the kiln in times past.

One of many converted oast houses in the countryside around Ledbury

LEDBURY

Ledbury is one of the loveliest of the market towns of Herefordshire, with a rich Georgian heritage almost matched by exceptional half-timbered dwellings throughout the central area. The floral street displays, brightly decorated shop windows and interpretation plaques on some buildings make it the sort of place where it is easy to linger. The Old Market House is a pivotal point for exploration of the town and the stroll to Ledbury's impressive church along a medieval street, whilst featured in every brochure, is as pleasant a picture as the publicity portrays. This is a town of literature, poets and philanthropy and is not to be missed on your travels.

Walking around town

Ledbury railway station is on the edge of town; it is situated snug between a magnificent viaduct built between 1859 and 1861 and a tunnel beneath Bradlow Hill. There's a 10-minute walk along Homend into town but this is sufficiently pleasurable. It was

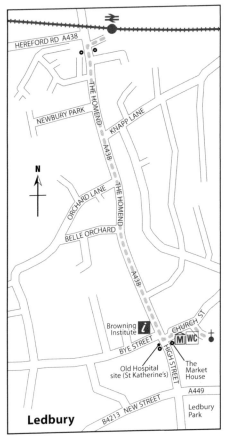

Ledbury

(Map labels: HEREFORD RD A438, THE HOMEND, NEWBURY PARK, KNAPP LANE, A438, N, ORCHARD LANE, THE HOMEND, BELLE ORCHARD, A438, Browning Institute, BYE STREET, CHURCH ST, HIGH STREET, M, WC, Old Hospital site (St Katherine's), The Market House, A449, NEW STREET, B4213, Ledbury Park)

herringbone timbers and white plaster infill are supported by sturdy wooden pillars between which there are stalls on market days. The building dates from the 17th century and this has been the meeting place for farmers seeking to buy and sell their animals for centuries. It is also one of the major bus stops in town, the other being across the road by the **St Katharine's Hospital almshouses**. These superb houses are on the site of a medieval hospital, sponsored by the Bishop of Hereford in 1232. It was built to care for the infirm and pilgrims seeking shelter. The site includes the remains of a master's house dating from a later century and a barn, as well as the remodelled 19th-century almshouses.

Across the road you'll also see the **Barrett Browning Memorial Institute** with its clocktower standing above all else around. This was dedicated to the poet Elizabeth Barrett Browning, who spent part of her early life near Ledbury. Some of her poems included references to the countryside where she spent her childhood. Her husband was the outstanding 19th-century poet, Robert Browning; they spent most of their life together in Italy until her untimely death in 1861. The building was opened in 1896 by Henry Rider Haggard, author of books such as *King Solomon's Mines*. It was dedicated as a public library in 1938 and on that occasion, it was John Masefield, son of Ledbury, who officiated over the opening. He was, by then, the Poet Laureate.

There are good views along High Street from this point, across to the Feathers Hotel, an old coaching inn with an elegant half-timbered frontage. From here you can see another important looking half-timbered building known as **Ledbury Park**. It stands majestically on the corner of Southend and Worcester Road, built for the Biddulph family in the late 16th and early 17th centuries and now a little isolated by the busy road junction.

one of the old medieval routes leading to a crossroads in the town, where the Worcester Road meets the High Street. These crossroads were strategic in the world of commerce. Ledbury also owes its existence to ecclesiastical patronage, especially the good work of the Bishop of Hereford, Richard de Cappella, in the early 13th century, which encouraged the growth of the settlement around the church. For the most part it is the Georgian architecture that entices you as you make your way to the Market House.

The **Market House** is a two-storey half-timbered building which has an immediate impact on passing visitors. The braced

Ledbury's Market House

The roofs of the Barrett Browning Institute – a solid and much loved landmark in the town but the architectural historian, Nikolaus Pevsner dismissed it as being an awful piece of architecture

The Feathers in Ledbury's High Street

Main attraction

From the Market House you might like to walk along **Church Lane**, a classic Tudor passageway, where the buildings over-hang the tiny cobbled thoroughfare to **St Michael's church**. On the left is a **Heritage Centre**, at one time the Grammar School, and now housing displays on local history and half-timbered dwellings. Just up from there is the Prince of Wales public house which also dates from the 16th century (and is a great pub to boot).

The church is in an imposing position above town and is the main attraction (along with the lane leading to it). The earliest parts of the building date from Saxon times but the Norman design is imprinted on both the exterior and interior of this fine parish church, although it has been much altered in later centuries. The 13th-century detached belltower is a marvel in its own right, with a carillon chiming a hymn every three hours during the day. The spire was added several centuries later. The church interior contains many preserved monuments to local notables, some dating from the medieval period, making this one of the finest collections in the Marches. There is a 12th-century font and many stained glass windows lighten the church considerably. The churchyard and cross paths make this a pleasant corner of town for contemplation or simply to rest awhile.

Much Marcle and the Big Apple

A few miles to the south and west of Ledbury is Big Apple Country. The intimacy of the apple orchard rarely fails to appeal, regardless of the season. There's no better place to take a closer look at the defining features of the orchard landscape than in the parishes of Much Marcle and Putley near to Ledbury. Row after row of apple trees, orchard upon orchard, hedgerows and leafy lanes make this place worthy of the name. The greatest pleasure is derived from the older orchards where standard trees, varieties such as Dabinett and Redstreak, stand tall. Since the 1930s farmers have tended, however, to intro-duce smaller trees of a bush variety that are far easier to handle, but these are pleasant to look at too. In the autumn, the fruit is shaken off the tree and driven down the road by the tractor load to cider and perry makers just around the corner, the likes of Dragon Orchards, Gregg's Pit, Lyne Down and Westons. Some farmers also grow dessert varieties for the making of pies, jams and juices alongside other mixed farming activities. At Pixley Court, for example, the emphasis is on berries grown in accord with nature rather the harshness of the herbicide.

It is a patchwork which encourages exploration on foot or by cycling down the lanes that pass by craft cider and juice producers that are well off the beaten track. All this lies within a few square miles to the east of the Woolhope Dome and south-west of Ledbury.

The Big Apple is also about a commitment to community life and conservation of the landscape. That is why, twice a year, the communities and commercial growers of the area get together to show off their orchards and to offer village teas or tastings for the visitor. Add to this a few walks, guided cycle trips and talks and you have the kernel of the event. These two weekend events are Blossomtime (early May) and Harvestime (early October), both well worth putting in the diary.

There's no link, by the way, with the other Big Apple, that well-known place across the water. It is just a matter of two Big Apples happening in a parallel universe. The origin of the other Big Apple is strikingly less obvious as there are no apple trees involved. US pundits have rummaged about among some obscure sources and it seems that the phrase relates either to race horses and prize monies, or to jazz venues in earlier decades. It has also been suggested that the name possibly relates to the old root and tree analogy referring to the wealth of the place. Not entirely convincing stuff but by the 1970s, the city fathers of New York had bitten the bullet and rolled out the brand big time. There's none of that stuff here; the Big Apple celebrates small time rural heritage.

Not that all is rosy in this part of the world. Nearer to Ledbury, the large scale use of polytunnels to assist the growth of soft fruit has caused a stir amongst local residents. Furthermore, the fruit processing plants near to Ledbury are now in the hands of a multinational giant. They have that heavy industrial look and sit uncomfortably with their beautiful surroundings.

Much Marcle

To enjoy this area you'll need to take the bus to Much Marcle. This can be done from either Ledbury or Ross-on-Wye

The shop at Weston's Cider at Much Marcle

but on Mondays to Saturdays only. The principal bus stop in the village is on the main road by the Walwyn Arms opposite the vintage garage and shop. The main attraction is **Weston's Cider**, producer of traditional cider and perry in accordance with traditional recipes and not given over completely to cider fizz. The visitor centre and plant is located at the Bounds, next to a 17th-century sandstone farmhouse, and tours of the cidery are available (charge made). There's also a small breeds farm and shire horses on the site so it is good for a family outing too. It is 10-minute walk from Much Marcle Garage or the Wallwyn Arms.

From the centre of Much Marcle it is also possible to visit the historic manor house known as **Hellens** (open Wed, Thurs and Sun afternoons, April to Sept); it is also a 10-minute walk from the Walwyn Arms or Much Marcle Garage along a drive lined with perry pear trees. This dwelling dates from the 11th century but is noted for being a Jacobean red brick house with stone mullioned windows. The walled knot garden is magnificent as is the octagonal dovecote dating from the 1640s, which was converted from the original defences. The house passed down to Radcliffe Coke in the 19th century, who was known as the Member of the House for Cider! He re-planted many cider and perry pear trees that are now mature.

The **church** is also worth visiting. Outside is an old yew believed to be 1,500 years old, and it possible to sit on benches erected inside its trunk, whilst inside the church is most noted for three of its tombs: to Blanche Mortimer, the daughter of the Roger Mortimer who was created the first Earl of March; to a yeoman, Walter de Helyon, who is commemorated with a rare painted wooden effigy; and to Sir John Kyrle, who fought in the Civil War, and his wife. The church also has six carvings of a Green Man; and there is much stained glass by Charles Eamer Kempe. Nearby are the motte and bailey remains of **Mortimer's Castle**.

Bromyard

There's another way to travel to and from Ledbury, one which takes in the market town of Bromyard and the Frome Valley. The principal bus 420 to Bromyard leaves Hereford via the Lugg Flats, superb untouched Lammas riverside meadows (hay meadows which can be grazed by stock but only after Lammas Day, 12th August, each year until a new hay crop begins to grow). It then proceeds through undulating countryside to Stoke Lacy, the home of the **Wye Valley Brewery**.

All buses arrive and depart from Pump Street in Bromyard, located just off High Street, with a mix of Georgian and Victorian fronts. The leaflet *Herefordshire Hop Country by Bus* outlines a short walk around the town, and it also a 'Walkers are Welcome' town (see www.bromyard.info). On Mondays to Saturdays it is possible to continue to Ledbury via the Frome Valley where Bishop's Frome is the main spot. **The Hop Pocket**, a craft centre and exhibition focusing on the hop, is located here; there are other shops in the complex too. Then it is a 20-minute ride through to Ledbury.

WALKING

Ledbury is a great base for a walking holiday. Not only does it provide access to endless walks into and along the Malvern Hills, but there are also local walks from Ledbury to Frith Wood and Wellington Heath. The **Herefordshire Trail** follows a route through to Big Apple Country in one direction and north of Ledbury towards Bosbury in the other. Catch the 417 bus (Mondays to Saturdays) to Bosbury for a 6 mile walk back into Ledbury.

Putley is the parish next door to Much Marcle. The best way to see it and to visit the Big Apple Blossomtide event is to catch the 476 bus to Poolend (daily service). Walk by Poolend Farm to a junction where you go right and then rise by Main Wood to a junction at Coldmoor Farm. Here you can join a lovely walk referred to as The Putley Orchards Loop walk (see Extras).

Bosbury church's tower

This offers a great introduction to the area. You can simply retrace your steps back to Poolend afterwards.

There is also a good short walk from Dormington to Tarrington featured in The *Herefordshire Hop County by Bus* leaflet produced by Herefordshire Council. There are also superb walks across the Woolhope Dome, an area rich in geological interest, by following a route along Marcle Ridge and/or through Checkley to Woolhope. These walks, however, require the use of the bus to Woolhope from Hereford (Bus 453, Mondays to Saturdays) if you are planning a day's walk.

CYCLING

There are a number of opportunities for cycling out of Ledbury. One is published in a leaflet *Herefordshire Cider Cycling Routes, Ledbury*, outlining a 20-mile ride to Much Marcle and Putley. There are also enjoyable rides and maps from the Ledbury Area Cycle Forum (www.lacf.org.uk). The main roads are fairly busy in Ledbury but elsewhere it is relatively traffic-free.

REFRESHMENT

Ledbury

Cafés and Restaurants
There's a wide selection so this may well not do justice to all of them:

Black Pepper, High Street: restaurant in 17th-century building which sources food locally.

Ceci Paolo, High Street: mainly dishes from different parts of world but deli sources local products.

Market House Café, Market House: friendly local café using local ingredients.

Mrs Muffins Teashop, Church Lane: great spot with organic/local food sources.

Pubs
Prince of Wales, Church Street: superb Good Beer Guide entry.

Severn Stars, Homend: homemade food using local ingredients wherever possible.

Talbot Hotel, New Street: friendly hotel in Good Beer Guide which is worth a visit.

Local Produce
Four Oaks Fine Foods: deli selling local products.

Handley Organics, Homend: emphasis on local and organic in this great shop.

Llandinabo Farm Shop, Homend: pies and home made sausages are made at this traditional farm shop.

GT Waller: Butchers that makes pies and sausages on the premises.

The Apothecary Shop, Homend: eco and ethical products mainly.

Big Apple Country

Cafés and Restaurants
Scrumpy House Restaurant, Westons Cidery, Much Marcles: quality home cooked food, much of it sourced locally.

Pubs
Butchers Arms, Woolhope: exceptional place using locally sourced food and beverages.

Crown, Woolhope: champion for real ciders and ales plus locally sourced food; lucky to have two great pubs in one village. Landlord produces bio-diesel to generate his own power.

EXTRAS

Big Apple: www.bigapple.org.uk.
Farmers' Market, St Katharines Walk: 4th Thursday in the month.
Tourist Information Centre: Masters House, St Katherine's, Tel (01531) 636147.

PUBLIC TRANSPORT

Trains
There is a daily service from Hereford to Ledbury. Approximately hourly with slightly less frequency on Sundays. Ledbury has a direct link to London and The Midlands. From the railway station it is a 10-minute walk into town.

Buses
Bromyard (Pump Street) is served by a daily bus service from Hereford Country Bus Station. 420. Hourly on Monday – Saturday. Four trips on Sunday. Travel time: approximately 45 minutes. Operators: First Midland Red and DRM.

Ledbury (Market Hall) is served by a daily bus service from Hereford Country Bus Station. 476. Hourly every day in summer; two hourly on Sunday in winter. Travel time: 33 minutes. Operator: DRM

Bromyard (Pump Street) to Ledbury (Market Hall). 672/673. Four buses per day Monday – Friday, only two journeys on Saturday. Travel time: 30 minutes Operator: DRM.

Hereford (Country Bus Station) To Woolhope (Crown) 453. Monday – Saturday. Travel time: 35 minutes. Operator: Yeomans Canyon Travel.

GARWAY AND LOWER MONNOW VALLEY

Ride to Garway
The bus journey from Hereford to Garway is one of the best in the borderlands. It winds its way through the lowlands of the Wye valley to Much Dewchurch and Wormelow before climbing up to the hamlet of Orcop Hill. It then follows a narrow lane to Saddlebow Common, where the views across to Orcop (left) and over to the Black Mountains (right) are superb, even better when there's a moody sky. You then rise through the hamlet of Bagwyllydiart to a remote area known as Garway Hill. It is then about ten minutes further on to Garway Common, and the views simply get better.

GARWAY

The parish of Garway offers a good example of a rural community which is dispersed across a wide area. Most of its dwellings are near to its four commons, two of which are readily accessible. The common opposite the Garway Moon public house stretches over some 23 acres and is used principally for informal recreation. There are seats to while away the time or for picnics, and the green bus shelter is easily spotted at the south-eastern edge of the common. The Garway Moon is one of the major hubs of this community. In the 1880s, the landlord at that time decided to call it the Garway Inn, hence the name on the outer wall. However, it soon reverted to the Moon and has remained so ever since.

Garway Hill Common is very different. It has a remote feel about it, mainly because it is windswept most of the time and wild on occasion. It amounts to over 200 acres of common land rising to 1,204 feet. Prehistoric sites have been discovered in this area but recent interest has been mainly in its role as a common during medieval times. Like most commons this was marginal land. Despite the 'common' name, these are private lands where commoners have rights to graze the poor quality, acidic grasslands. In earlier times there would have been more extensive woodland on the common, as commoners were also were entitled to collect wood and furze; wood was cut hereabouts for ship-building and charcoal burning. There was also small-scale clog-making in the area until the early 1900s. The four commons in Garway technically fall within the jurisdiction of the Lord of the Manor and that is how it is to this day. In reality, the Parish Council is the dutiful custodian. There are well used footpaths onto the common from the settlement at Garway Hill (through which the 412 bus passes). Not far from here is the Woodland Trust site known as The Jockies, which has a number of paths threading through it.

Main Attraction

The main attraction, other than the hauntingly beautiful scenery, is **Garway church**. Alight from the bus at the first junction at the edge of Garway village. There's no particular landmark here; it is simply a junction, signposted left to Monmouth and right to Pontrilas. From here, it is little more than five minutes' walk to the church. Once off the bus, go right in the direction of Pontrilas, but as you descend towards a dwelling, cut left through a kissing gate into a field. The church stands in the foreground and the Monnow valley is beyond; this is a moment to savour the lie of the land. Head slightly right across the field and then enter the graveyard by way of another kissing gate. From this vantage point you'll catch sight of an ancient dovecote (private property) that has 666 nesting holes.

The 12th-century church, with its detached tower, is very unusual. It was founded by the Knights Templar in the 1180s and following their demise in the 14th century, the church was passed to Knights of St John until the Dissolution in 1540. The original quest of both organisations (Knights Templar and St John) was to secure safe passage for pilgrims to the Holy Land. In reality it became a prolonged funding exercise to fuel a series of military campaigns. On the part of the Knights Templar this was resourced by a support network (of monastic-style groups) spread across Europe. In this way a pervasive

Garway church with its once detached tower now connected to the nave

Some of the many carvings made on the outside walls of the church

financial and social structure emerged, one which enjoyed considerable privilege and held allegiance only to the Papacy. Garway church was the home of one such grouping in the network; it was a preceptory, where valuable items were held on behalf of wealthy lords abroad, fighting the Christian cause in the Holy Land. Not everyone would return to reclaim their wealth.

It is still possible to discern the foundations of part of the circular nave of the Templar church on the ground immediately to the north of the church. Most visitors also notice markings on the outer walls, including the Cross of Lorraine, a swastika, the Lamb of God and a winged gryphon. According to the architectural historian Nikolaus Pevsner, these are not the work of medieval craftsmen but were later additions perhaps added when the church was being restored in the 17th or 18th centuries. In more recent times, the church has been associated with the book *The Da Vinci Code* and featured in an episode of the TV series 'Bonekickers'. This created a stir of interest among aficionados and visitor numbers have crept up since. The interior has a chancel arch noted for its Saracenic look, which also contains a capital with a green man carving. After your visit, you may simply wish to proceed to Garway Common. That is easy enough; you retrace your steps back to the road, go right and walk ahead until you reach the Garway Moon public house. If you have a map with you, there's also a footpath via The Gwyn which is clear on the ground. Either way, it is a 30-minute walk.

THE LOWER MONNOW VALLEY

However, there's also an opportunity to explore the Monnow valley from Garway. The Monnow, described by one early guide book writer as the merriest of rivers in the Marches, rises in the Black Mountains near Craswall. It flows for about 40 miles in a south-easterly direction to its confluence with the river Wye in Monmouth, through borderland country that is hard to beat. The river has always had a reputation among fly fishers for its brown trout. There have been renewed efforts in the past decade to improve habitats along the Monnow by removing tree shade, reducing damage to the river banks by stock and cutting back the dreaded, invasive Himalayan Balsam. This has been to good effect: wildlife is coming back including otters, kingfishers and sandmartins. There are also improved spawning grounds for trout and grayling.

Admittedly, the Monnow valley is not easy to explore by bus as there is no service at all between Monmouth and Llangua (near Pontrilas), some 17-18 miles, other than a pre-book community facility designed for residents. Given this poor state of affairs, it is interesting to note that in the 1860s there was a proposal to run a railway right through the valley. The project actually got off the ground and a tunnel entrance in Monmouth was built. The railway entrepreneur, Thomas Savin, then promptly declared his company to be bankrupt and no further work took place. Market day buses took hold some 50-60 years later but have not survived into the 21st century.

However, the village of **Skenfrith** can be accessed from Garway on foot; it is a 30 minute walk from Garway church. Go to the main church gateway and walk ahead along the drive to the road. Turn left and descend for over a mile into the valley bottom to the B4521 in Skenfrith. Turn right, cross the bridge and pass by the Bell, at one time a coaching inn, and now a hotel. Keep ahead for the village. **Skenfrith Castle** was originally a motte and bailey castle with a wooden palisade built to guard a fording point on this early trading route between England and Wales. The wooden structure was replaced in the 13th century by a stone castle, much of which has survived, including the superb round keep and the five towers on the curtain walls. Adjacent is the **church of St Bridget** with its solid tower topped out with a wooden belfry. Inside the church is a rare cope, an embroidered garment similar to a cape dating from the 15th century; it is now preserved in a glass case.

The village of **Grosmont**, on the other hand, is best accessed from Llangua (reached direct from Hereford on the X4 Bus) rather than Garway (ask for the first stop after the bridge over the river Monnow, a mile south of Pontrilas). You can either follow the lane off to the left

The curtain walls of Skenfrith Castle behind which stands a round keep

to Grosmont or take to the fields on the Monnow Valley Walk which is waymarked. It is a 2 mile walk each way. Grosmont is derived from the Norman French, Le Gros Mont, presumably referring to the brooding mass Graig Syfryddin, a steep hill overlooking the village. Grosmont was, in past times, the main market place in these parts. It was also home to the local manor and possessed its own town hall in later centuries. The **castle**, however, is an indicator of its huge importance. It is one of three in this area. It shares much in common with its counterparts, Skenfrith and White Castle (at Llanvetherine) as the architects of these formidable fortresses shared in the design and build. Grosmont was built under the auspices of the powerful William fitz Osbern and then remodelled, as was Skenfrith, in the early 13th century. The later additions at Grosmont were to make it liveable and the Great Hall and grand internal chimney can still be seen.

The **church of St Nicholas** in Grosmont was built originally to serve the garrison, hence its grand size for a relatively small village. It has many fine medieval features including a large and unusual nave. Grosmont and Skenfrith remain as fairly isolated outposts in the Marches. Perhaps that is why they have, like Garway, such strong community character. Grosmont, for example, takes pride in having its own resident octogenarian poet and numerous artisans around the place. It also has a number of local organisations including a pig-rearing club. There's a post office and superb café in the centre of the village for those needing provisions. But many share the opinion that there's no better place to sample the collective spirit of the place than at the Angel, a 17th-century inn which is one of the liveliest traditional pubs in the Marches.

Kilpeck

Not that many miles away lies the small village of Kilpeck, best accessed by the X4 bus from Hereford to St Devereux (ask for the Kilpeck turn between Didley and Wormbridge). It is an easy walk from this turn of less than a mile to Kilpeck along a road lined with perry pear trees, across

Kilpeck church – notice the line of carved corbels that encircles the building below the eaves

the railway by the old station and then by the lovely **church of St Devereux**, with its late 13th-century nave and well preserved 17th-century monuments of William and Ann Goode. It has an unusual dedication to Saint Dubricius, a Celtic saint of local origins who is supposed to have presided at the crowning of King Arthur. As the road bends and rises you catch a first glimpse of **Kilpeck church**. Go through a kissing gate on the right and then head up the field, the site of a deserted village, to enter the churchyard of one of the borderland's finest churches.

Over the years this out of the way place has enjoyed a constant trickle of visitors searching out the little church of St Mary and St David and you can see why. It is one of the best preserved Romanesque churches in the Marches (probably in England) illustrating the stylised carvings and stone masonry of the Herefordshire School of Romanesque Sculpture (see Extras below for the definitive work on this topic). The church has not been altered much since its creation in the 12th century, which is nothing short of a miracle.

Not only is the church doorway adorned with fine carvings but there is a sophisticated artistry exhibited beneath the church eaves in the shape of 85 corbels. Here, shades of Celtic and Saxon are intermingled with Norman Christianity in many forms, comprising the green man, soldiers, dragons, monster heads, tendrils, foliage and alongside these an occasional touch of lewdness and humour. Many have commented on the Sheela-na-gig, a woman displaying her genitalia for all to see. The dog and rabbit sitting together adds a different touch of humanity to it all. However, the most powerful aspect of the master craftsmen's work has to be the south doorway, with snakes, a green man, figures on the columns and various tendrils and birds. There is just so much going on in this work. It is best for you to make your own interpretation for historians do not have conclusive answers regarding the imagery and allegory wrapped into these carvings.

The south doorway at Kilpeck

The interior of the church is simple and it is this simplicity that draws the eye to the chancel arch figures and the carving of heads in the round apse. The early font is Norman in style but nothing like as elaborate as those at Eardisley or Canon Frome, also attributed to the Herefordshire School. Historians are not certain as to why this is the case. All this exceptional work was funded by Hugh de Kilpeck in 1140, William the Conqueror's forest warden for the area and the son of William fitz Norman. It was probably completed in two or three years. What would the community of Kilpeck have said at this time? They had their own exposition of life and death, sin and goodness writ large in their place of worship and in very centre of their world. Lords and peasantry alike must have been taken by this good fortune.

Adjacent to the churchyard are the scant remains of **Kilpeck Castle** among the scrub and tree cover. It was brought into existence by William fitz Norman in the 11th century and strengthened in the

12th century. However, Kilpeck became a castle of lesser significance in the tensions between the English and Welsh, and was dismantled at the end of the English Civil War on the orders of Parliament. A walk around the village brings you to the Kilpeck Inn, at one time known as the Red Lion and closed for many a year, before its re-birth in 2010.

WALKING

For the walker there's an excellent route, which is not that well known, the **Monnow Valley Walk** (the logo is a heron which is perhaps not a good omen for the fish stock). From Skenfrith it is possible to walk to Monmouth (about 9 miles) or to Llangua (about 8 miles) as tasters. The walk incorporates a diversity of landscapes from riverside sections to alpine style upper meadows and broadleaved woodland.

There is a superb walking trail, the **Three Castles Walk**, between the three Norman outposts of White Castle, Grosmont and Skenfrith. It is 19 miles in length and perhaps it is best to do this in two days with a stay in either Grosmont or Skenfrith (as these have pubs, cafés or shops). The **Herefordshire Trail** passes through Wormelow Tump (Buses 412/416) and offers a lovely walk through to Kilpeck, where you can peel off to St Devereux or walk onward to Pontrilas. If you choose the latter it is the best part of a day's walk. Catch the X4 or 440 bus back into Hereford.

CYCLING

Grosmont is accessed from **National Cycle Route 46** between Hereford and Abergavenny. It is possible to then divert from Grosmont to Skenfrith; the road is lightly trafficked but hilly. NCN 46 also passes through Kilpeck so is a good way to visit this historic village. A cycle ride out of Hereford to Kilpeck and back makes for a lovely day. The back lanes of the Garway Hills see little traffic and the vistas are a fine reward for the keen cyclist but you need stamina for cycling in this part as there are some harsh gradients to encounter.

REFRESHMENT

Cafés
Gentle Jane Tearoom, Grosmont: homemade food with seasonal, local ingredients. Green Dragon Standard (achieved by businesses in stages) recognising sound environmental management practices.

Seal-y-Pant Tea Rooms, Grosmont: organic food served here in lovely setting.

Pubs and inns
The Angel Inn, Grosmont: excellent community pub.

The Bridge Inn, Kentchurch: sources food locally and local beers.

The Garway Moon, Garway Common: good food and ale.

The Kilpeck Inn, Kilpeck: local beers and quality food available.

EXTRAS
Bailey, T. (2000) *The Parish Church of St Mary & St David at Kilpeck*, Five Seasons Press (available from the church and a must if you are to get the best from the visit).

Tapper, Audrey (2009) *Knights Templar and Hospitaller in Herefordshire*, Logaston Press.

Thurlby, Malcolm *The Herefordshire School of Romanesque Sculpture*, Logaston Press.

PUBLIC TRANSPORT

Buses
Garway is served by bus service from Hereford Railway Station. 412. Monday – Saturday. Four buses per day. Travel time is 1 hour. Operator: Stagecoach Wye and Dean.

Kilpeck is a mile walk from St Devereux on the X4 route from Hereford Country Bus Station. Monday – Saturday. Travel time: 20 minutes. Operator: Stagecoach in South Wales.

HAY-ON-WYE (Y GELLI)

The ride to Hay-on-Wye
The bus ride out of Hereford can be a little exasperating as there's a lot of traffic south of the city to Belmont but from there onwards the run is clear. There's a succession of views across to the Black Mountains for most of the route. The bus passes through the large villages of Clehonger and Kingstone (and Madley on Sundays) then rises up across Stockton Hill into a different world, the **Golden Valley**, a place that deserves a visit in my book – see below. Once in the valley the road pretty well runs straight between settlements. Firstly you'll notice the beautiful little church of Vowchurch on the left and then in the next village the tall (fibreglass) spire of St Peter's church at Peterchurch. Once out of Peterchurch there's usually a sprint to Dorstone where the road twists and narrows to the vintage village green and from there onwards the run is through sparsely populated territory to the Welsh border at Cusop on the very edge of Hay-on-Wye.

HAY-ON-WYE

It takes a little time to get to know a place but much longer to know it well. Hay-on-Wye happens to be a good case in point. Every time you visit Hay another part of its rich borderland heritage unfolds. For some it retains the lingering vestiges of an old world in Wales, a nudge to nostalgia as in the phrase 'Kilvert Country', based on a vicar's diary of rural life in the 1870s. Hay was, after all, a principal crossing place of the river Wye (afon Gwy), where drovers cajoled their cattle, geese, sheep and horses through the tightly-knit streets to market. Until the 1960s the farming community still drove ponies and sheep down from the hills on fair days. Hay is literally a border town (the border is the Cusop Brook) but it belongs to Wales for sure, surrounded as it is by those haunting hills. Trekking and canoes, multi-lingual road signs and

rain-washed slate roofs are other tell-tale signs of Welshness.

For some Hay is the town that re-awakened in the 1960s when hippies and hippie look-alikes were attracted to the countryside nearby. In many respects it still holds to bohemian ways; music, street artists, tarot cards, fairs and festivals are integral to Hay. These comings and goings have interfaced well with the old ways although not without some resentment. But during the past few decades Hay has moved on; it has become the world's first book town and attracts thousands of visitors each year.

Main attraction
The re-invention of Hay-on-Wye as **the leading book town** has served as the engine of change. The principal protagonist of the movement was Richard Booth, who came back to his home town to set up a secondhand book empire. He encouraged others to join him in the crusade to put Hay well and truly on the map. By 1977 a new tourism phenomenon had been born; it has since caught on in over 60 destinations across the world. Mr Booth proclaimed himself as King of the independent Kingdom of Hay and his mastery of public relations has managed to keep him, and more to the point Hay-on-Wye, in the limelight ever since. In effect, the commercial lifeblood of the town runs red with the printed word. Four decades on and there are over 30 booksellers established in a variety of buildings around the town with some million or so books to peruse.

For whatever reason, the book world somehow sits easy with the slow pace of the town. Many would now admit that there's a vibrant feel here that somehow beguiles the visitor. It is very much the place to stay over, to buy a book from one of the specialist shops, to slump into an armchair and drift into the pleasure of reading for hour after hour. That is the main attraction of Hay, and this little borderland town by the Wye beneath the foothills of the Black Mountains deserves more than a passing glance.

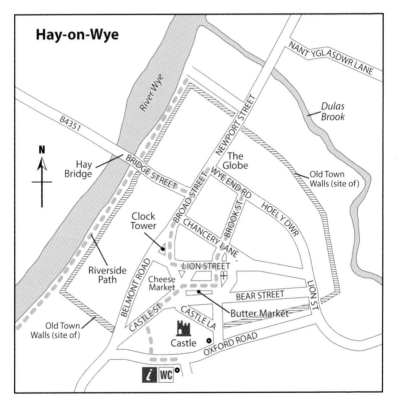

Walking around town

The main bus stops are in Oxford Road. Buses from Hereford arrive by an expansive car park sloping down into delightful countryside. Buses from Brecon arrive on the other side near Bell Bank. A good first move is to call into the tourist information centre (by the car park) to pick up a copy of the leaflet *A walk around Hay*. Follow the route towards **Hay Castle**, which stands back from the opposite side of Oxford Road. Cross the pedestrian crossing and walk ahead down the narrow Back Lane part lined with shops and cafés to Castle Street where you turn right. The castle dates from the early years of the 13th century and is associated with Matilda de Breos. It was subject to a barrage of skirmishes between the Welsh and English throughout the Middle

Ages and Henry III decided to invest in rebuilding it in the 1230s after a damaging attack by Llywelyn ap Iorwerth. It was substantially damaged again and again by Welsh warriors and especially Owain Glyndwr and his men in the first part of the 15th century. The 17th-century Jacobean manor house attached to the old castle has also seen rough times; it has been subject to two major fires but restoration has always followed.

Wander along Castle Street to the Old Butter Market and Cheese Market, both rebuilt in the 19th century and very much a centre point of Hay. The sculpture on the end of the **Cheese Market** is of Henry VII, also known as Henry Tudor. A series of streets radiate out from here and it is best to wander at will to soak in the range of shops, cafés and pubs that radiate out from the open space around the **Butter Market** down to the Clock Tower of 1881. This is where stalls are set out on market day and

other events take place. Intermingled in all this are several bookshops selling every conceivable book under the sun. Probably the largest general collection is at the Hay Cinema on Church Street, but there are specialists too. Nearby, in Brook Street, for example, is the Poetry Bookshop, devoted to poetry only.

From the Clock Tower, continue ahead along Belmont Road / Broad Street to a junction with Bridge Street. Turn left here but before the bridge it is possible to walk down to a riverside cycle and walking path from where you can watch the canoeists go by on the river Wye.

Hay festivals
The town has also become something of a venue for events. The Hay Festival is the major annual literary landmark in the Marches. It began as a small-scale affair in 1988 but has grown to a point where it had to move out of town to a greenfield site. People walk about the site at a snail's pace in the utter pedestrian congestion that occurs between the auditoria, but once inside and listening to

The book town of Hay-on-Wye

a top line speaker, it is a different world. There's always an impressive line up of celebrities, politicians, academics and authors. Critics say it has become too corporate (with *The Telegraph* and Sky currently – 2011 – being the main sponsors) and disconnected from the town. On the other hand, the shuttle buses into town and nearby villages, and the almost permanent walking bus along the Brecon Road suggest otherwise. Listening to the speakers and artistes is the prime reason for attendance; the chatter and debate is best reserved for the fringe events, coffee shops and inns of Hay itself. There are other events in town too including Hay on Fire, Hay Food Festival and How the Light Gets In philosophy festival.

For places of refreshment in Hay see pages 185-186.

The Golden Valley

En route to Hay is the Golden Valley, one of the least spoilt areas of Herefordshire. Sheltered to the north by the wooded Merbach range, it retains an air of tranquillity that seems almost to have been nurtured since the late middle ages. The community has resisted industrial activity despite the arrival of the Golden Valley Railway in the 1880s, built to transport agricultural products to market. The line has long since gone. This broad valley, stretching from Pontrilas in the east to Middlewood in the west, is one of the quietest parts of Herefordshire and well worth the detour by bus or cycle.

It is also a slow travel route to the foothills of the Black Mountains, especially if you'd like to explore the parishes of Craswall and Michaelchurch Escley. This area is very Celtic in nature, typified by the small

---

THE BLACK MOUNTAINS

Hay is the best place to access the Black Mountains, a sombre looking group of ridges and valleys made shadowy by passing clouds. It is high ground with stunning views but requires stamina and proper kit if you are to venture forward into them. There are four options to access the mountains. The easiest is to use the Offa's Dyke Flyer bus (see p.184) for this little bus allows you to sit back and enjoy a panoramic view.

Walking
Offa's Dyke National Trail traverses the Black Mountains and it is possible to walk to Pandy in one day (17-18 miles) if you are into solid day walking. Otherwise, you can drop down into Llanthony or Longtown for an overnight stop if you prefer to take it easier. There is a strenuous climb out of Hay to Hay Bluff and from then onwards you follow a broad spine for most of the way before a couple of miles' descent through pastures into Pandy. The bus stops are near to the Pandy Inn.

Cycling
National Cycle Route 42 follows the road over to Capel-y-ffin and onward to Abergavenny. Like Offa's Dyke National Trail, it affords superb views but requires considerable stamina and experience as the lanes are narrow with high hedges and meeting a convoy of 4x4s can be a pain when you are on two wheels.

On Horseback
There are two routes for horse-riders which encourage exploration of the Black Mountains. The first is the Three Rivers Ride, which can be accessed at Dorstone, in the Golden Valley, through to Brecon. Another ride is the Black Mountains loop. In each case there are several experienced stables to support the venture and some cooperative bed and breakfast outlets catering for horses too – see page 16 for more information.

Looking towards Peterchurch in the Golden Valley

fields, large hedgerows and woodland cover reaching up to the spring line. Sheep farming remains a distinct way of life and there are isolated farms and rubble-built cottages, sometimes whitewashed, which give the area a distinctive feel.

The derivation of the name, Golden Valley, is not as you might expect; it comes from the Welsh word 'dwr' (or Celtic 'dur') which sounds like the French 'd'or', meaning golden. The river Dore is minuscule in relation to the nicely rounded and wide valley. This most probably was carved out by post-glacial melt-water. The fertile soils of the valley have been put to good use through the centuries. At Turnastone Court Farm near Vowchurch some of the ancient meadows have not been ploughed for centuries and their preservation is in the hands of the Countryside Restoration Trust.

The main attraction is walking. Whilst the footpaths are not manicured this is superb walking territory; you'll not meet many others en route. The Herefordshire Trail between Ewyas Harold and Dorstone makes for an ideal introduction to the valley, possibly planning a day walk or several shorter walks between villages, all of which are served by bus. It is also possible to design your own circular walks from the larger settlements of Ewyas Harold, Peterchurch or Dorstone.

The upper reaches of the Escley brook and Monnow valley are great places to be if you'd like to get away from it all and for walking expeditions. It allows an opportunity to call at some of the remotest pubs in Herefordshire, for example, the Bridge at Michaelchurch Escley, or the Bull's Head at Craswall, the Cornewell Arms at Clodock or the Carpenter's Arms at Walterstone. Each has many endearing traditional features. They all retain a character of their own. Camping is possible at the Bull's Head and the Bridge Inn, which makes it feasible to plan a two-day walk from Pandy (X4 bus) to Hay-on-Wye (Buses 39/39A) stopping off overnight en route. On summer Sundays the Offa's Dyke flyer links three of the four pubs and this provides another option for a day walk (see www.slowtraveluk.com.

The village of **Dorstone** is a Norman settlement laid out between the motte and bailey castle and church founded, so it is said, by the errant knight Richard de Brito. He was one of the assassins of Thomas à Becket and returned here to repent his sins. Near to the immaculate village green and cross is the Pandy Inn where refreshment is close at hand. But if you really do have a deep-seated urge to explore more historical sites, then follow in the footsteps of an old Dorstone custom of climbing (how does 600 feet sound?) up to the remains of the early burial chamber known as **Arthur's Stone** on Merbach Hill. How did Dorstone folk have enough breath left to take part in celebrations held up here?

Ewyas Harold and Abbeydore
There are two villages located at the south-eastern end of the Dore Valley that are also worth a visit. They are best accessed by bus from Hereford on the X4 bus to Pontrilas with a shuttle minibus 440 into the villages. If you enjoy walking then a visit to the two villages with a walk in between makes for a great day out. Ewyas Harold is the largest of the villages in the Dore Valley. It stands at the confluence of the Dulas brook (home to a rare crayfish) and the river Dore which in turn tips out

into the Monnow less than a mile downstream. Ewyas Harold grew up beneath the castle of Ewyas and there's a pub, fish and chip shop and shop to stock up here before or after your ramble.

There's a lovely walk over Ewyas Harold Common to Abbeydore. It is said that the Cistercian monks used to make their way up to the common on these old paths so as to harvest meadow saffron used in the production of dyes. These crocus-like flowers, at their best in autumn, are one of many rare flowers found in this fairly wild place. It is still owned by the Lord of the Manor so tread carefully as you make your way in the footsteps of those early Christians. The **church of St Mary**, which was formerly **Dore Abbey**, suffered badly in the Dissolution and stood in ruins for nearly 100 years before restoration in the 1630s. On entering the church, the high ceilings and superb wooden vaults around the southern transept are immediately appealing to the eye. The stained glass windows, some from the 16th and 17th

---

OFFA'S DYKE FLYER

This is something of a misnomer as the flyer, B17, rarely has an opportunity to get up speed on this amazing back lane meander from Hay-on-Wye to Pandy via the Gospel Pass, returning via the Upper Monnow Valley. The origin of the name Gospel Pass points to it being used by Christian preachers, but differing tales credit the preacher being one of the Apostles (unlikely), an early Celtic saint (possible) or someone drumming up support for one of the crusades (more likely). The small bus climbs remorselessly out of Hay up to the flanks of Hay Bluff with Lord Hereford's Knob to the right (don't ask; it is also known as Twmpa). At the summit of the pass it weaves its way into the Vale of Ewyas. The lane narrows in places and the bus squeezes between sinewy roots of trees and a canopy of branches that envelop the road. It soon arrives at the hamlet of **Capel-y-ffin** with its little white chapel and onward to **Llanthony**. Here the ruins of the Augustinian priory are open for visitors; given the endless furious fighting along the border it is a wonder that so much of it is preserved. Soon after, the bus passes through Cwmyoy and you should just be able to catch sight of the leaning tower of St Martin's church beneath Hatterill Hill; it leans at an angle greater than Pisa.

On the return leg the bus passes through the historic villages of **Llanvihangel Crucorney**, with its ancient Skirrid Inn, said to be one of the oldest in the land, and then on to **Longtown**, where you'll see the castle ruins. It passes near the Olchon Valley and in sight of the Black Hill before reaching the isolated parish of **Michaelchurch Escley**. Finally, it rises to the legendary Bull's Head at **Craswall**, then across open moorland before descending once more between luxuriant hedges into Hay-on-Wye. The Flyer will pick up and set down at any spot where it is safe to do so. You need to put your hand out to get the driver to stop.

The screen in the former Dore Abbey

century, are simply beautiful (and have been restored in recent times). There are wall paintings of biblical text and the grim reaper. But there is far more to be told and a real atmosphere to experience and you'll need to get hold of an excellent history of the abbey, edited by Ron Shoesmith and Ruth Richardson (see Extras), if you are to spend some time here.

WALKING

Hay is also a great place for walking holidays. **Offa's Dyke National Trail** and the **Wye Valley Walk** cross here. For an easy river valley walk, catch the bus to Glasbury and walk back along the Wye Valley Walk to Hay. If you are seeking a harder day walk, catch the bus to Dorstone and climb up to Arthur's Stone and Merbach Hill on the **Herefordshire Trail** then join the Wye Valley Walk back into Hay-on-Wye.

There are also numerous local walks in and around Hay. A lovely short walk is via St Mary's church and the small waterfall on the Login Brook to the Warren meadow leading down to the river. Another is to admire the waterfalls of the Dulas Brook in Cusop dingle.

CYCLING AND HORSE RIDING

The **National Cycle Route 42** (Lôn Las Cymru) runs through Hay, partly utilising the old railway trackbed, but then follows back lanes through to Glasbury where it

is lovely to sit by the River Wye or to take refreshment at the River Café. There's also access to nearby **NCN Route 8** running through to Talgarth, where there are some great projects on the boil, including one to renovate the old mill. There's been a recent restoration of nearby Bronllys Castle which makes for a good outing.

Amazingly, Route 42 in the other direction uses the old drovers' road through the Gospel Pass to Capel-y-ffin and Abergavenny. This is a very strenuous ride best suited to experienced cyclists, but those who make it say it is an experience to be remembered.

There is a substantial bridleway network in the foothills of the Black Mountains which is ideal for those seeking off-road cycling. These bridleways are extensively used by trekkers from local stables such as at Tregoyd. The area is a stronghold for pony trekking and the **Three Rivers Ride**, near Hay, has been designed for cross country horse riding.

REFRESHMENT

Glasbury
The River Café: good food in informal surroundings. In the Green Dragon scheme (effective environmental management).

Hay-on-Wye
There are several places to take refreshment in Hay-on-Wye including:

Cafés
Globe at Hay, Newport Street: offers locally sourced food and has a programme of arts events.

The Granary, Lion Street: is a long-standing café and restaurant which offers a wide range of vegetarian dishes (and caters for vegans).

Old Stables Tearooms, Bear Street: homemade food and special preserves made by the owners.

Oscar's Bistro, High Street: sources organic produce wherever possible.

Shepherds Ice Cream Parlour, High Street: coffee and homemade cakes too.

Pubs

Three Tuns, in one of the oldest buildings in town (16th century) and at one time used to be called Lucy's after a long standing landlady, but since her time has been much altered. Good food and ales.

Kilvert's, Bull Ring: sells locally produced ales.

Local Produce

Golden Valley ales: brewery is located in Peterchurch and sold at the Boughton Arms in the village.

Gwatkins Cider: award winning cider and perry made at Moorhampton Farm, near Bacton (no bus to the farm but ideal cycling and walking in this part of the Dore valley).

Golden Valley

Cafés

Abbey Dore Court: tea rooms open from April to October with delicious organic food available.

Pubs

These very rural pubs are where many people head when walking and cycling:

Bridge Inn, Michaelchurch Escley: riverside pub in an idyllic location which offers local beers.

Bull's Head, Craswall: legendary historic drover pub which sources some local ingredients for the kitchen, plus local cider and beers.

Carpenter's Arms, Walterstone: ancient pub and restaurant using local ingredients wherever possible

Cornewell Arms, Clodock: very traditional pub worthy of a visit. Local bottled beers and ciders

Crown at Longtown: cheerful inn prides itself on sourcing local food from nearby farms.

Dog Inn, Ewyas Harold: a community pub that is a must for lovers of real ale and homemade food.

Pandy Inn, Dorstone: old inn which sources food locally where possible and offers local real ales.

White Haywood Farm Restaurant, Michaelchurch Escley: sources produce from its own farm.

EXTRAS

Countryside Restoration Trust: see www.livingcountryside.org.uk for details.

Drover Holidays, Oxford Street, Hay-on-Wye: organises walking and cycling tours and bike hire. see www.droverholidays.co.uk.

The Globe at Hay, Newport Street: Arts centre and home to the Institute of Arts and Ideas. It created the 'How the light gets in' festival combining philosophy, debate and music.

Hay-on-Wye Tourist Information: Oxford Road, Tel (01497) 820144.

Haymakers, St John's Place: long standing cooperative shop selling the wares of several local craftspeople and with changing gallery to view.

Shoesmith, Ron and Ruth Richardson (1997) *A Definitive History of Dore Abbey*, Logaston Press.

Talgarth: for more detail about the mill project, green energy, walks and cycle rides around Talgarth see www.visittalgarth.co.uk.

PUBLIC TRANSPORT

Buses

Hay-on-Wye is served by bus service from Hereford Railway Station. 38/39A. Daily. Travel time 50-55 minutes. Operator: Stagecoach in South Wales on Monday – Saturday / Yeomans Canyon Travel on Sundays.

Vowchurch, Peterchurch and Dorstone are also served by this bus.

Ewyas Harold and Abbeydore, in the south of the valley, are served by the X4 from Hereford Country Bus Station with a guaranteed connection from Pontrilas to the villages. X4/440. Monday – Saturday. Travel time approximately 40 minutes. Operators: Stagecoach in South Wales / Nick Maddy Coaches.

ROSS-ON-WYE

Ride to Ross

There are two direct ways to travel to Ross-on-Wye (Ross) by bus from Hereford. The main route (Bus 38) is via Kingsthorn, where the views across the basin of Herefordshire to the Garway Hills, Skirrid and Black Mountains are divine. The bus then passes through gently rolling countryside where big-time fruit production is in evidence. Descend through Much Birch, home to Sir Roy Strong's **Laskett Gardens** (open occasionally to groups and those staying at The Folly cottage – managed by the Vivat Trust, a charity dedicated to restoring derelict historic buildings and often then offering them for holiday lets). Soon afterwards, on the left, is Llandinabo Farm. This fine looking farm dates from the 17th century and the nearby church, uniquely dedicated to St Dinabo, dates from an earlier century. The bus runs through the hamlet of Harewood End, then by elegant Pengethley Manor Hotel on a hillside surrounded by sweeping parkland.

The other route (Bus 37) takes a very different, back lane route to sleepy **Hoarwithy**, a village renowned for its sandstone red Italianate church, situated on a south-facing slope (see p.193). It is worth a visit to simply sit awhile at this beautifully tranquil spot. The bus then passes along-side the wandering Wye, before rising up past the Lough Pool inn (recently closed) and onward through Bridstow to Ross.

If you choose either route, the last section into Ross-on-Wye crosses the **Wilton Bridge**, first built in 1597 but since strengthened and widened. It was where many of the early romantic movement began their Wye Tour. You might be able to catch sight of a sundial, on the right parapet, dating from the 18th century with an inscribed epigram:

> Esteem thy precious time
> Which pass so swift away
> Prepare thee for eternity
> And do not make delay.

On the left you might be able to glimpse Wilton Castle (see below). The bus then rises beneath the sandstone cliff into Edde Cross Street (there was once a preaching cross here) and through the edge of town to Cantilupe Road where all buses call. This is the place to change buses.

ROSS-ON-WYE

Ross-on-Wye has been involved in tourism for over two centuries. The view of the sandstone buildings overlooking a large meander in the river Wye has been a picture postcard for decades and its charm

The classic view of Ross-on-Wye across the river Wye

has not faded. The focal point of the town is marked by an historic market house which is both heritage centre and still a market place for produce stalls on market days. Packed with interesting buildings, an inspiring church and walks down to the riverside, Ross attracts the visitor who enjoys a perambulation around a place. The Civic Society has worked to improve interpretation of the town and there are information plaques sited at different locations as you make your way around.

Walking around town

In Ross-on-Wye vistas are everything. One of the town's most notable sons, John Kyrle, set about to beautify the place for the benefit of its residents. In the latter decades of the 17th century and the first quarter of the 18th century, Kyrle had a hand in numerous projects which certainly improved the quality of the place. His achievements have endured for three centuries despite the considerable change around the town in that time.

Two decades after John Kyrle's death, tourism came to Ross-on-Wye in the form of the Wye Tour. This was unwit-

The plaque to John Kyrle near the Market House

tingly pioneered by the vicar of Ross, the Reverend John Egerton, who lived a comfortable existence here during the 1740s. He was known to entertain his guests by taking them on a boat trip down the Wye to Monmouth. It was essentially a two-day experience with an overnight stay in some riverside inn. It caught on; within 30 years, the Wye Tour had become a commercial proposition. It was all the rage with the affluent mercantile classes taking time out to experience the journey; to pen words or paint pictures of the passing scenery at a pace that made them pioneers of slow travel.

The Market House at the centre of Ross

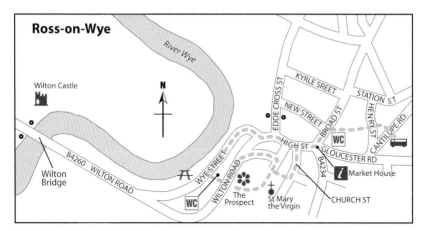

From Cantilupe Road, it is possible to cut through to Broad Street, via a walkway, which runs between the library and a small taxi office, across Henry Street and ahead on a pathway through a shopping quarter. On arrival at Broad Street, cross the road, and turn left to walk up to the **Market House**, built of rich red sandstone and very appealing to the eye. Market stalls are laid out here each Thursday and Saturday and it is also home to a **heritage centre** which displays a changing exhibition throughout the year. Look at the gables of the hall, for at one end is a medallion of King Charles II and at the other end an oval tablet that highlights the letters F and C intertwined with a heart. This may seem a hint over the top to us but it was essential for Kyrle to display his public allegiance to the Crown. This is how he showed it; the letters translate into *Faithful to Charles in heart*. On the left, below the hall, can be found a half-timbered building where Kyrle lived most of his life; it is now a stationer's shop.

From the Market Hall, go right into High Street, where there are many traditional shops, and then left into Church Street. On the left are the Rudhall almshouses, founded in the 1570s, with mullioned windows adding character to the buildings. Go right through the iron kissing gate, attributed to a local foundry, Perkins and Bellamy, at one time based in Nottingham House in nearby Broad Street. Enter the churchyard and on the right is the very fitting Church Row, a neat cluster of buildings, overlooked by the church. Pass by the Plague Cross, originally dating from 1637, since restored and a long-standing reminder of the harsh realities of life in times past.

Main attraction

The church of St Mary the Virgin and the public garden known as **the Prospect** make this quarter of Ross-on-Wye very special, and indeed the main attraction of the town. The church spire is one of the tallest in the Marches and can be seen from some distance. The church dates mainly from the 13th and 14th centuries and includes numerous monuments including many ascribed to the influential Rudhall family, dating from the 17th and 18th centuries and, of course, there's a magnificent monument to John Kyrle. There are also examples of 15th-century stained glass. One curious aspect is the number of depictions of the hedgehog. Ross was, in Saxon times, one of the main settlements in an area known as Ergyng (translated as the land of the hedgehog). It later became Archenfield. Even so, logos and crests associated with Ross have continued to include this much admired little spiky animal, which in real life has suffered decline in recent times. In fact, there's a group determined to save it from extinction; a British Hedgehog Preservation Society has been established with its HQ near Ludlow in the Marches.

Step back outside and make your way to **the Prospect**, entered by way of the south gate, replete with elegant pillars and triangular pediment dated as 1700. John Kyrle leased the land from the Marquess of Bath in 1796 and laid out the gardens for public use. There are a number of mature trees which date from that time. A part of the plot was sold off to the adjoining Palace Hotel (on the site of the present Royal Hotel) in 1870 and this caused ructions in town. Fortunately, another Ross philanthropist, Thomas Blake, stepped in and bought the gardens freehold (as they remain now) and sanctioned the area for societal use. Walk through the gardens to the viewpoint. Spread out before you is a wonderful vista of the Wye valley and the Black Mountains beyond.

Excavations on the Prospect have unearthed evidence of use by Bronze Age tribes and the Romans so the view has been an inspiration for a very long time. On your return, look for a second remaining gate with Grecian vases adorned with spiral scrolls; it is a splendid piece of work. This leads into the old burial ground. However, keep to the left of the church and enter Palace Yard where the old fire station has been converted into the Phoenix Theatre. Pass by the long-standing Royal Hotel on the left, built in 1833 and frequented by famous people such as Charles Dickens and Lloyd George. But you'll be distracted by the historic quarter to the right. These medieval-looking sandstone walls and tower actually date from the 1830s. They were built when the Wilton Road was being re-modelled by no other than that prolific road and bridge engineer, Thomas Telford.

Drop down to the Wilton Road, cross over and turn left. Pass by the restored, six-storey **Ice House**, which was built, as its name suggests, to store ice blocks hewn from a frozen river Wye during the depths of winter. The ice would last for months. As you descend the slope, look for a gap on the right that leads across the parkland to Wye Street. Turn right to walk up Wye Street to The Man of Ross public house.

Wye Street is packed with interesting buildings including the British and Foreign School (1837) and you'll notice the memorial gardens (1908) dedicated to Thomas Blake, a major benefactor to the town in the late 19th century. Adjacent to the gardens is the Ropewalk, steps leading down to the riverside. It was at one time where a local rope works stretched and dried their rope. By the Dutch-gabled Man of Ross pub, you will see a sculpture of leaping salmons by local sculptor, Walenty Pytel (there's more of his work in the meadows by the Wye on the footpath to Wilton). There are many works of art around the town; it is another endearing aspect of Ross.

If you wish to walk out to **Wilton Castle**, follow the banks of the Wye, cross over the bridge, where the **Herefordshire Trail** heads off to the right and passes round part of the castle. Originally an earth and timber motte and bailey, in the early 14th century the castle passed to the de Grey family who substantially rebuilt whatever existed at that time so that it then consisted of a rectangular keep and a curtain wall

Leaping salmon sculpture by The Man of Ross pub

Wilton Castle

Keep ahead along High Street with many examples of 17th-century buildings, some of which have much older interiors. At the Market Place you can either retrace your steps or walk ahead along Gloucester Road to Cantilupe Road.

GOODRICH AND SYMOND'S YAT

The bus for Goodrich (Bus 34) runs through the Wye valley and crosses the river at Kerne Bridge. On the right stands the 14th-century Flanesford Priory, now restored as apartments. The bus into this part of the Wye valley, i.e. between Ross, Goodrich, Symond's Yat (West) and Monmouth, runs on Mondays to Saturdays. What is more, **Goodrich** is by far the most enchanting of the villages in this part of the Wye valley. It has been much loved by artistic and literary circles and it is easy to see why. It even attracted the Wordsworths on more than one occasion. Early tourists on the Wye Tour adored it, inspired by the man who gave a new meaning to landscape, the Reverend Gilpin, who described Goodrich as 'correctly picturesque'. The views from the castle, in particular, are (or were)

with several towers and a twin-towered gatehouse. In the 16th century, Charles Brydges built an Elizabethan mansion within the walls but this was attacked and burnt during the Civil War by the Royalists while he procrastinated over which side he would support.

Across Edde Cross Street is the old Swan Hotel. This hotel was up until 30 years ago, one of several clustered around here, most of which have now closed.

Tents pitched by the walls of the White Lion inn just over the bridge in Wilton

WYE VALLEY AREA OF OUTSTANDING NATURAL BEAUTY

The Wye Valley Area of Outstanding Natural Beauty (AONB) covers an area of beautiful countryside around the river Wye from the south of Hereford to the north of Chepstow in the counties of Gloucestershire, Herefordshire and Monmouthshire. It was designated as a special area in 1971 and seeks to conserve the special nature of the environment. The AONB has become a paradise for walkers and those using the river. Now infrastructure is improving for cyclists and there is a sound rural bus network allowing access to most places except on a Sunday when only Ross, Monmouth and Tintern enjoy a basic service. For more detail see www.wyevalleyaonb.org.uk.

some of the finest in the Wye Valley Area of Outstanding Natural Beauty. Why past tense? There's an almighty row brewing over landscape here. Some say it is a bad case of landscape blight. Acres of polytunnels have been assembled. This enables a longer season to grow soft fruits (strawberries in supermarkets come to mind). But these polytunnels are right bang in this 'correctly picturesque' landscape, right in the centre of an Area of Outstanding Natural Beauty, and very close to a river which happens to be a Site of Special Scientific Interest.

The bus arrives at a stop by Jolly's, a local shop in the village and it is a five-minute walk to the castle's visitor centre (English Heritage) from there. It is another five-minute walk through to **the castle** along an ancient oak-lined path. The earliest castle was first built by a nobleman, Godric Mapson. His early fortification was superseded by an extensive stronghold funded by Richard 'Strongbow' de Clare and then embellished later by Walter Marshall. Unlike many of the other Marcher castles, it did not suffer the exhaustive and continued assaults by the Welsh. As a consequence, the domestic quarters were made more liveable and there were several periods of enhancement. Collectively, the domestic quarters have been cited as being pretty unique, given that they have survived relatively intact.

What is striking about the castle is the sheer thickness of the sandstone walls, not only the 12th-century keep, but the 13th-century outer curtain and towers. It was only in the last throes of the English Civil War that they were breached by

a Parliamentary force from Hereford, led by the veteran commander, Colonel Birch. The Royalist forces were somewhat beleaguered by the siege but held on for some weeks. Birch soon tired of this and commissioned a heavy-weight mortar, Roaring Meg, to finish off the job. After a few days of bombardment the castle duly surrendered. The cannon and some recently rediscovered cannon balls are on display. Recently discovered? Evidently, a dozen or more cannon balls had been sitting under the stairs of the keep for the past 35 years. They were found again in 2010 much to the surprise of the curator. This is a majestic Marches masterpiece and deserves our utmost attention, cannon balls and all.

The bus continues to the next village, Whitchurch, where there's a stop at the roundabout for **Symond's Yat** (West). Thus, you might well decide to travel on to Symond's Yat to take a closer look at the Upper Wye Gorge. Unfortunately, it is not a particularly pleasant walk from the bus stop to the riverside; it takes about 20 minutes. Symond's Yat (East and West sides of the village are on located on either side of the river Wye) attracts huge numbers of visitors on high days and holidays, so that's also a point to consider. On the plus side, there are a number of exceptional features here that make a detour worthwhile. The rope ferry (pulled by hand) across the river Wye is something else. It operates all year except when the river is high with flood waters. This beautiful link allows access to the east bank and Symond's Yat East, and there are superb riverside walks south-west of Symond's Yat to the **Biblins** (where there's a footbridge across the river). From Symond's Yat East you can walk on to Monmouth (about 6 miles) or walk back along the riverside to Symond's Yat West using the bridge at the Biblins (about 2 miles). It is also possible to follow the Wye Valley Walk back to Ross-on-Wye from Symond's Yat East. Some may prefer the climb up to the Yat, a high rockface above the deeply incised and wooded Wye valley. What a view! This stunning scenery was one of the key film locations for *Shadowlands,* a story about C.S. Lewis and writer Joy Gresham, released in 1993.

Hoarwithy

The village of Hoarwithy can be accessed by bus 37 from Ross as well as Hereford, although it is not a very frequent service. You can also cycle from Ross (see below). There's a pub, The New Harp, under the shade of a large tree and plenty of local walks, including to the nearby hamlet of

Looking up the approach to the Italianate Hoarwithy church

Carey with its picture postcard pub and to King's Caple; the church spire is seen for some miles. The Herefordshire Trail offers a lovely linear walk back into Ross (see below) via Sellack Bridge, Sellack hamlet and the church of St Tysilio. Those in search of good food should look no further than Aspen House, a rather special bed and breakfast (www.aspenhouse.co.uk).

The church of St Catherine is approached by way of large shaded steps to a cloister that evokes the warm feeling of southern Europe even on a wet day. It is a very Mediterranean affair; the church exudes that certain Byzantine and Romanesque style. Yet, this church was still in the making in the 1880s, evidently a commissioned rebuild of an earlier, more modest church dating from 1843. The effect is stunning and the decoration, with ample tiling, mosaics and stained glass of exceptional quality, cannot fail to draw your attention as you stand in amazement at one of the most unusual churches in the Marches. It is a place that every slow traveller will want to see, to linger in the cloister and reminisce about travels to warmer climes.

WALKING

Ross is a Walkers Are Welcome town and it is keen to encourage public transport. It has partnered with Stagecoach Wye and Dean to publish a leaflet *Bus Walks in and around Ross-on-Wye* which sets out 14 local linear walks. Herefordshire Council has also published a beautifully produced leaflet *Ross-on-Wye and The Wye Valley* which includes a superb short walk from Peterstow (Bus 38, daily) through orchards to the cider makers at The Broome farm and by the ruins of Wilton Castle to Ross-on-Wye.

The Herefordshire Trail and the **Wye Valley Walk** pass through the town. It is possible to use these for several longer linear walks back into town. For example, catch the 37 bus to Hoarwithy (Mon – Sat) from Hereford or Ross then walk back into Ross, some six miles. Another good walk is facilitated by catching buses 34 or 35 (Mon – Sat) to Kerne Bridge and following the Wye Valley Walk back into Ross.

CYCLING

There are a limited number of cycling routes from Ross-on-Wye as many of the exit roads are heavily trafficked and hence unpleasant. One good ride is to follow the Wye upstream via Hole-in-the-Wall, How Caple and Hoarwithy, returning by a similar route. That is the only way to avoid the M50/A40 highway horror. The cycle route is based on the *Herefordshire Leisure Cycle Guide* (Wye Valley) but the return route via Wilton roundabout cannot be recommended.

However, the nearby Forest of Dean is a paradise for cyclists seeking traffic-free routes and offers a number of excellent cycling opportunities, with cycle hire readily available at Cannop. It is possible to cycle out from Ross-on-Wye on the B4234 to Kerne Bridge and then through Lydbrook to Upper Lydbrook to join the off-road cycle route network. These roads are feasible if you have some cycling experience and cycle hire is available at Ross from Revolutions in Broad Street. They can offer good advice.

REFRESHMENT

Cafés and Restaurants

There are many to choose from in Ross but these two are favourites:

Caffe Eleganza, Broad Street: sources local food.

Nature's Choice café, Broad Street: friendly vegetarian café and restaurant.

Pubs

Kings Head, High Street: has a good bar with local real ales as well as restaurant.

There are fewer cafés out of town but some pubs in the area offer good food and stock local beverages.

Hoarwithy

New Harp Inn: keen on sourcing local and organic where they can.

Symond's Yat

Ye Old Ferrie Inn (West) and **The Saracen's Head** (East) offer local ales and ciders and source food locally wherever possible.

Local Produce

Field Fayre, Broad Street, Ross: offers wide range of organic food and drinks.

Pengethley Farm Shop, Pengethley Garden Centre (on Bus Route 38): has a wide variety of local food and beverage products available.

Ross Cider, Peterstow: traditional cidermaker who welcomes people to view his orchards and taste ciders and perries made in a time honoured manner – see www.rosscider.com for details.

EXTRAS

British Hedgehog Preservation Society: www.britishhedgehogs.org.uk.

Farmers' Market, Market Hall: 1st Friday in the month.

Hurley, Heather & Pat Hughes, *The Story of Ross*, Logaston Press 2010. Lots of information about the town's history.

PUBLIC TRANSPORT

Buses

Ross-on-Wye (Cantilupe Road) is served by bus service from Hereford Country Bus Station. 38. Monday – Saturday, hourly. Sunday, two hourly. Travel time: 35 minutes. Operator: Stagecoach in Wye and Dean.

Ross-on-Wye (Cantilupe Road) to Goodrich (Castle Lane). 34 Monday – Saturday, two hourly. Travel time 16 minutes to Goodrich; Whitchurch (for Symond's Yat West) is 5 minutes beyond. Operator: H&H Coaches.

Ross-on-Wye (Cantilupe Road) to Hoarwithy (New Harp). 37 Monday – Saturday, every two hours but last bus is early afternoon. Travel time 15 minutes.

ABERGAVENNY (Y FENNI)

The Sugar Loaf is the haunting mass that is prominent from wherever you happen to be standing in and around Abergavenny. It serves as a reminder that this is hill country offering exceptional walking and riding. The Brecon Beacons National Park lies just beyond the town, and that is what makes Abergavenny an attractive place; it is a good spot for discovering the central and eastern parts of the Brecon Beacons. On walking over the footbridge from the railway platform there's a very good view of another brooding massif, Blorenge Hill; this is a sheer climb from the Usk valley below but has endless exquisite views. The freshness of these hills is one of the lasting appeals of Abergavenny.

Abergavenny is located between the confluence of the Gavenny tributary and the Usk. It has a rich history steeped in Welsh, Roman and Norman tradition. The Romans built a fort on a central site. The town was known as *Gobannium* and from AD 55 onwards Publius Ostorius Scapula led numerous campaigns to quell the Welsh tribes who were thwarted by Roman precision and power. This fort provided a core link in a major supply route between Kenchester, Caerleon and Y Gaer near Brecon. Excavations in the last century unearthed several Roman artefacts (now lodged in Abergavenny museum) and mapped out the extent of the fortress lying below the town centre. Centuries later, the Normans took advantage of the Roman development by building a castle on one part of the Roman enclosure. The Norman empire left a strong imprint across the area and in Abergavenny this is manifested in the castle ruins and medieval street pattern. The town walls have long since gone.

Many of the town's monuments can be visited but much of the old Welsh farming feel about the place has gone; it has been lost to the humdrum noise and fumes of its main streets. Nevertheless, step away from these highways and there are some quieter corners where you can readily appreciate the town's heritage. In the last century, the town had a number of literary and musical associations including Ethel Lina White, who penned a best-selling novel *The Wheel Spins* (1936) which inspired Hitchcock to make the thriller *The Lady Vanishes* in 1938. In more recent years the poet Owen Sheers, who hails from Abergavenny, was listed by the *Independent* as one of Britain's top 30 young writers. The singer Marina from Marina and The Diamonds also comes from Abergavenny, a far cry from the Marty Wilde song of the 1960s about 'Taking a trip down to Abergavenny'. The town is currently building a reputation for its food through an annual festival and the perseverance of up and coming chefs in nearby inns. It is destined to become a foodie paradise.

A train journey to Abergavenny is easy from Cardiff and South Wales. There are connections at Newport from Bristol and London. It is also well served by buses from Cardiff, Cwmbran and the South Wales Valleys. There are other services from Hereford and Brecon and an amazing number of market day buses on a Tuesday. It is possible to travel to Raglan and Monmouth on Sundays and to Brecon in the summer months. Admittedly, Abergavenny suffers from a seemingly endless circulation of traffic in its central core, but it provides an excellent hub for gaining access to the Brecon Beacons National Park and Usk valley.

Walking around town
Abergavenny railway station is just under a mile out of town and there's no useful bus link. There are always taxis standing by. There is a back way down into town, signposted as a walk or cycle ride through a housing estate along Holywell Crescent and Road, but it just as easy to walk down Station Road. At the bottom, turn right to

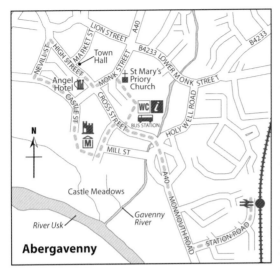

Abergavenny

century. Many of these are located in the Herbert Chapel. There are also wood carvings including a large image of Jesse from the Tree of Jesse and choir stalls dating from the 14th century.

As part of a renewed restoration process, the 12th-century Tithe Barn has been refurbished to house a food hall, café and exhibition featuring the church's history. It is home to a tremendous tapestry, painstakingly created by Abergavenny residents over the past decade. If you follow the path alongside the church you'll gain access to the walled **abbot's garden**, designed to exhibit a range of the fruit and plants that would have been grown 900 years ago by the inhabitants of the priory.

From St Mary's Priory Church, head along Monk Street to a crossroads, where you'll see the Angel Hotel, an elegant looking Georgian coaching inn of old. Go right to walk up Cross Street to the Victorian **Market Hall** where stalls are set out on most days, although the main market is on Tuesday with smaller markets held on Friday and Saturday. To the right

descend along Monmouth Road to the bus station. This is a good first stop, for the Brecon Beacons National Park and tourist information centre is located here and there's a public convenience. The bus station itself is spartan with little cover against the elements. It occasionally gets crowded out by bikers who meet up for a brew at the Oasis snack bar, which is a friendly port of call for a slow traveller waiting for a bus.

From the entrance to the tourist information centre, turn left to pass by the toilets, and then slightly left again through the car park to the lovingly restored courtyard at **St Mary's priory church**. This was originally part of a Benedictine priory, established in the 11th century by the first Norman lord of the manor, Hameline de Balun. However, the priory was abandoned at the Dissolution. From that time, the church was re-designated as a parish church for wider community use. It has suffered periods of neglect and even partial destruction prior to restoration work in the 19th century. Despite this, it houses many exceptional monuments dating from different periods, including effigies of local notables such as Eva de Braose dating from the 13th century and Sir John de Hastings from the 14th

The sign for the Angel Hotel

is Market Street, also known as Traitors Gate, being the place where an insider allowed the Welsh Prince, Owain Glyndwr, to slip within the curtain walls during the 1404 campaign. His men duly followed him and proceeded to ransack the town. There is a row of buildings here with overhanging jetties supported by posts; this provides a glimpse of what medieval Abergavenny may have looked like. Continue up Cross Street, which soon becomes a traffic-free thoroughfare known as High Street. You can take a look at St John's Street on the left where the old grammar school stands in the place of the earlier St John's church. The school was established following the dissolution of the priory.

However, take the next left instead to walk along Nevill Street, leading into St John's Square. The street was associated with the making of periwigs, a wig fabricated with goat hair that was fashionable from the 17th century until the mid 19th century. There are some Georgian properties of note in this street; it was also home to a number of hostelries including the Cow Inn (you can see cow's horns and ornate lintels and sills here above the Trading Post café) and further along is the 16th-century coaching inn, the Kings Head. Take a look at the 19th-century coat of arms on the wall, depicting the inn's association with

The Victorian Market Hall and assorted stalls

hunting lodge dating from the early 19th century, built in honour of the Marquis of Abergavenny, stands pretty firmly on the site of the old motte; this is where the keep once stood. This is home to the **Abergavenny Museum**, which offers a curious mix of re-assembled historic settings such as a Welsh farmhouse together with contemporary exhibitions. It is well worth a perusal as you also gain a feel of the castle from within its walls.

Other attractions

From the castle it is easy enough to descend to the **Castle Meadows**. These amount to 21 acres of water meadows alongside the river Usk where it is lovely to picnic and while away the time watching the sandmartins nest in the red earth banks opposite. It is possible to turn left to walk back to Mill Street (the old mill wheel still exists), passing by the Tan House, at one time a centre for tanning in Abergavenny in the late 19th century. The town was also a manufacturer of flannel. You can walk back to the bus station from here.

royalty in the past. Turn left into Castle Street and as this bends left, go ahead into Castle Meadows.

Main attraction

The main attraction is **Abergavenny Castle** which is accessed by way of a 15th-century gatehouse. The castle was established in the 11th century by Hameline de Balun. It was inherited by the de Braose family. Richard de Braose has a questionable reputation as in 1175 it is written that he invited local Welsh warriors into the castle for a banquet only to slaughter them when unarmed. The surviving Welsh tribesmen took revenge and the castle and town were both severely damaged. In fact, this was a recurrent theme throughout the medieval period here, despite the castle being strengthened by the Normans in the 13th century. It remained, however, the focal target of attack from the river crossings on the nearby Usk. There was an outer defence in the form of a town wall, spanning out from the battlements, but this was often breached. Little or nothing remains of this fortification.

Nevertheless Abergavenny was held for the most part by the Normans throughout the 13th and 14th centuries, but like many other borderland castles it was damaged in the English Civil War. Held by the Royalists, it was actually torched by them to prevent its use by an overwhelming Parliamentarian army that came to seek its surrender. From then onwards it fell into a spiral of disrepair. However, a

Part of the walls of Abergavenny Castle

SLOW FOOD

Slow food was a term first used in the 1980s by Carlo Petrini, one of the founders of a movement that sought to counter a growth of fast food in Italy. The focus of the movement has been the same for the past 30 years: locally sourced ingredients, traditional recipes and taking time to prepare and enjoy food are core values. This has been expressed more recently as food that is good (tastes good), clean (respects environment, human health and animal welfare) and fair (provides a fair wage for producers). There are two slow food groups in the Marches: Herefordshire Slow Food, and Ludlow and The Marches. See www.slowfood.org.uk,

Taste Real Food is another non-profit organisation that champions good food for everyone and campaigns to encourage food that is produced with minimal environmental impact, increased biodiversity, and linked with local cultures. Its HQ is in Ludlow and more details are available from www.tasterealfood.com. There are other schemes and projects such as Flavours of Herefordshire and the Taste of Wales which encourage local producers and retailers to provide food and drink which has its roots in the locality, such as Bara Brith from Wales, Shropshire Fidget pie or Herefordshire perry. Mouth-watering stuff.

WALKING

Abergavenny makes for a great base for a walking holiday. The **Usk Valley Walk** passes nearby, at Llanfoist, on the Monmouthshire and Brecon Canal. This can be accessed by a walk across the Castle Meadows to Llanfoist Bridge. There are also narrow boat holidays from a basin near to the village. There are also direct walks to the Blorenge from the town using this route. Perhaps the main appeal will be to walk to the Sugar Loaf or the Skirrid. It is possible to go for either in a day's walk. The **Beacons Way**, a linear walk of 101 miles across the Brecon Beacons, starts at the Skirrid near Abergavenny. However, a useful taster for the Beacons Way would be to catch the X43 bus to Bwlch and walk back to Crickhowell via Tretower. It is about 5-6 miles with one big climb.

CYCLING

NCN route 46 goes through Abergavenny from Hereford and **route 42** through to Usk and Chepstow. The route follows quiet lanes through the countryside but joins busy roads in Abergavenny so care needs to be taken. Abergavenny is not a good place to cycle around as it is seems to encourage frenetic traffic movements,

The Great Western Hotel,
one of several backpacker hotels
in the area

but a local cycle group is campaigning for more and better routes for residents and visitors. The group has also produced a leaflet featuring easy cycle routes around Abergavenny, but many of these include either hilly sections or some main roads which are less than desirable.

Route 46 south of Abergavenny is more promising. It crosses the Castle Meadows to Llanfoist then follows a traffic-free route through to Govilon and the Clydach Gorge. This makes for a good day's cycling in inspiring countryside. There's also cycle hire at Govilon (3 and X4 buses on Mondays to Saturdays).

REFRESHMENTS

Cafés and Restaurants

Abergavenny is home to an annual Food Festival held each September, followed by a Christmas Fair in December. It has been described as the Glastonbury of Food Festivals and the spread across different venues in town makes for a great foodie stroll. This momentum has created considerable interest in slow food in the southern stretches of the Marches, with several gastro pubs out in the sticks. Back in Abergavenny, there are a number of cafés and restaurants; listed below are a few that seem particularly good.

Angel Hotel, Cross Street: uses local ingredients and has signed up to the Green Dragon environmental management scheme.

For the Love of Cake, Frogmore Street: A small café that specialises in locally made cakes.

Tithe Barn Food Hall, Monk Street: A food hall that truly represents Wales in homemade dishes offered to the visitor.

Trading Post, Nevill Street: A traditional style coffee house in a house once owned by the Vaughan family, one of whom was the 17th-century Welsh poet, Henry Vaughan.

Pubs

The Crown at Pantygelli: this pub lies a mile to the north of the town (on 43, X4 bus routes) on the Hereford Road. It seeks out locally sourced food and local beers.

The Kings Arms: an inn that prides itself on sourcing local food whenever it can; it is also home to a micro brewery, the Tudor Brewery.

Local Produce

There are three butchers in town and fresh local vegetables are sold in the market.

Deli-Delicious, Nevill Street, sources Welsh foods wherever possible.

St Mary's Bakery, sells products baked in Brecon.

EXTRAS

Abergavenny tourist Information, Bus Station: (01873) 857588.

Farmers Market, Town Hall: 4th Thursday of the month.

M&D Cycles, Frogmore Street: sales and repairs.

Pedalabikeaway, Hopyard Farm, Govilon: cycle hire available, www.pedala-bikeaway.co.uk, 01873 830219.

PUBLIC TRANSPORT

Trains

Abergavenny is served daily by direct trains from Cardiff, Manchester, and Shrewsbury as well as trains from north Wales.

There are no buses into town from the station forecourt; it is a 10-minute walk to Abergavenny Bus Station.

Buses

Abergavenny is served by bus from Hereford. X4. Monday – Saturday. Operator: Stagecoach in South Wales.

Buses also run to the following towns on weekdays (+includes Sunday journeys):

Brynmawr	Brecon+ summer only
Cwmbran	Monmouth+
Ebbw Vale+	Pontypool

There are several local Abergavenny town services.

EXCURSIONS FROM ABERGAVENNY

BRECON (BRYCHAN)

Ride to Brecon
The bus to Brecon sweeps through the grass-green landscape of the Usk and Rhiangold valleys. It takes about 50 minutes and in that time you are offered cinematic views over the Black Mountains, to Llangors Hill and the summits of the Beacons including the mighty Pen-y-fan. The highlight has to be when the bus rises out of the Rhiangold valley to the hillside village of Bwlch ready for a gentle descent into the Usk valley.

In contrast, there are also more homely horizons, a chance to peep into gardens full of runner beans, leeks, cabbage and different fruits growing in the town houses of each and every village en route. The heritage of the valley is unfolded on this trip. You catch sight of the rickety remains of Crickhowell Castle (on the left), the

solitary Norman tower at Tretower (on the right) and the sheer serenity of the Monmouthshire and Brecon Canal at Pencelli. The ride through to Brecon is as pleasant as they come.

BRECON

The small and distinctly Welsh town of Brecon has an appealing air. The central area from the Bulwark leading into High Street Inferior has a range of Victorian (and some Georgian) buildings with local shops that make it an engaging place to walk around. But the restoration of the Monmouthshire and Brecon Canal and the riverside promenades along the Usk are an equal match and deliver quiet recreation away from it all. Brecon Cathedral is slightly out of town whilst Brecon Castle is not open to the public, but given their proximity, the two combine to form the basis of a heritage quarter that is charming to walk around. Brecon's role as a market and service centre, in addition to the military presence, has encouraged the retention of facilities such as its town

BRECON BEACONS NATIONAL PARK

The work of the National Park is often taken for granted. Established in 1957, the Park has a prime aim to conserve natural beauty, wildlife and cultural heritage of an area approximating 1,344 square kilometres so that future generations can enjoy the very best of the scenic splendour that it has to offer. That is easier said than done. There is a resident population of 32,000 and a visitor count of 3.8 million each year and the most popular activity is sightseeing by car.

The good news is that the Park is working hard with the tourism sector to encourage sustainable development and its work is beginning to take effect. For example, businesses are becoming ambassadors for the Park; these are guest house proprietors, taxi drivers and publicans who know a fair amount about the Brecon Beacons, its landscape, natural habitats and how you can get the best from the area. There's also a guide to eco-friendly accommodation which highlights those providers working with the Green Dragon scheme to reduce resource use and lessen environmental impact. A third major plus is the Beacons Bus network.

The Beacons Bus network is unique in the Marches and shows what can be done. Beacons Bus is the banner brand name for specially commissioned buses, supplied by a range of bus companies, that run on Sundays and Bank Holidays (May to October); the network is designed specifically with the visitor in mind but obviously is there for residents too. There's also a range of booklets available from the Park as to how you to make the best of local buses too, from walks, to family outings and heritage by bus. For more details take a look at www.breconbeacons.org.

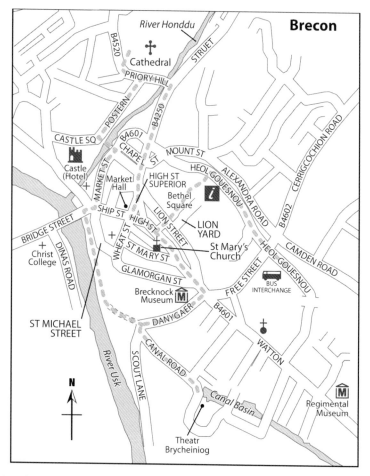

Brecon

River Honddu

Cathedral

STRUET

B4520

PRIORY HILL

POSTERN

B4250

CASTLE SQ

B4601

CHAPEL ST

MOUNT ST

CERRIGCOCHION ROAD

Castle (Hotel)

MARKET ST

Market Hall

HIGH ST SUPERIOR

HEOL GOUESNOU

ALEXANDRA ROAD

B4602

Bethel Square

i

SHIP ST

HIGH ST

LION STREET

LION YARD

BRIDGE STREET

DINAS ROAD

Christ College

WHEAT ST

ST MARY ST

St Mary's Church

HEOL GOUESNOU

CAMDEN ROAD

GLAMORGAN ST

Brecknock Museum **M**

FREE STREET

BUS INTERCHANGE

ST MICHAEL STREET

DANYGAER

B4601

WATTON

River Usk

SCOUT LANE

CANAL ROAD

Canal Basin

N

Theatr Brycheiniog

Regimental Museum **M**

centre cinema and a waterside theatre that make it a good place not only to visit but to stay awhile.

It is also by far the best base to discover the western and central areas of the Brecon Beacons National Park across to Llandovery via Trecastle, to Craig-y-nos and Dan-yr-Ogof caves, as well as rides through to Builth Wells and Hay-on-Wye. It is also ideal for those looking for some serious walking, cycling, or other outdoor activities, as there is a range of equipment suppliers and activity organizers in town. If it's rough stuff adventure you are after then Brecon is a great base.

Walking around town

Brecon has always been at a cross-roads. Sited on the hills above the town are prehistoric camps and nearby is the Roman settlement of Y Gaer, built in AD50 and in existence for well over 200 years. However, the layout of the town is that of a Norman stronghold, with a castle and church on higher ground, overlooking track-ways that once led to the fords across the Usk and Honddu. Before the 19th century, it was a stopping-off point for coaches en route to Aberystwyth, Bristol and London. These links were replaced by the railways and Brecon became a centre for train services in mid Wales. The lines from Neath, Merthyr Tydfil and Hereford ran into nearby Tal-y-llyn Junction and it was literally all change. But the political clout in Brecknock was not sufficiently resilient to resist the Beeching cuts that swept the UK in the 1960s and the railways have been removed from the map.

In the five decades since that era, Brecon's rail links have been replaced by a bus network from Abergavenny, Cardiff, Hereford, Llandovery, Newtown and Swansea. Some of these are part of the Traws Cambria network designed to link towns and railheads across Wales by bus; it is a really good idea and there are plans to make it even better, so that will be a bonus for the slow traveller. There's a new interchange that's neat enough, but it's a little anonymous and also a little out of the central zone beyond Morrison's supermarket. That is where the walk begins.

Go left to walk along Heol Gouesnou, across the lights and ahead to steps on the left to the tourist information centre (and toilets) situated at the car park. Continue ahead from the TIC into a shopping quarter known as Bethel Square, where Beacons Craft shop is located and Boots the Chemist has re-used the old Bethel Chapel of 1852. From here, cross Lion Street and keep ahead again into High Street Inferior by the old Guildhall, dating from the 1770s but much restored in the late 19th century. Across the road is a plaque to commemorate the Reverend Coke who was a founder member of the Wesleyan church. You might also notice, on the right, the Sarah Siddons public house, the birthplace of the famous actress of the same name. There have been many names associated with Brecon but Sarah Siddons has to be top of the list as she became the undisputed diva of Drury Lane in the late 18th century. Frances Hoggan was also born in Brecon; she was the first British woman to graduate as a medical doctor in 1870. Another first for Brecon was the civic advances made by Gwenllian Morgan; she became the first Welsh female councillor and mayor of

Brecon in 1912. In more recent times two sons of Brecon are Roger Glover of Deep Purple and Peter Hope-Evans of Medicine Head, two fine rock bands of the late 20th century.

Go left into the Bulwark by the church of St Mary, with its solid 16th-century tower; it is a real presence in the town centre. But what catches the eye at street level is the impressive statue of Wellington standing, very appropriately, in front of the Wellington Hotel. The statue was given to the town by the well-known local sculptor John Evan Thomas in 1852. Keep ahead towards the junction between Glamorgan Street and Watton. On the right is the old Shire Hall, now the **Brecknock Museum** (see below). Just beyond, go right into Dan-y-gaer and follow this around to the **Monmouthshire and Brecon Canal terminus**, where the Theatr Brycheiniog stands on the right. The canal was opened at the turn of the 19th century. It has been beautifully restored and there are boat trips and boat hire from the basin.

Retrace your steps along Dan-y-Gaer to a terrace of houses. Go left on a path where town walls stand to the right and you will pass some enchanting gardens. The path also allows you to observe the gravel pools of the river Usk; these beds make the river attractive for salmon spawning. Across the bridge, take a look at Brecon Christ College on the left, founded in 1541 but the late Gothic school buildings tend to dominate. Next to the collegiate buildings is the **chapel of Christ Church**, much of which was part of a 13th-century Dominican friary. It houses many monuments including misericords featuring lions, an angel and a skeleton and an 18-branch candelabrum dating from the 17th century.

Go right into Ship Street, across the lights into Market Street. Look for a footpath on the left which crosses the river into Castle Square. To the left stands the remains of **Brecon Castle**, most of which is situated in the private grounds of a hotel. Go right into Postern, which would have been the site of the postern gate to the castle, a back gate to sneak in and out of while the enemy wasn't looking. It is an old quarter and there's sometimes an old gentleman sitting alongside his flowers and produce offered for sale, near to the old gaol house. On reaching the much busier Priory Hill, go

left and at the corner cross over to enter the grounds of the cathedral.

Main attraction

Pevsner describes **Brecon Cathedral** as 'pre-eminently the most splendid and dignified church in Mid Wales'. Who could argue with that? It stands serenely on the site of a former Benedictine monastery established in 1093. The benefactor was the Norman lord, Bernard de Neufmarché, keen to develop both the fortification of Brecon and its spiritual welfare. The famous scribe, Giraldus Cambrensis, became its Archdeacon in 1172, and under the patronage of a succession of Norman lords the priory continued to flourish until an abrupt end at the Dissolution. Fortunately, not all was destroyed and it became a priory church, serving the town for almost four centuries. However, in 1923 the Church set up a diocese of Swansea and Brecon and Brecon priory church was given cathedral status.

It is a small cathedral but there are some exceptional ecclesiastical features and it is far less busy and given over to tourism than

Brecon's Market Hall

many other cathedrals. From the Norman period, there remains only the nave (or at least part of it) and a large 12th-century font decorated with gruesome masks, beasts and birds, very reminiscent of the font at Eardisley church in Herefordshire. Much of the interior architecture dates originally from the 14th century, but there was a major restoration in the 19th century, although there are a range of tablets, effigies and monuments from several centuries. One fascinating feature is a stone cresset with 30 round holes that once stored oil for the lamps of the cathedral.

The Havard chapel was adopted as the Regimental Chapel for the South Wales Borderers, a place for peaceful contemplation and reflection on the many military campaigns with which it had been involved. There is also a cathedral organ of note, installed in 1886 (but since restored and augmented), which accompanies the various choirs that visit. Some of the surrounding buildings were also associated with the priory. They have survived in one way or another, altered perhaps, but still extant and put to good use. These include the Tithe Barn which is a **heritage centre** that displays the history of the cathedral and houses a tea room.

From the cathedral, it is possible to leave by way of a path which drops down by the Deanery to a small gate into Priory Road. Cross over and go left. At the junction, go right along Hay Road, which becomes the Struet, where there are several late Georgian and early Victorian buildings. This leads to High Street Superior where there's a humble entrance to the 19th-century **Market Hall** where markets are still held. Continue into High Street Inferior. Then cut left into Lion Street and right and left into Lion Yard to get back to the tourist information centre.

Other attractions

The **Brecknock Museum** started life in 1928 in a less ostentatious building, an old chapel down the road, before being moved into the rather grand Shire Hall, at one time also the site of the assizes court in Brecon. There is a wide variety of displays in the museum and you might decide to concentrate on a few as you wander up and down the different floors. The first to grab your attention might be the Roman remains from the Y Gaer fort and some fascinating early crosses including the 10th-century Pillar Cross from Maesmynys. The courtroom does not have quite the same effect as that of the Judge's Lodgings in Presteigne but elsewhere in the museum there is superb photographic material of past times in Brecon which makes every penny of the small entrance charge worthwhile. Whatever you decide to look at, don't miss the boat retrieved by a local man at Langors lake in 1925. The dugout is estimated to date from somewhere between AD120 and 760.

We are sometimes reminded of the sacrifice of the armed forces in wars throughout the world. The **Regimental Museum**, located in Watton by the barracks, represents the history of several Welsh regiments including the Royal Welch Fusiliers and the South Wales Borderers; these are all now part of the Royal Welsh regiment. Of particular note is a section on the history of the South Wales Borderers' involvement in the Anglo-Zulu wars and their heroic defence of Rorke's Drift against all odds.

Crickhowell (Crug Hywell)

En route to Brecon, you might like to stop off at Crickhowell, a 20 minute ride from Abergavenny. The bus stops in Beaufort Street, opposite Crickhowell Resource and Information Centre and by Castle Garage in the other direction. Crickhowell lies near to the banks of the River Usk beneath Pen Cerrig-calch and Llangattock scarp. Its ancient buttressed bridge has stood the test of time well; it replaced a ford a little downstream that was used throughout the medieval period. However, the name is not derived from this time. Crug Hywell is associated with an earlier existence, the Iron Age fort lying on a hill of the same name, but also known as

The remains of Crickhowell Castle

Table Mountain; it can be seen to the north above the town.

Crickhowell was developed by the Normans under the stewardship of the Mortimers, gaining its own borough charter as early as 1283. The Normans, however, chose to build only a modest **castle** here. It was known as Alisby's castle after the first lord to start work on it. Later, it was developed by the Turberville and Pauncefoot families. Needless to say, like Abergavenny and Brecon, this was contested territory, and the castle suffered badly as a consequence. Owain Glyndwr, in one of his many ferocious onslaughts, ransacked the place in 1403 and from then onwards the castle was allowed to fall into a ruinous state. It is possible to walk around the stone remains of the castle.

The hub of the town is centred on the market cross. It is a fairly pleasant spot despite the endless flow of traffic. Nevertheless, the local community has done its best to enhance the appeal of a town that enjoyed considerable prosperity in the 19th century. There are a few shops clustered on the High Street. What becomes immediately obvious is that Crickhowell is a bastion of good food with a local bakery, two traditional butchers, dairy farm ice-cream from nearby Rheld

and apple juice made a mile away at Graig Barn, using rare varieties of apples some of which are grown organically. There are good cafés and inns in the locality.

Look for the old **market hall**, a covered market place beneath Grecian columns dating from the 1830s which once housed a magistrates' court, but it is now home to a café. Stalls are still to be found there on Fridays and Saturdays. Cut down a lane on the right to the **church of St Edmund**, a 14th-century building which has been extensively altered. It contains a number of interesting monuments, including effigies of Sir Grimbald and Lady Sybil Pauncefoot, from the late 13th and early 14th centuries. Retrace your steps back to the High Street. Further along, on the left, is Tower Street where there are the remains, surprisingly in someone's garden, of a small tower which is presumed to be part of an old castle gateway. High Street leads down to Bridge Street and the lovely 17th-century bridge just past the Bridge End Inn. It is a short walk which highlights an old quarter of the town and you can then retrace your steps back to the castle grounds.

Tretower Castle and Court

A couple of miles beyond Crickhowell is the hamlet of Tretower. The bus will pull up at Hoel-draw where there's a half mile walk, if that, to Tretower Castle and Court. It is worth stopping off, for there's not a better place in the southern Marches to illustrate the way in which castles gave way to fortified manor houses between the 14th and 17th centuries. The first impression of this site, managed by CADW, is the dominance of the 12th-century round keep and the closeness of its surrounding bailey walls. The keep was no doubt strengthened in the 13th century by the Picard family who occupied the premises for centuries. The stonework that survives is on the site of an earlier wooden palisade motte and bailey castle. The round tower is the landmark for some distance, but within the outer bailey there's all the paraphernalia of a farm, including rusted corrugated barns, which makes the place look very tranquil now. It seems that Tretower was not a major player in borderland warfare but it had its moments. Amazingly the Norman-English held off the onslaught of Owain Glyndwr in 1403, for example, and the skirmishes moved on, down the valley and across to Mitchell Troy and Monmouth.

Tretower Court, built alongside the castle, dates from the 14th century onwards. It was definitely new build rather than an extension of the old medieval castle and this may have been its saviour when the castle was eventually sacked by Glyndwr's men. The Court was developed by the Vaughan family and illustrates an emerging style of architecture that favoured enhancement and comfort rather then defence. It served generations of that family and in turn they continued to gentrify it. In the 18th century, the Vaughans let it to the Parry family and it became more of a working farm than at any time hitherto; this was also a period of deterioration. It was only through the efforts of the Brecknock Society in the 1920s that the site was saved for posterity.

The recent restoration by CADW, including the recreation of a late medieval garden, is superb. Some 90 years ago, the entire place was in danger of collapse. The craftsmanship is much to be admired, meticulous and fitting for a Welsh fortified manor house that sits in such a sumptuous setting. On entering the courtyard, you cannot fail to note the genteel first-floor balconies to the right and the magnificent 17th-century classical windows ahead. The Great Hall is perhaps the most dramatic feature on the tour as you begin to absorb the significance of the superb woodwork throughout the building, some of which dates from the 15th century. You'll need to allow two hours if you are to do justice to walking around the court, castle and medieval garden.

WALKING

Brecon is a brilliant centre if you want to make the most of activities in the Brecon Beacons National Park. Opportunities to walk are manifold and there are dozens of leaflets and booklets describing rambles and expeditions that can be undertaken. If you fancy something on the less strenuous side, walking alongside the **Monmouthshire and Brecon Canal** to Tal-y-bont makes for an ideal afternoon stroll, perhaps calling in at the Star Inn before catching the bus back (or the walk can just as easily be made in the other direction).

From Crickhowell, you can have a great day's walk on the **Beacons Way** by catching the bus out to Bwlch then

Tretower Court

walking back via Cwmdu, perhaps resting awhile at the Farmer's Arms for lunch, then following the flanks of Pen Cerrig-calch before dropping into Crickhowell. There are also gentler walks along the Monmouthshire and Brecon Canal either to Llanfoist (for Abergavenny) or by catching the bus to Tal-y-bont then walking back to Llangattock and across to Crickhowell. But there are dozens of local walks, for example, into Grwyne Fawr and the villages of Llanbedr and Llangenny with their snug traditional pubs that way-lay the slow traveller. In Talybont there's a short stroll, *Vaughan Walk*, bedded into the historic and poetic landscape of the valley and following the footsteps of Henry Vaughan, 17th-century poet and doctor.

CYCLING

The Brecon Beacons has recently improved considerably as a place for leisure cycling. It also has a deservedly good reputation for off-road cross country and mountain biking. There are more companies in Brecon than anywhere else in the Marches offering cycle hire, serv-icing, delivery and pick up and cycling packages, so it is fast becoming a mecca for cycling. Even Beacons Bus includes a popular cycle carriage facility on the run up from Cardiff and through to Abergavenny.

Cycling on Lôn Las Cymru to and from Tal-y-bont or to Llangors are two ideal casual cycle rides utilising quieter roads out of Brecon. The Grwyne Fawr valley, from Crickhowell, also offers a quiet cycling circuit, somewhat hilly, but nevertheless very enjoyable.

REFRESHMENT

Brecon
There are many places that offer refresh-ment in Brecon. Some favourites include:

Cafés and restaurants
Bridge Café: caters especially for cyclists and walkers, open in the evenings for meals (Thursday – Saturday) and Sunday mornings for breakfasts. Signed up to the Green Dragon environmental management scheme.

The Hours Café, Ship Street: read and sip café and bookshop.

Pilgrims Tea Rooms, Brecon Cathedral Close: Tea rooms and restaurant which specialises in Welsh cooking.

Pubs
Boar's Head, Ship Street: Breconshire Brewery pub tap, part of the Green Dragon environmental management scheme.

Crickhowell
The town is packed with places which pride themselves on offering good food.

Cafés and restaurants
Askews Family Bakery, High Street: bread, cakes and pies baked on the premises, café and shop.

Court Room Café, Market Hall: café located in historic building, offering home-made food.

Number 18 Café and Brasserie: aims to provide organic and locally sourced food wherever possible.

Gilffaes Country House Hotel: this lovely hotel has embraced the ideals of the slow food movement. It is just a little over a mile of quiet road walking from the turning to Tretower on the A40.

Pubs
Bear Hotel: A 15th-century coaching inn that sources food locally for its bar and restaurant.

EXTRAS

Abergavenny Cycle Group: *Easy Cycling Around Abergavenny* and *A Ride Around Abergavenny* highlight routes. There's a small charge for these leaflets available at the Tourist Information Office.

Adventure Cycling Wales: based in the Brecon Beacons, this company can deliver or pick up as well as offer cycle for hire plus cycling and walking packages. See www.adventurecyclingwales.co.uk.

Bikes and Hikes, Brecon: bike hire at www.bikesandhikes.co.uk.

Biped Cycles, Brecon: bike hire and servicing at www.bipedcycles.co.uk.

Brecon Beacons and Radnor loop horse riding trail: 4 day circular hack at www.bennettthewern.vispa.com.

Brecon Beacons Park Society: aims to encourage the enjoyment and protection of this very special landscape and environment. Its members designed the Beacons Way. www.breconbeaconsparksociety.org.uk.

Brecon Tourist Information, Cattle Market car park: Tel (01874) 622485.

Brecknock Wildlife Trust, Bethel Square, Brecon: see www.brecknockwildlifetrust.org.uk for information on nature reserves and for opportunities to volunteer or join events.

Farmers' Market, Market Hall: 2nd Saturday of the month.

Ride and Hike, Brecon: a delivery or pick up service and lightly packaged breaks – see www.rideandhike.com.

Stay somewhere green: very useful booklet listing eco-friendly accommodation in the national park. See details on www.greendragonwales.com.

PUBLIC TRANSPORT

Buses

Brecon (Interchange) is served by bus service from Abergavenny Bus Station. X43. Monday – Saturday. Travel duration is 50 minutes. On summer Sundays and Bank Holidays, Beacons Bus operates a limited service. Operator: Sixty Six Coaches.

Brecon has bus links to the following towns on weekdays (+indicates Sunday service):

Abergavenny	Hereford+
Builth	Llandrindod Wells
Cardiff+	Llandovery
Hay-on-Wye+	Merthyr Tydfil+

USK (BRYNBUGA) AND RAGLAN

Ride to Usk

This outing requires two buses from Abergavenny. It takes about 45 minutes. The first stage is a 25 minute ride to Raglan (Beaufort Arms) where you change onto another bus for Usk. The 83 bus to Raglan runs through pleasant but unspectacular countryside. It branches off the old main road to Clytha Pit where you catch a glimpse (to the left) across parkland to Llanarth Court with its grand Palladian portico dating from the 1770s. It is now a hospital. The bus soon reaches Raglan where you step across the road to catch the 60 bus to Usk, reached after a 10-minute ride through Gwehelog Common.

USK

Usk lies within a tourist area known as the Vale of Usk. It is a pretty and unassuming town that welcomes the visitor to stay awhile and enjoy what is on offer. There's a museum and a number of riverside walks that are enjoyable but the real attraction stands above the town. Usk Castle is both charming and redolent of a Welsh border culture that makes Usk really worth a visit. It is a wonderful place to be when the sun is shining.

Usk (known in Welsh as *Brynbuga*) was in Roman times a significant settlement with accommodation for up to 6,000 soldiers at a fort known to the Romans as *Burrium*. This evidently means the 'place of the knobs'. This was not meant to be a Pythonesque comment about the legion but recognition that Usk is surrounded by knobbly hill tops. The fort was under the jurisdiction of Aulis Didius Gallus and excavations indicate that it was constructed between AD54 and 55. This was not a long-standing affair, however, as the entire camp was evacuated some ten to twelve years later. Nearby Caerleon became the main Roman settlement from then onwards. There are small sections of

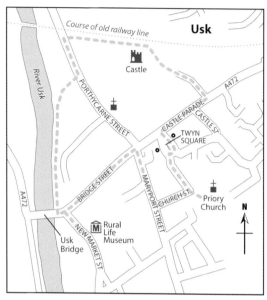

Walking around town

The centre of the town is Twyn Square where the bus sets down. The brick clock tower, dating from 1887, is an iconic feature located in the centre of the square that is essentially medieval but now faced out with Victorian rebuilding. What immediately strikes you is the floral display around town (unless you happen to visit in the depths of winter). Usk is one of the best floral towns in the Marches and continues to win prestigious awards, year after year, for the local people's superb and sustained effort in decorating the place with flowers, including the Usk Bridge.

Many of the buildings in the town look Victorian although several have clearly been rebuilt from earlier shells that date back to the 16th and 17th centuries. It is worth a wander

the Roman earthworks at the edge of town and information plaques embedded in the pavement where remains lie beneath the modern urban fabric. Since those early days, the population of Usk has barely exceeded 2,500 people at any one time. Even now, it prides itself on being a tranquil backwater in the borders.

Thus, the town itself has grown little beyond the grid pattern laid down by the Normans. It lies between the high ground of the castle and a strategic crossing of the river Usk. An ancient bridge still exists where there was previously a ford. This is one of the reasons the Welsh and English fought so much over the town; it was a strategic place to cross the Usk. This fighting came to an end when Owain Glyndwr's forces were heavily defeated at the Battle of Usk in 1405, despite his having ransacked the town three years earlier. On the day of the battle, the English troops gathered under the flag of Harry of Monmouth and repelled the invading Welsh forces. Glyndwr must have been truly dispirited as he lost his brother at the battle and his son was locked up in the keep of Usk Castle where he subsequently perished.

The clock tower in Twyn Square

and there are plaques throughout the town to let you know some facts about different buildings. Walk down Priory Street to take a look at the impressive **priory church**. Its origins lay in the foundation of a Benedictine nunnery dating from the 1160s and following the Dissolution it became a parish church to serve the township. The current church occupies only part of the original nunnery which was far more extensive. In medieval times it had a shrine dedicated to St Radegund, a saint created in the 6th century in Poitiers. The shrine at Usk priory attracted pilgrims throughout the medieval period. The church, as it exists, is known for its stained glass and two 15th-century porches of note. It has a number of other interesting features including a magnificent organ adorned with Spanish trumpets and coloured pipes, brought from Llandaff Cathedral in 1899. The equally ornate rood screen, spanning the two naves of the church, is also very impressive as it is set against a vaulted wooden ceiling.

It is said that Adam of Usk lies buried in the priory church grounds but the exact

Usk priory church: one of the porches, and the highly decorated organ and screen

location of his burial is not known. There is, however, a small rectangular brass memorial to Adam on the eastern side of the screen. The inscription is in an old Welsh language. Adam of Usk gained notoriety as a controversial chronicler of events in Wales during the late 14th and early 15th centuries and he often found himself in difficulties with the monarch as a consequence. The chronicles he penned are held in the British Library.

On leaving the priory church you will see the memorial laid down in 1994 to commemorate St David Lewis, a priest who was tried and hung in Usk for pursuing his Catholic beliefs at a time when Jesuit activity was viewed as dissension and in some cases conspiratorial. His execution was very much against the will of local people who had considerable respect for the man; he became their martyr.

You might like to continue past the church, through the extensive churchyard to Four Ash Street. On the way you might catch a glimpse of the old priory house (private property) which exhibits original stone mullion windows from the 16th century and is a marker of the extent of the priory in medieval times. On reaching Four Ash Street you will see on the left across the road a building called the Black Friars, a private dwelling of late medieval origin.

Retrace your steps back through the churchyard to the gates leading into Church Street. Pass by the ivy-covered Priory Gatehouse on the left and walk ahead to a road junction.

Turn right here to walk up Maryport Street. At the top turn left into Bridge Street where most of the shops are located. Across the road is a traditional coaching inn with its historic sign 'Three Salmons Livery and Bait Stables', the bait referring to feed for the horses. Continue along Bridge Street towards the Usk Bridge. Just before you reach it, there is New Market Street leading off to the left. It is worth a detour here to take a look at the town's small museum, the **Usk Rural Life Museum** and the Rural Crafts Preservation Society. The museum

is located in an old malt storage barn; its main aim is to tell the story of rural life in Monmouthshire from the mid 19th century to the Second World War, and that it does well. There are a wide range of displays of all things rural – models of horse-drawn vehicles, agricultural tools of past years and artisan products such as corn dollies and the like. There are also exhibits of rural skills practised in decades past, such as butter making in the dairy, cooking in the farmhouse kitchen and the work of the wheelwright. These displays add greatly to the atmosphere of the place.

You might also like to walk a little further down **New Market Street** to gain a feel of Usk as in past times for this is now a far quieter quarter than hitherto. There are many fine houses to admire in this sleepy street. New Market Street leads to the old **Market Hall**, originally designed with open arcades for the exchange of market goods. It was used in later decades as a town hall and now belongs to the British Legion. On the right of the Market Hall is the handsome **Royal Hotel**, sadly currently closed and in need of restoration. It was built in the late 1830s for a local poet and dilettante, John Trelawny, who fought with Lord Byron in the Greek War of Independence against the Turks in the 1820s. Trelawny was equally passionate about Italy, and stayed with Shelley on many occasions. He used to bring back seeds of cedar trees from the Protestant Cemetery in Rome, where Shelley's ashes were buried and which became Trelawny's final resting place too. Some of the cedars remain in Llanbadoc churchyard across the Usk. There are many other fine Georgian and early Victorian buildings on the street, such as Wellesey House and the Lawns.

On returning to the bridge, cross over the road (not the bridge) and follow Coniger Walk, alongside the banks of the Usk at first, and then through to Porthycarne Gateway where you turn left. Before the railway bridge, cross the road and go right up a track leading up to the site of the old station on the Coleford to Pontypool Junction railway, built in 1856 and closed to passengers 99 years later. There's a nature trail across the bridge to the west and through the old tunnel to the right. This was opened up through the efforts of the Usk Conservation and Environment Group and is a very good local amenity. However, on this occasion take the lesser path off to the right, climbing up steps to a track. Go right to descend to the entrance to Usk Castle.

Main attraction

There two main attractions on this outing. Both are the **castles**, one at **Raglan** and the other at **Usk**; they could not be more different. At the gatehouse of Usk Castle you are invited to place a pebble from the bowl into a pot (for data collection purposes) and to leave a donation in lieu of a charge. A visit to the castle is worth a generous donation, for it really is a classic romantic ruin with a great view across to Wentwood Forest. Usk Castle was commissioned by William fitz Osbern in the 12th century and then passed to the Norman de Clare family. The de Clares continued to fortify the castle in order to repel the onslaught of the Welsh, but the castle (and town) changed hands several times in the ongoing tussle. This came to an end with the Battle of Usk in 1405 and the slaughter of 300 Welsh soldiers beneath the castle walls. From then onwards, the castle played a lesser part in borderland history.

It is said that Usk Castle was modified to afford more comfortable living conditions by William Herbert in the 15th century. Catherine Parr, the sixth wife of Henry VIII, came into the ownership of the castle in the 16th century but it is unlikely that she spent any time here. Catherine had a busy but short life; she had four husbands and unfortunately died of childbirth at the age of 36. From her demise until 1908 the castle simply fell into a ruinous state. It was not until the 20th century that fortunes changed when the Humphrey family took over ownership in 1933. They have maintained the fabric of the castle since for the public to

enjoy. It is very unlike most castles open to the public as it has that lived-in feeling; there are two guardian geese wandering around, whilst cockerels, hens and sheep graze the inner courtyard. Interpretation is limited but there is a leaflet with a brief history and site map to help (although you can acquire *Usk Castle, Priory and Town* edited by Jeremy Knight and Andy Johnson from the house if anyone is in).

After your visit, continue to walk down the lane, past the car park, to the Monmouth Road. Go right along Castle Parade to Twyn Square. The bus stop for Raglan is by the Nag's Head pub.

RAGLAN

Raglan is a smaller settlement than Usk but is also very floral and brims with blossoms for part of the year. The town is also associated with the design world through a feature known as the Raglan Sleeve, developed for Lord Raglan who lost his arm in the Crimean War, the sleeve stretching from the underarm to the neckline. The town's main street is lined with nearly as many inns as there are shops. This is no doubt a legacy from the days when Raglan was a main route from London through to this part of Wales.

At the crossroads stands the Beaufort Arms, an old coaching inn, and **St Cadoc's church**. This would have been a very busy location in the days of turnpike roads. The earliest church had origins in the 6th century but the existing structure is from the 14th century with many additions and modifications undertaken in later centuries. The North Chapel was funded by the Somerset family, who resided at Raglan Castle for several centuries, and there are many monuments reflecting their heritage. The clock on the tower is a curiosity as it has only three faces. It was presented to the church by a local benefactor, Miss Bosanquet, some time in the 1860s, but she was so incensed about the arrival of the railway that a face for the side facing the railway was omitted as a protest.

The **main attraction** is **Raglan Castle**, and the railway brought thousands of visitors to the castle, regardless of the missing clock face. They would walk up from a halt, known as Raglan Footpath, direct to the ruins. Not that the railway was the start of tourism for Raglan. An increased flow of visitors had already been noted some 50 years earlier and a visit to the castle ruins became a fashionable thing to do for the romantic movement of the time. The activity prompted the Duke of Beaufort to appoint a keeper to look after the ruins and make them more presentable to visitors.

The castle lies about half a mile to the north of the village and the walking route involves crossing the busy A40 so is far riskier now than a train trip would have been in the 19th century. From the Beaufort Arms, go left to walk along Castle Street to a point where it runs alongside the A40. There's a seat here for people to watch the traffic go by and, astonishingly, some people do, regardless of the noise. Go through the barrier and cross when safe, but don't be tempted to chance it. Once across, walk ahead along the lane to the castle entrance. The walk should take no longer than 15 minutes.

Raglan Castle is considered to be the finest of the late medieval castles: it is the last grand castle to be built before nobility opted instead for fortified manor houses. It was built as a treasured possession rather than a defensive fortification. The site is managed by CADW and the entrance and shop leads to the Great Gate, a magnificent piece of architecture that combines beauty with the functional necessity of repelling unwanted guests. This was most probably commissioned by William Herbert in the 1460s. He was the son of the castle's founder, William Ap Thomas, who commenced building the castle during the 1430s. There's a mixture of medieval magic, of gargoyles adorning the towers and Tudor tracery that make this an enchanting place. There's also a touch of the French about it, perhaps best illustrated by the hexagonal towers, reflecting the owners' interest in the increasingly fashionable design of fortified houses on the continent.

As you walk around you begin to appreciate both the solidity of the structure, for example the thickness of its walls and the deep moat around the substantial keep, and the refinement of the interior layout. The castle was made for luxurious living

Raglan Castle

as seen in the state apartments, the space given over to the kitchen and pantry, the cobbled court, and hall for banquets and court gatherings. These embellishments were introduced by the Somerset family, who inherited the castle through marriage ties, and it reached its zenith in the 16th century. Disaster came with the prolonged siege of the castle by Parliamentarians in the English Civil War, and they proceeded to dismantle as much as they could after its capitulation. From then onwards, it suffered a period of continuous decline into an ivy covered ruin. Fortunately, the State has since restored this exceptional monument. If this castle was built as a statement, it worked. Nearly 600 years on it still stands as a moving tribute to the ingenuity and skill to those who spent their lives building it.

WALKING

The main walking route in the area is the **Usk Valley Walk** (48 miles in total from its source in the Brecon Beacons to Caerleon). There are opportunities to sample the route in the Usk area. It is possible to travel down to Usk by bus and walk back to Llanfoist near Abergavenny, a distance of 12-13 miles with a short detour (or bus ride into Abergavenny).

Raglan is not a particularly good walking area as it is hemmed in by two four-lane highways. There are, however, two local walks written up in a local tourism booklet *Raglan Past and Present*, which facilitate a little more discovery of the area on foot.

CYCLING

National **Cycle Network route 42** runs between Abergavenny and Usk. This utilises back lanes for most of the way and is gently undulating so not too exacting. A round trip would be approximately 30 miles. Otherwise, this is not particularly good cycling territory unless you are an experienced cyclist willing to use busier roads.

REFRESHMENT

Usk
There are a number of cafés and pubs in Usk but none that stand out.

The Three Salmons Hotel: offers locally sourced food wherever possible for bar snacks and meals in the restaurant.

Raglan

Beaufort Hotel, Raglan: long standing Good Beer Guide entry that is popular for dining too.

EXTRAS

Farmers Market, Memorial Hall, Usk: 1st and 3rd Saturdays of the month.

Raglan Twinning Association and Cheryl Morgan, (2010) *Raglan Past and Present*. A nicely produced booklet, focusing on Raglan, available locally.

Knight, Jeremy H. & Andy Johnson (eds) (2008) *Usk Castle, Priory and Town*, Logaston Press

Usk Civic Society, (2010) *Usk Town Trail*, available at tourist information offices, a detailed walk through the town packed with historical detail.

PUBLIC TRANSPORT

Buses
Raglan (Beaufort Hotel) is served by bus from Abergavenny. 83. Daily. Two hourly weekdays. Four trips on Sunday. Travel time: 26 minutes. Operator: Veolia on Monday – Saturday, Stagecoach in South Wales on Sunday.

Usk (Twyn Square) is served by bus from Raglan (Beaufort Hotel). 60. Hourly on weekdays, four trips on Sunday. Travel time from Raglan 10 minutes. Operators: T. Ward on Monday – Saturday, Stagecoach in South Wales on Sunday.

MONMOUTH (TREFYNWY) AND THE LOWER WYE VALLEY

Ride to Monmouth

The run from Abergavenny to Monmouth takes you through to the ancient cross-roads of Raglan (described in the outing to Usk). From Raglan, the bus follows the Trothy valley via Dingestow to Monmouth. **Dingestow** was at one time a Norman stronghold and the motte still survives but little else remains. You can see St Dingat church when the bus reverses in the village. There's an old preaching cross of note in the churchyard. It then passes the Somerset Arms and alongside the wooded slopes of Mitchel Troy. Unfortunately, the arrival at Monmouth's bus station is something of a disappointment; to describe it as basic would be an overstatement.

The ride from Monmouth into the Lower Wye valley, however, lifts the spirits. It is as picturesque as they come, even on the old bus that is turned out daily for this run. The bus travels beneath canopies of woodland to Redbrook and then over the Bigsweir Bridge into Wales. You'll catch sight of a toll house on the right and the remnants of the one-time Wye Valley Railway on the left here. It then passes through **Llandogo**, where the Sloop Inn is a reminder of those days when boats sailed on the tide to tie up here. The village was known for the building of flat-bottomed trows suitable for shallow waters. Then you by pass Brockweir, an historic village nestled across the bridge in Gloucestershire, before reaching the turn for Tintern Station, and a little further into Tintern village alongside the river's edge.

MONMOUTH

Monmouth has a bustle about it. Its main thoroughfare, Monnow Street, leads up from the unique Monnow Bridge and Gateway to Agincourt Square. This is the heart of the town. That is where you'll find the tourist information centre and just

beyond is an old quarter around the parish church with old priory buildings which are delightful. But what makes Monmouth especially intriguing is its curious association with Admiral Horatio Nelson. The Nelson Museum, the Nelson Garden and the Kymin offer clues to the town's infatuation with one of the nation's favourite heroes. Monmouth is a good centre for those who love the outdoors; it has a growing reputation for the provision of outdoor activities, particularly canoeing, but also walking and cycling in the Wye and Monnow valleys. It's a good little place from which to explore these localities.

Walking around town

Before you head for Agincourt Square, turn right out of the bus station, over the Monnow Bridge and through the Gatehouse into St Thomas's Square. Here you can admire the Norman architecture of **St Thomas The Martyr church** dedicated to Thomas à Becket. A fine chancel arch and font are the main features of the church, which has been restored extensively in the past 200 years. The **Monnow Bridge Gatehouse** dates from the 13th

The medieval gated bridge across the Monnow

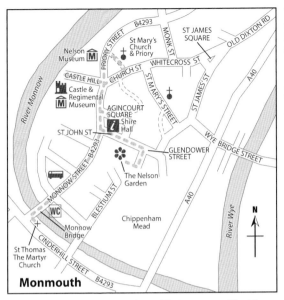

Monmouth

from 1792; it has been cleaned up beautifully. In 2010, the gold-painted scroll which Henry holds proudly in hand was stolen, much to the amazement of the town's residents. There followed some good old-fashioned community policing and the scroll was handed back pronto. It was repaired and has been duly placed back where it belongs. A statue of Charles Rolls stands on the forecourt (Rolls as in the Rolls-Royce partnership). He lived a good part of his life in Monmouth and was laid to rest at Llangattock following an aviation accident in the early part of the 20th century.

century. It is a very rare survivor of its type in that the gatehouse is actually built on the bridge. At one time, the gatehouse was inhabited, and early paintings also show a dwelling attached to the bridge. Historians suggest that it was not particularly good as a defence but may have fared better as a toll gate. Needless to say, it looks the part, in fact it looks great.

Make your way back along Monnow Street, a wide but gradually narrowing thoroughfare packed with parked cars and traffic; there is talk of making it more pedestrian friendly and it certainly needs it. At the top, the Shire Hall stands proudly in **Agincourt Square**, thus named to reflect the acclaimed victory of King Henry V (who was born in Monmouth) against the French at the Battle of Agincourt in 1415. The Shire Hall was built as a court in 1724 but it also doubled up as a market hall and general purpose public rooms. This impressive building has been restored on numerous occasions since, but the latest restoration really does merit praise. The first clock was mounted on the building in 1765 but the one *in situ* dates from 1880. Beneath it is the finely carved statue of Henry V dating

The Monmouth assizes, held for many a year at the Shire Hall, became the scene of intense judicial interest in 1840 when John

The recently restored statue of Henry V in Agincourt Square

The historic Punch House in Agincourt Square

Frost of Newport and other chartist leaders were tried here. The scene was a sombre one when the judgement was made; the black cap was donned and the accused were sentenced to be hung, drawn and quartered for the act of treason. For whatever reason, this harsh sentence was changed to transportation for life to Van Diemen's Land (Tasmania). John Frost was eventually pardoned, and in due course he returned to Bristol to live out the remainder of his life – and what a life that was! He lived to be nearly 100 years old. Adjacent to the Shire Hall is Beaufort Court, where one of Monmouth's many lost historic inns, the Beaufort Hotel, was located.

Walk along cheerful **Church Street**, passing by a amazing survivor, the **Monmouth Savoy theatre and cinema** which is over 150 years old. There are a range of boutique shops in the street so you'll possibly be tempted to browse. The flagstones in this thoroughfare add to the character of what is an older core of the town. This gives out into a Georgian quarter where there are many fine dwellings. **St Mary's church** stands at the top of Church Street, rebuilt on the site of a Benedictine priory. Go left to walk through the churchyard. The tower is of Norman origin, but most of the church was damaged and rebuilt in the 18th and 19th centuries. Next door is the remainder of the old priory building, now a conference/meeting venue. If you continue through to Priory Street, go right for a few steps and you will see Geoffrey's Window, an oriel window adorned by gargoyles said to honour the 12th-century scribe, Geoffrey of Monmouth. Cross the road and go left.

Main attraction

On the right is the river Monnow, minding its own business below the parapet and overlooking the Vauxhall water meadows. The first building on the right is the old market hall dating from 1840 and this is where the **Nelson Museum and Local History Centre** is located. This is something of a curiosity given that Monmouth is landlocked and Horatio Nelson was born in Norfolk and buried in St Paul's Cathedral, London. It seems that the good people of Monmouth had nothing but admiration for Nelson. Lady Llangattock, the mother of Charles Rolls, collected hundreds of items associated with the admiral's life and these were given to the town in 1924. They formed the basis to establish a museum.

The museum is charming. It houses a varied collection of items, from personal letters to one of Nelson's trusty swords. Nelson, of course, led a colourful life. He had certainly earned a place in history and, at the time, was the number one national hero. By all accounts, he led his men into battle, on each and every occasion, without fear and concern for his own life, which explains why he was near mortally wounded on more than one occasion. At Calvi, during the Corsican campaign, he lost the sight in one eye which led to the common idea that he wore a patch. That was not the case as the eye could still detect light and shade. Nevertheless, a Welshman made an authentic glass eye, and the rumour that Nelson wore it became so rife that a Welsh entrepreneur set up a production line to make the fake glass eyes to be sold to unsuspecting people. One of those manufactured Nelson glass eyes is on show here in a display case along with all manner of artefacts which were made in Victorian times to commemorate the life of Admiral Nelson.

The museum also provides insights about the man as a lover. His affair with Emma Hamilton was laid bare through Nelson's prolific letter writing, and the gathering of many of these letters was something of a scoop for Lady Llangattock. There are other displays in the museum about the Rolls family and the social history of the town. So, the museum is a joy.

On the right, just along from the museum, is Castle Hill, which leads to the ruins of **Monmouth Castle**. The castle was part of the fitz Osbern empire, presumably built on this site to protect nearby river crossings. It was the birthplace of young Henry in 1387 who soon earned his place in history as King Henry V. As with so many of the borderland fortresses, Monmouth Castle was dismantled in the English Civil War, but fortunately parts of the Great Tower and Hall remain. The splendid **Great Castle House**, built in 1673, stands to the right, guarded by a Russian cannon donated following the Crimean War. There are other pieces of military hardware on the forecourt, standing by the entrance to the castle and **Regimental Museum**. Castle House is now the HQ of the Royal Monmouthshire Engineers, the museum being located in part of the old stable block and devoted mainly to explaining the regiment's illustrious past. Behind

Castle House

the museum is a lovely little herb garden packed with herbs and plants what would have been grown during the years when Henry V was on the throne. There's also a serene memorial garden by the castle which offers a tranquil spot for quiet reflection.

A visit to Monmouth would not be complete without mentioning two other places which illustrate the town's adoration for Nelson. The **Nelson Garden**, a half acre hidden behind red brick walls, is to be found behind Glendower Street. From Castle Hill turn right along Monnow Street, then cross over into St John's Street. This leads to Glendower Street and, in turn, to Glendower Gate Street. The path runs right alongside the flood defence bank on Chippenham Mead, a well laid-out recreational ground. You arrive at a small black door leading into the garden; it is not very noticeable. In the summer of 1802, Nelson accepted an invitation to dine at the Beaufort Hotel. Nelson arrived in Monmouth by boat, and disembarked at the old quay area near the Wye Bridge, so there was a touch of nautical etiquette involved. The formal meal was served late one afternoon, followed by an evening of refreshment at what was simply known then as the town garden. By all accounts it was a very successful day for the town. The summerhouse in which the party took tea has long since been demolished, though plans are afoot to try and reconstruct it. A later pavilion was erected in 1958. Over the years the town garden became known as the Nelson Garden and it has been restored in recent decades by volunteers. It is open in the afternoon during summer months, but you are advised to first check current details at the tourist information centre to avoid disappointment.

On stepping back out onto the flood defences, you can catch sight of a white building gleaming on the hillside ahead, between the tree cover above the Wye. This is the 18th-century **Round House** at the Kymin where Nelson and Lady Hamilton, on another visit, took breakfast one fine morning. It was a favourite picnic and luncheon spot for the well to do of Monmouth. Alongside is the **Naval Temple** monument, funded by public subscription, to give recognition to Nelson's heroic role in the Battle of the Nile and to 14 other admirals, as well as offering praise to the navy in general. Both buildings are now in National Trust ownership.

TINTERN AND THE LOWER WYE VALLEY

In his immortal *Lines Composed A Few Miles Above Tintern Abbey* William Wordsworth eulogised about the place, with its 'steep woods', 'lofty cliffs' and 'green pastoral landscape'. In a similar vein, the Reverend Gilpin, the man who put the picturesque into the rural landscape dictionary, wrote of Tintern in 1782:

> A more pleasing retreat could not easily be found. The woods, and glades intermixed; the winding of the river; the variety of the ground; the splendid ruin, contrasted with nature; and the elegant line

formed by the summits of the hills, which include the whole; make all together a very enchanting piece of scenery.

His best-selling book undoubtedly boosted tourism to the valley. In the early years of the 19th century there were at least eight pleasure boats plying up and down the river and many more tourists came by horse-drawn carriages. Amongst the literary cognoscenti who came to paint or write about the place were Coleridge, Southey and Turner, who continued to give the impression of a rural idyll not touched by a rapidly encroaching industrial world.

The reality could not have been further from truth. In Tintern and the Angiddy valley the furnace, forge and waterwheel were all well established. By the romantic ruins stood an early works that manufactured wire for the best part of three decades. But no one seemed to mind; tourism and industry sat alongside one another. There was another side to all this too. Gilpin complained about the begging brought about by tourism, and guidebook

Tintern Abbey

writers well into the 20th century wrote of the overselling of tourism at Tintern. A particularly good book on the subject is Julian Mitchell's *Wye Tour & its Artists* (see below),

Most people still come primarily to visit the magnificent ruins of **Tintern Abbey**, a Cistercian monastery built in the 1130s under the Norman benefactor Walter de Clare, who resided at Chepstow Castle. The abbey flourished in a valley so rich in resources but this came to an end, as elsewhere, with the Dissolution. From then until the late 18th century it was left more or less to decay, but with the rise in tourism, the ivy-clad ruins became valuable once more. Basic maintenance was applied to keep the monument intact for all to see until CADW, the official guardian of heritage in Wales, inherited and managed the site to good effect for the nation. The centrepiece is without doubt the 13th-century church; it looks so impressive in this sylvan setting.

Tintern is a linear settlement with a range of shops strung along the main road. There's a wide range of accommodation providers and inns here too so it could well be the place you choose to pause from your travels. The restored **Tintern Station** on the Monmouth to Chepstow line once served this early tourism resort. It lies about half a mile north of the village along a riverside path. Nearby is the Tintern Parva Farm vineyard, which welcomes visitors, as do the Meadow Farm Shop and Kingstone Brewery, both of which are a short walk from Tintern village. The latter is on the Wye Valley Walk. A little further up the valley above Brockweir is Orchard's cider; the owner is actually a Mr Orchard. He uses his own and local fruit from standard cider apple and perry pear trees, and employs traditional methods to produce very drinkable cider and perry.

But the most surprising part of Tintern is the Angiddy valley, once a hotbed of industrial activity and now recaptured by nature. The remains of the mills are all but gone. However, a recent project by a group of innovative locals is set to install a micro

The signal box at the restored Tintern Station

hydro power generator on the brook. This will supply green electricity to the grid and will probably become a visitor attraction in its own right. The valley can be explored by woodland walks (see *Walk this Wye*) and to top it all, there's a great place to take refreshment off the beaten track at the Cherry Tree Inn, which is a welcoming pub.

Chepstow
Some may wish to travel on to Chepstow. Tintern is almost equidistant between Monmouth and Chepstow and the latter has a railway station on the Newport to Gloucester line for those at journey's end. Unfortunately, Chepstow is besieged by traffic, and a walk to the railway station necessitates a dive into a subway beneath the A40. If you alight from the Wye valley at the bus station in Thomas Street, you might like to walk to the station in a circuitous manner. Go ahead into Moor Street, then left through the town arch, part of the medieval town walls, to walk down High Street, which has been the subject of a greatly appreciated regeneration project. It includes poetry paving, stone columns exhibiting poetry and the eye-catching *Boatman* sculpture by André Wallace. Keep ahead into Beaufort Square and the relative tranquillity of St Mary Street. Then go left and right into Bridge Street.

Chepstow Castle

The main attraction in the town is **Chepstow Castle**. This revered riverside fortress must have been one of the earliest stone castles to be built in the Marches. No sooner had William the Conqueror established a firm base after 1066, than he devolved power to no lesser person than William fitz Osbern, earl of Hereford and granted him permission to build a major fortress here. The result was a powerful fortification that not only resisted the onslaughts of Welsh warriors but also became a seat of Norman entrenchment in the southern tip of the borderlands.

As you make your way through the double gateway you can almost feel the power. The Great Hall still stands some 800 years on, surrounded by towers and curtain walls strengthened by subsequent Norman occupations. This was only undone by the heavy cannon fire of the Parliamentarians in the English Civil War which brought about the ultimate demise of a Norman castle, which they considered as one built to last.

The tourist information centre is located in the castle car park and opposite is **Chepstow Museum**, which houses a wide range of local displays including one about the Chepstow wine merchants. A good way back to the railway station is to follow the heritage town trail down to the old bridge over the Wye. From here you can admire the design capabilities of the Norman overlords; the view of the castle is exquisite. Then retrace your steps back to the Bridge public house, where you turn left onto a path alongside the river. It is hard to believe that this was once a thriving port and a national shipyard, established here to rebuild the British fleet during the First World War. The path leads to a road called The Back, which you follow around to a junction. Turn left into Lower Church Street and this leads up to **Chepstow church**. This was founded as a Benedictine priory by William fitz Osbern, and the nave and western end remain from the Norman building, with a wealth of Romanesque decoration. There are several tombs inside the church, including that of Henry Marten, a signatory of Charles I's death warrant who was long imprisoned in Chepstow Castle. Once you are through the churchyard, cross the road and walk ahead along Nelson Street. When you reach the subway, follow the signs for the station, or walk along Station Road; there's a café in the station buildings.

WALKING

Monmouth is a hub for walkers. **The Offa's Dyke National Trail** and the **Wye Valley Walk** offer a series of truly classic walks in the Lower Wye Valley. Another local walk is out to the Kymin on Offa's Dyke National Trail. You can continue onward to Redbrook. Here you cross a footbridge alongside the old railway bridge to Pennallt, where a stop at the legendary Boat Inn is obligatory, before walking back on the Wye Valley Walk back to Monmouth. Alternatively, you can catch bus 69 to Llandogo or Tintern and make a day walk of it back to Monmouth. There is also a superb walk along the Wye (on the Wye Valley Walk) from Symond's Yat and the Biblins. Catch Bus 34 out to the Whitchurch roundabout for Symond's Yat West then follow the riverside path to the Biblins where you join the Wye Valley Walk.

The Monnow Valley Walk begins at Monmouth and offers a three or four day walk through to Hay-on-Wye. For those seeking a short taster, you can walk out to Ancre Hill Vineyard, which is only a mile out of town across Vauxhall meadows and then back along the bridleway, Ancrehill Lane, to Osbaston where there's a chance to call into the cemetery; pick up the excellent cemetery trail leaflet that explains aspects of social history in the town. It is a little on the morbid side but well worth the visit.

By far the best walks publication (small charge) is *Walk This Wye*, which outlines 12 walks using public transport in the Wye Valley and packed with information. It is available from the Wye Valley Area of Outstanding Natural Beauty or bookshops in the area.

CYCLING

After years of resistance from landowners and conservation groups, a mainly traffic-free cycle route, the **Peregrine Path**, is now in place between Monmouth, Symond's Yat and Goodrich. It has a rough surface in places and the Symond's Yat to Goodrich Castle section can be busy with traffic.

There are plenty of quiet lanes that lead from the Rockfield Road into the Monnow and Trothy valleys, although expect to climb several hills. The scenery is exquisite.

REFRESHMENT

Monmouth

Cafés and restaurants
There's a wide range of cafés in Monmouth:

Maltsters Coffee shop and **Wigmore's bakery**, St Mary's Street: a little off the main drag but it is worth the short detour.

Nigel's Baker Fayre, Beaufort Arms Court (by the Shire Hall): local ingredients and homemade cakes.

Bistro Prego, Church Street: uses locally sourced food.

Local Produce
Organic produce is sold by **Wyedean Wholefoods** located in Monnow Street. Look out for the **Mon Cacao** shop on Monnow Street, a chocolatier that uses local, organic and fairtrade ingredients wherever possible.

There are also two local butchers, **Hancocks** on Monnow Street and **Le Gourmet** on Church Street.

Lower Wye Valley
The Boat Inn at Pennallt: a must for lovers of old inns where good food and beer are served.

Brockweir and Hewelsfield Village Shop and Café: eco design café and shop which sources many local products and organic items wherever possible.

Cherry Tree, Angiddy valley: friendly, great beers and locally sourced food wherever possible.

EXTRAS
Farmers' Market, Old Monnow Bridge: 4th Saturday in the month.

Kenny's Taxis: will transport cycle and canoes too: 07828 882432, www.kennystaxis.com.

Monmouth canoe and Activity Centre: Ideal for booking a canoeing trip on the Wye: 01600 713461, www.monmouthcanoe.co.uk.

Monmouth Tourist Information, Shire Hall, Agincourt Square: (01600) 713899.

Pedalabikeaway: Cycle hire for rides on the Peregrine Trail or Monmouthshire back lanes: 01600 772821, www.pedalabikeaway.

The Nurtons near Tintern is an organic bed and breakfast near to the Wye Valley Walk. There is also a beautiful garden which has been tended with organic principles for the past 40 years: 01291 689253, www.thenurtons.co.uk.

Mitchell, Julian (2010), *The Wye Tour and its Artists*, Logaston Press.

PUBLIC TRANSPORT

Buses

Monmouth is served by buses from Abergavenny. 83. Two hourly on Monday – Saturday. Four trips on Sunday and Bank Holidays. Travel time: 46 minutes. Operator: Veolia Transport Cymru on Monday – Saturday, Stagecoach in South Wales on Sunday.

The bus from Monmouth to Chepstow via the Wye Valley is two hourly on weekdays and four trips on Sunday. Travel time to Tintern is 37 minutes. Operators: Chepstow Classic on weekdays, Stagecoach in South Wales on Sunday.

Monmouth also has links on weekdays to the following towns (+indicates a Sunday service):
Coleford
Hereford
Ross-on-Wye
Usk+
Newport+

Index

A selection of other books on the Marches from Logaston Press
(for the full list and details see www.logastonpress.co.uk)

Castles and Churches

Ludlow Castle, its History and Buildings £14.95 (pbk), £22 (hbk)
St Laurence's Church, Ludlow; The parish church and people, 1199-2009 £12.95
Castles & Moated Sites of Herefordshire £10
Herefordshire Churches through Victorian Eyes £12.95
Leominster Minster, Priory and Borough c.660-1539 £10
Castles of Breconshire £8.95
Usk Castle, Priory and Town £12.95 (pbk), £17.50 (hbk)
Chepstow Castle: its History & Buildings £17.50 (pbk), £24 (hbk)

Prehistory

Prehistoric Sites of Montgomeryshire £7.95
Prehistoric Sites of Breconshire £7.95

History

Regime & Religion, Shrewsbury 1400-1700 £12.95
The Lead, Copper & Barytes Mines of Shropshire £12.95
Shropshire Almshouses £12.95
The Origins of Ludlow £10
The Fitzalans, Earls of Arundel and Surrey, Lords of the Welsh Marches (1267-1415) £12.95
Knights Templar & Hospitaller in Herefordshire £4.95
Herefordshire Place-Names £12.95
Leominster Revisited £10
The Story of Ross £12.95
The Book of Hay £6.95

Art & Architecture

Artisan Art: Vernacular wall paintings in the Welsh Marches, 1550-1650
£17.50 (pbk), £24 (hbk)
The Walled Gardens of Herefordshire £10
The Dovecotes and Pigeon Houses of Herefordshire £12.95
The Wye Tour and its artists £12.95
Landscapes of the Wye Tour £14.95

Folklore

The Folklore of Shropshire £12.95
Herefordshire Folklore £12.95
The Folklore of Radnorshire £12.95
The Folklore of (old) Monmouthshire £12.95
Merrily's Border: The Marches share their secrets £12.95 (pbk), £20 (hbk)
Arthur, Louise and the True Hound of the Baskervilles £10

General

The Essence of Herefordshire £3.95
Around and About Herefordshire and the southern Welsh Marches £12.95